THE CIRCLE GAME
BOOK 3

LIAM FARRELL

blaw wearie books

Published in 2018 by Blaw Wearie Books

Copyright © 2018 Liam Farrell

Liam Farrell has asserted his right to be identified as the author of this Work in accordance with the Copyright, Designs and Patents Act 1988

ISBN Paperback: 978-0-9954905-4-3
Ebook: 978-0-9954905-5-0

All rights reserved. No part of this publication may be reproduced, stored in a retrieval system, or transmitted in any form or by any means, electronic, mechanical, photocopying, recording or otherwise, without the prior permission of the copyright owner.

A CIP catalogue copy of this book can be found in the British Library.

Maps © Ordnance Survey data © Crown copyright and database right 2018.

Published with the help of Indie Authors World

ACKNOWLEDGEMENTS

My special thanks goes to Kim and Sinclair MacLeod at Indie Authors World, without whom this book would most likely never have seen the light of day.

Also a great gratitude is given to the Ordnance Survey open data for the maps, without which the book wouldn't be the same.

CONTENTS

Acknowledgements 3
Introduction 7
Basic Equipment 9
Following The Routes 12

Route 1
The Cree Run Route Map 13
Route Summary 14
The Cree Run 15

Route 2
Stirling Castle Route Map 41
Route Summary 42
The Stirling Castle Run 43

Route 3
Carron Valley Route Map 73
Route Summary 74
The Carron Valley Run 75

Route 4
Falkirk Run Route Map 107
Route Summary 108
The Falkirk Run 109

Route 5
Forth Run Route Map 139
Route Summary 140
The Forth Run 141

Route 6

    Loudoun Valley Route Map   165

    Route Summary   166

    Loudoun Valley Run   167

Route 7

    Douglas Run Route Map   183

    Route Summary   184

    The Douglas Run   185

Appendices   215

Local Training Runs   217

The Bike   220

Essential Equipment   221

Saddle Height   222

Cleat Position   224

Saddle Fore-Aft Position   226

Stem And Handlebars   226

Saddles   227

Heart Rate Monitor Info   228

Hypnosis Downloads   231

Injuries   232

Data   232

Photography   234

Workshop   235

Further Reading   236

About The Author   237

INTRODUCTION

A most warm welcome to this, my third book, based around the cycle runs that I do from my home in Glenburn, South Paisley. These are trips that I do to anywhere I can reach and return from in a single day, without the need for assistance or overnight stops. The trips that I cover in the book are mostly old acquaintances of mine, and most have been done many, many times over the past 14 or 15 years, since I started my passion for road cycling.

Let me make one thing clear right from the start. I am no natural athlete. Nor one lucky enough to be born with the genes of a champion cyclist, or a champion anything for that matter. I have never won a damn thing in any sporting event in my life, nor am I of a competitive nature; far from it. I should have said I have never won a damn thing in my life. I am just a guy, that's how I regard myself, just a guy. I enjoy the outdoors, mostly on my own, and I only undertook the challenge of doing fairly long cycle runs for the sheer pleasure and personal feeling of achievement.

I came to the world of biking in adulthood by what is often regarded as chance, or more accurately adverse circumstances, when on a raw spring day in 1997 I was climbing a couple of remote Munros that lie to the west of the Linn of Dee, just south of the Cairngorms. At this point I had been climbing Munros for a good eight years, all on foot and without the assistance of pedal power. On that particular day the weather turned very nasty indeed and I was a long way from the car. For once I was slightly under-equipped and the trudge back to my vehicle was a very long one, of extreme cold and wet misery.

When I say misery, I mean bloody misery. In fact, I still rank it as about the worst day's walking in the mountains that I have ever had in 20 years, and that is bloody saying something. The vast majority of the approach to those two hills was along Land Rover tracks that I knew would be greatly shortened by the aid of a mountain bike. And, vowing never to suffer like that again, I went straight out the same week and invested in a nice wee GT Talera, which was at bargain price as it was painted in the previous year's colours.

That was the start of it. I soon found that the remote hills in the Cairngorms and Grampians were now a pleasure rather than a drudge to approach, and I was hooked. Soon not only was I riding rough but also hitting the tarmac and regularly covering the Clyde Coast run, where the extra enjoyable exercise made a total difference to my weight and fitness level. Being a naturally wee stocky guy – 5' 7 inches tall – weight loss does not come easily to me. And having the bike meant that there was no need to do a long drive north to get a big dose of weekly exercise, now I could simply open the door and away I went.

For the first time in my adult life my fitness went up to a good standard and the remaining Munros and the following nine years of climbing the Corbetts were a damn sight easier than the first seven years of hillwalking. During that period I was a heavy smoker, easily doing in 40 cigarettes a day; this would rise to around the 50 mark if I was having a small carry-out (bevvy) in the evening after finishing work. This was occurring far too often, and I was getting close to slipping into addiction. So on a drunken night in October 1996, I decided that it would have to stop, as my lifestyle was not sustainable. I have been smoke-free and completely teetotal since that night.

The point I am trying to make is a very simple but important one to anyone reading this book and wondering if the cycle runs here are beyond them. If I can do these runs then anyone can, including you. A lot of guys who you meet on the road were introduced to the sport by their father or uncle or older brother, but if you have no-one to mentor you, don't worry. I didn't either. My old man's passions in life were Celtic and drink, but not in that order. I abandoned being a football supporter when I left school and became a passionate trout fly fisherman, which was enjoyable but very sedentary. When I finally took to the hills in January '89, I was only 24 and as unfit as a young man that age could be.

I struggled – and I do mean struggled – on for about seven years, before that fateful day west of the Linn o' Dee, which was when it all turned around. Often in life I have learned that the real blessings can come in disguise; the great energy of the Universe lends its guiding hand to steer you in the right direction. But only when you are ready, of course, there's no point in trying to rush it.

Let me tell you something else I discovered: a lot of what you do or don't do is all in the mind. The law of attraction plays a major role in all our lives and the early conditioning we get can be very limiting and difficult to overcome, but it can be overcome.

"If you think you can or you think you can't, you're probably right." Henry Ford said that, and he knew what the hell he was talking about. If you have a negative mindset, or you don't value your self-worth, or lack confidence, or have any other negative program running your subconscious, including that major adversity of fear, then it can be difficult to accept challenges and embrace and get the best from life.

However, the early negative programing, with all its ills, can be overcome by installing a new program into your subconscious mind, much the same as you would do a computer. Computers and brains both work the same way at certain levels, and by using proven techniques like positive self-talk or confidence-building CDs, a lot of unwanted baggage can be gotten rid of. Constant, constant, constant repetition of the positive is the key.

Add to that the motorcar that just about every one of us now owns or aspires to own, and which a lot of us use for even the shortest of journeys, and it's easy to see why a lot of people would regard it as being nigh impossible to cover 100 mile runs or more on a bike. I can assure you that if the bike turns out to be your thing, it will be damn near impossible to stop yourself doing them, not the other way round. And this will take place in a fairly short period of time, which is good news if you are a human, as we are not a very patient species.

Bonnie Scotland is a most stunningly rugged, beautiful country. I rarely holiday abroad unless it's a cycle tour of the battlefields of France, but that's a different story. However, whenever I meet people in the remote highlands and islands, over 90% of them are from south of the border; very few people I meet are actually Scots. I don't have a problem with that per se, as there are so many of us heading south looking for work while they come north looking to escape the rat race, so it's a fair swap in my book. But what is disappointing is the fact that so many of us stay in the central lowlands and holiday abroad chasing the sun, so have no idea just how beautiful our country really is. That is a real crime, and one I'd like to redress.

I recently climbed Tinto Hill with a big mate of mine (Scotty Kirkland) who had travelled the world as a chef on board numerous sea-going vessels, including the QE2. But that day was the first time he had ever visited the top of the Clyde Valley, and he was struck by the serene greenness and beauty of the place. He'd no idea it was like that, and this was a man in his sixties.

I am in my late forties now and still going strong on both hill and bike. As I was taking a break on my last trip round the tough Arran run, one bike rider who flew by me turned out to be 72 years old and he was still in great shape. The health benefits of cycling are awesome.

I had to ask myself just who am I aiming this book at, as most established riders will know and most likely have done most, if not all, the runs in this book. They are, for the most part, either well-worn training runs or classic standards of long standing. So really I'm hoping to reach as many people who have either recently bought a machine and are looking for runs to do, or others who are thinking about getting fitter and don't fancy gyms or crunching their knees on concrete.

If the statistics are correct, then I might awaken the sleeping giant. For they say that there are as many bike owners in Britain as there are car owners, with the vast majority buying them with good intentions and using them once or twice before relegating the new machines to the back of the garage or garden shed, where they lie gathering dust.

So maybe if some clean up their hidden gems and get active again, it might help in some way towards us losing the unenviable tag of the sick man of Europe. This is despite the fact we are an undoubted rugged and hardy breed who, along with the Irish and Norwegians, have always had the toughest job in all of Western Europe in trying to eke out a living. Mind you, the weather doesn't help and I admit that it's easier to get motivated and look forward to a cycle in warm sunshine than it is in the rain and damp. But as Irish hardman Shaun Kelly once said, "You don't know how cold and wet it is til you're out there", as it often looks worse than it is.

Take it from me, the good days will come. And when they do, then boy, oh boy. Fancy it? Then just read on

Liam Boy.

BASIC EQUIPMENT

If you are completely new to the game, here is some advice on what you need to get you started before we dive out the door for our first run together. Starting with clothing and starting at the top, a helmet is a very good idea. It's personal choice as to whether you wear one or not, and I know some guys who are very experienced road men who never wear one. Personally, I don't get out of bed without mine, and recommend you do the same.

Only once in a blue moon, if I am on a really quiet road round the back of an island, for example, will I take it off – and only then if it's a scorcher. In its place I will put on a cycling cotton cap, one of which I always carry to keep the sun off my head. The cotton cap's peak is also good under a helmet for stopping both hail and rain from battering into your eyes when it's so wet you have to remove your glasses to see where you're going.

The glasses themselves are also essential, and the ones with interchangeable lenses can be changed to suit the conditions. Some of these can cost the earth, but you don't need to pay top dollar for a good set. About £40 will get you a good quality pair.

Now although you don't actually need a cycling specific top, if you look the part, you'll act the part (or so they say). Cycling team jerseys do have the advantage of having three rear pockets, which are good for keeping essentials in. They come in short or long sleeves, and although most of us buy too many, probably two of each will be more than sufficient. For the short version, it's a good idea to buy a pair of arm warmers that go with them. I also have a couple of short-sleeved performance t-shirts that I wear under my cycling top on all but the warmest days.

You will also find most serious riders have more than one waterproof jacket – a heavyweight one for winter riding, and a lighter one for summer. The summer one can be rolled up and stuffed into one of the rear pockets, along with the cotton cap. Both rain jackets I have are yellow in colour to maximise visibility, which is a good safety idea. My helmets are always yellow for the same reason.

Having a pair or two of track mitts (padded fingerless gloves) stops hands becoming sore when pressed against handlebars for long periods. On top of this they protect the ulnar nerve, which runs from your palm to your arm and becomes painful if pressured and damaged.

Next comes probably the most important item of clothing – the shorts. Don't skimp on price here. The one thing that can really put you off cycling early doors is saddle soreness. Get a pair that retails for around the £40 mark to start with; anything cheaper I have found doesn't quite do the job. I like the Campagnolo brand, but any reputable brand will do. You don't have to go more expensive than that at first, but if you start doing really long endurance then a really well padded top-end pair is recommended. A pair of leg warmers is also a good addition, particularly for spring and autumn; they're not required on summer runs, and for winter ones more substantial leggings are worn.

Cycling socks are basically just short cotton socks; some do claim to have beneficial properties like improving ventilation, but most just sport team logos or the like. They help you look the part, so it's good to have them, even if only to match your track mitts and jerseys. Cycling specific shoes are now mostly a must, with the cleat and clipless pedal system now in use, and some models go up to about the £200 mark. These are only needed by the top end racers, however, both professional and amateur. The level entry shoe that all manufacturers make will be more than adequate to get you going. Correct fitting and alignment of the cleats is real important, so I will give you the technique for that at the back of the book. If you get that wrong, your knees will hurt like hell, so it's important to get that one spot on from the word go.

So too is saddle height and handlebar stem length; again, I will give you an accurate and easy to perform technique at the back of the book to leave you millimetre perfect. Remember, it's very easy to spend every penny you earn on equipment, so at first just buy what you need and take it from there.

Next the bike itself, which is of course the main piece of equipment and the biggest outlay. Now you can cover a lot of distance on tarmac riding a hybrid or even mountain bike, but life will be easier and more pleasant if you're on a racing machine. Thinner tyres, less weight, the right tool for the job, will make it a lot easier and faster. What bike, or rather standard of bike, you use doesn't really matter on most of these runs, with the possible exception of the five ferries.

I started off back in 99 with a Lemond Reno. It was steel-framed, a Greg Lemond-made bike, which was the bottom of Greg's range. The Reno's group set (gruppo), was also bottom range, being Shimanos SRX. Nowadays they call it Sora (Japanese for sky). Despite being bottom range, Greg made a good bike and I did just about every run in the book with it, including Edinburgh and back in a day. On that occasion they actually refused to let me into the castle with a bike and even refunded my money. I vowed never to go back there again and, true to my word, haven't done that run since.

So to get you going, any half decent road bike will do. It can be a difficult decision as to how much you want to spend, as you don't know how far you want to take things. To be sensible about it, don't break the bank early on. You can get a lot of bike for your money nowadays, with a road bike in the £500 range being more than adequate for the job. The Government Cycle to Work Scheme is ongoing, which is a good idea in itself and you can get a machine to your liking for almost half price. You will have to source that one out for yourself to see if your employers do it, and if so, the guys in your local bike store will be happy to help on all matters, including sizing, and bargains.

Don't forget about Gumtree and eBay, where there are great deals to be had once you know what you're doing. But it has to be said that riding a real top-end machine is a pleasure and can make a lot of difference on a long run and also when hitting the climbs. It can even make the difference as to whether you can catch a ferry or not when doing the famous five.

The frame of the bike is the most important and costly item, and determines how a bike handles and performs. Next in line of importance are the wheels, then the gruppo itself. You'll soon learn that most serious riders have a good machine that they don't ride in the wet. For that, they have their training bike, armed with mudguards and a lower-end gruppo.

It's not always that easy to tell the standard of a bike by its frame; obviously the price is a giveaway, but so too will be the gruppo. They usually team up a top-end frame with a top-end group set. Shimano and Campagnolo are the two big name component providers, with Sram also now coming onto the market with a range.

Campag make some lovely gear, and a lot of guys like to ride with it. It tends to be more expensive than Shimano for two reasons. First, you pay for the Italian styling, and secondly, Shimano produce more so can do it cheaper. It's the same with a lot of Italian produce in general, including their bike frames.

I don't believe you get the same value for money from a Pinarello frame, than you would for say an Eddy Merckx or a Trek. If you start off by buying a lower-end machine and decide to further invest in a high spec model, that's great. Just put mudguards on your original and use it as your wet weather bike. My training bike is a Terry Dolan carbon fibre, with the Shimano gruppo comprising a mixture of 105 and Ultegra components. My top machine nowadays is an Eddy Merckx Cima with a Shimano Dura Ace gruppo. To ride the Merckx is a pleasure, despite the fact it's 11 years old and has a 9-speed set-up. The more modern have at least 10. It's all about justification here.

If you graft hard and want to splash out and treat yourself, why not? Some guys change their bikes every couple of years or so, but not me. I buy real good and keep it a lifetime if I can, that way I get quality and value for money.

Living in the west of Scotland will mean a lot of rain, of course, and a lot of wet weather riding. So having a good standard of training bike will be very beneficial as the majority of the miles you do, even in the summer, will be done on it. I then recommend having a bike with at least a mid-range group set. As for a real top-end machine? Well, only you can justify spending the money. Very few can justify Campagnolo top-end set, with some guys saying Shimano's Ultegra is the thinking man's gruppo, compared to the higher priced Dura Ace. You'll have to figure that one out for yourself.

Other on-bike essentials are a pump, saddle bag for carrying a spare tube, puncture repair kit, tyre levers, a multi tool, some dough, and your house keys. A more substantial track pump for blowing up tyres in-house will also shortly be required, as will some specialised cycle tools as you become more proficient in the art of cycle maintenance, along with your cleaning and lubeing kits.

The techniques required for correct saddle height (very important), correct stem length (nearly as important), and correct cleat positioning (helluva important), will all be given at the back of the book.

Don't let that lot jumble your brain. It will all come quite naturally to you in time. And with that, we are about ready to go. So it's on with the show.

FOLLOWING THE ROUTES

The whole point of the book is to get people fired up enough to make them want to go out and ride the routes and enjoy the challenge that they present. So I hope that you will read the whole run through, and get in the mood to give it a real good go. I have, therefore, described the runs in great detail, much more so than most other guide books do. I also hope that the photos of our beautiful country and the history included will act as a spur to get you going and to keep you going.

To keep you on track to a certain extent when doing a route, I hope you will find the accompanying map and the route place names summary enough to guide you, for the most part. However some runs can become a little bit tricky in places, particularly when using country back roads for a few miles. Before you start out on any particular run, it might be worth checking with the relevant O/S map (if you have one) or even a large road atlas to give you a better idea of which roads to take, but that's only if you want to follow my way blow-for-blow, of course.

Remember that my route description may be only one way of many, and you might find a different approach road much more suitable for your needs. I am aware that everyone will be starting from a different location, bearing in mind that most people will begin the majority of the runs from their front door. Please don't forget that you are setting out on an adventure here, so a bit of trial and error on the road is more than acceptable and must be expected. If you don't get a route right first time round, that's fine, just check the map and correct your mistake the next time out.

Some cycling guide books give a brief description of a route and then provide a fairly long, though very accurate, set of instructions on how to follow the route. You know the sort of thing: turn left here, it's signposted such and such. However, I didn't want to do that, as it would mean constantly stopping to check you are on the right road, and that is the last thing you want to do on a bike ride. For me, flowing movement is the key to fun.

Just having the knowledge of your intended destination and some of the place names in between should get you there.

Bear in mind at all times that I personally just made tracks for any given place and made the route up as I went along, although I did use the O/S maps for guidance before I set out on most of them. So remember it can be done ad hoc and it all adds to the fun. Good luck to you all.

NOTE

Please note that when the idea for The Circle Game cycling book was first thought up and planned, it was my intention to produce only one book. It was not until it was just about finished that I realised just how big it was, and that it would therefore have to split into three books. Despite this, I have for the most part kept the original text for authenticity. Therefore, if for example you are reading about a run in book three and it mentions something that I have previously talked about and you have not come across it in book three, then it means that it is contained in an earlier book.

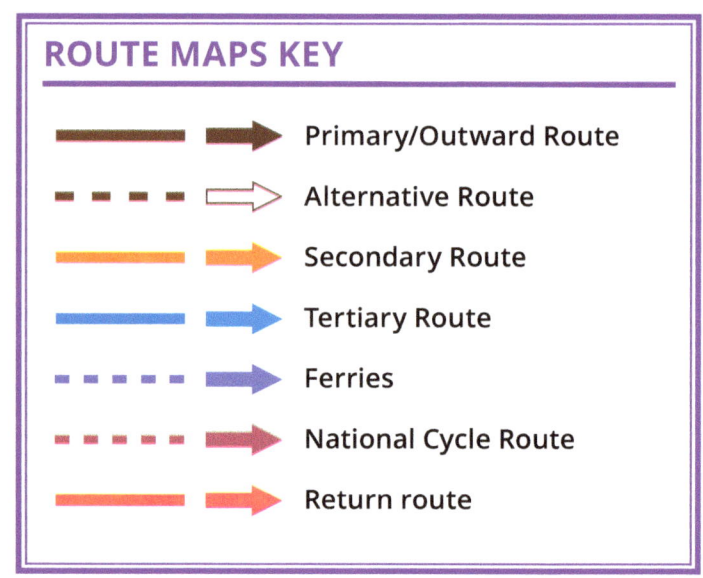

ROUTE MAPS KEY

- Primary/Outward Route
- Alternative Route
- Secondary Route
- Tertiary Route
- Ferries
- National Cycle Route
- Return route

THE CREE RUN

122.5-125.5 MILES
7.32-7.44 HOURS
ASCENT 4180-4400 FEET
CALORIES BURNED:
3978-4107

OS LANDRANGER MAPS
64, 57, 51, 50, 56, 63.

ROUTE SUMMARY

Renfrew Ferry
Yoker
Drumchapel's Kinfauns Dr &
Peel Glen Rd
Baljaffray Rd
Stockiemuir Rd A-809
Carbeth
B-843 (Killearn)
Blane Smithy
A-81(North)
Ballot Junction A-81

ALTERNATIVE ROUTE

Buchlyive A-811 — A-81
Arnprior — Port Of Menteith
Thornhill B-822 — Callander
Callander A-81
Lochearnhead A-84
Lix Toll A-85
Crianlarich
Tarbet A-82 (South)
Balloch
Alexandria
Bonhill Bridge
Bonhill
A-82 Or Dumbarton
Bowling
Old Kilpatrick
Erskine Bridge
Paisley

THE CREE RUN

The Cree run is another classic for any Greater Glasgow-based cyclist. It's known and feared by many, which I say a little tongue in cheek. That's because it's the longest run in the book, and I remember how big Donald Thompson[1], as he held court in his Lawn Street cycle store (sadly no longer there), would tell of how the old boys would threaten one another with it by saying, "Right, next year we're going wheel about on the Cree." "Take no council of your fears" (Stonewall Jackson[2] said that), just build up the miles, and then go out and enjoy this wonderful mountain-filled ride.

This one has plenty in store for you, which is hardly surprising as it's over 120 miles long, and specialises in mountains, more mountains, and lochs. Great, grand, wild scenery awaits you once you reach round about Callander,

---

1 - Sadly, the Big Man died during the writing of this book.

2 - He was a Confederate General in the American Civil War.

from where the rest of the loop back round Glen Dochart to Crianlarich and then down Loch Lomondside, runs you through some equally inspiring terrain. Thoroughly recommended whichever way you do it, my preference has always been to go anticlockwise and head for Callander first. That's the way we're going this time round. So, grab your helmets, grub up – you'll need it – and get settled in for some serious endurance on this one.

Now, the Cree is basically just a big loop, and for the vast majority of the route there is only one road option to take, which keeps it nice and simple. But on the stretch between Milngavie and Callander, there is scope for quite a bit of variation. This can add 2 or 3 miles to the route and, for me, miles can also be added to the run by using the Erskine Bridge both ways as opposed to using the Renfrew ferry on the outward leg. The ferry can be reached by going directly down the Renfrew Road, but that great wee boat can also be reached by taking the Inchinnan Road and then Abbotsinch Road out of town, and after heading down beside the airport, using the famous swing bridge and entering Renfrew that way.

I can access that route by either Paisley town centre or the west end, but prefer the west end option, as it's a bit quieter and more flowing. So, after my morning stretches, I'm out the door as early as possible, as there's a long day ahead of me. Shortly, I'm rolling gently past the shieling and warming up on the Gleniffer and Moredun Roads. Down through Maxwellton, as we've been several times before, and then at the bottom of the newish Gallow Green Road, we don't turn left for the new Saint Mirren Park this time, but instead head for the old one on Love Street. Passing this means you're heading north out towards the airfield, where another well positioned wind sock lets you know just what's what with the blowy stuff.

As always, it's good to be informed early on as to wind direction and strength, and the old sock beats a flag for that purpose any day. It's a long, open, drawn-out affair the Abbotsinch, running all the way from the entrance to the airport to the T-junction at its end, which allows access to either Inchinnan (left) or Renfrew (right). Flat as a bloody pancake is the landscape here, as you have Glasgow Airport left side, and on the other, flat, furrowed fields leading off towards the enormous sheds that once were part of Babcock's Engineering. Out of sight, the River White Cart separates the two. So, for about the best part of a mile you try and keep low on the bars if you're heading into a north east wind, as you have no shelter from the bugger on this stretch.

It won't take you long to cover it, as it's long but fast, especially as the top half has been retarred and you sail down that. When you get to the T-junction, turn right and almost instantly you pass through the Renfrew swing bridge. An A-listed building, if that's the correct terminology for this rather splendid structure, for years I always assumed it swung to the side when it was doing what it was meant to do. But no, it actually tilts up the way. The reason being is that this bridge is a replacement for the original bridge, which *did* swing to the side. This one, built in 1923, is in fact a bascule[3] bridge, and therefore tilts. Both bridges were so designed to allow ships upstream to either Paisley Harbour or Babcock's. A recent garish red paint job has somewhat spoiled the classic look of the bridge, and even – quite rightly – attracted local protests.

3 - Bascule is French for seesaw or balance.

Having turned right off the wonderful A-81 at the big straggly Ballot junction, you then encounter the equally wonderful A-811 with all its lovely, soft, pastoral views and pretty little villages. The first one of these that you come to is Buchlyvie, whose quaint houses and pubs will enchant and delight you. This is very pleasant easy riding at this point.

Regardless of the colour, it does its job and gets us over the Cart into Renfrew and on our way. There is next to nothing in the town now to tell of its early weaving days, as the later and much larger heavy engineering came to totally dominate the industrial landscape. So much so that at the height of its powers Babcock's used to employ 13000 people alone; nowadays this has dwindled to about 200. The size of their yard is enormous, and I speak from experience here, because on one occasion when I was taxiing in Paisley, I picked up a lad who was doing his night watchman in one of the sheds that a small company rented in Babbies[4]. After passing through the main gate, the lad said to me, "Just keep driving, mate, and I'll tell you when to stop." Well, I drove, and I drove, and I drove, and eventually – and I do mean eventually – he said, "Here's fine." I'll never forget it.

There is no need to hit Renfrew Cross from this direction, as the ferry can be reached by turning first left after the Juniors Football Park (Bell Street) and weaving your way round mucho boozers and gaining the old cobbled slip that way. Once again, we await our chance to cross, as have many thousands before us, and have used a different route to get here this time. We won't be using a different route when we alight on the north bank on this occasion, though, as we will be following the exact same course we took on the Trossachs run up to the Ballot junction on the A-81.

4 - Babbies was the local nickname for Babcock's.

THE CREE RUN

Just to refresh your memory: either cross the Clyde by the Erskine Bridge or Renfrew ferry. If it's the bridge, then head east along the A-82, before breaking off left onto the A-810, and follow it through Duntocher all the way to the Langfaulds roundabout at the start of Baljaffray Road.

This point is reached from the ferry by crossing Dumbarton Road at Yoker Ferry Road, and then by turning left at the roundabout at the end of Kelso Street. Continue to follow Dunreath Avenue into Drumchapel housing scheme, which leads you onto Kinfauns Drive, and leave this only when you climb up and past the police station, where you turn left onto Peel Glen Road. This is climbed, leaving behind the scheme, and leads up to the Langfaulds roundabout that way.

From there, climb over the Baljaffray and head out north on the Stockiemuir Road, the A-809, just like we did in both the Rowardennan and Trossachs runs, till we meet with the Killearn road, the B-834. Dive down it, over the Blane Water and up to the Blane Smithy roundabout. Phew! That was some descent (on the Stockiemuir, that is). No matter how many times it's done, it always catches you out with just how good it is.

From Blane Smithy, the plan is now to reach Callander. And as stated in the opening paragraphs, there are several options open to you to do this. The most direct route to take is the A-81 all the way there, by heading for the Aberfoyle roundabout and then climbing up and past Loch Rusky. We took this route, albeit in the other direction, when doing the Callander loop in the Trossachs run, so I will just do a quick recap this time. From the Ballot junction (4 miles up the A-81 from Blane Smithy), as always enjoy the long, gentle, rising straights that draw you towards the higher ground that guards the Trossachs front. Enjoy even more long, gentle, angled straights that drop you down beside the Gartmore roads, before you ride through the meadows and trees that lead up to the Rob Roy Motel roundabout.

Turn right here, and climb up fairly easily past the golf course. Ride mostly flat through the trees and curves, then mostly long and straight and fairly hemmed in till the approach to the Port of Menteith. There, the lake and fields afford views away to your right, and as for the Port itself, well, let's just say it's small. Absolutely magic is the next stretch of road that you take from the hamlet, up until you turn hard left to stay on the 81 and begin the climb up to Loch Rusky. It's a smooth, tree-lined bit of tarmac that just gently wanders up to the turn, though this is in complete contrast to the road that takes you steeply up to the loch. It is actually more pleasant to climb than to descend, so rough is its surface.

Now, as this is a main road, don't expect a horrendous gradient on the way up. It's straights or bends, though it's hard enough, and prepare to enjoy the luscious curves on the high stretch that follows, despite the devastated surrounding tree-felled landscape. Likewise, you will enjoy the twists and bends on the descent, which are slightly technical and very fast. Get low and attentive. They finally come to an end when you reach the bottom at the hard left-hand bend that begins the long straight down into Callander. The tall conifers are no longer standing here, and coming in from the right beside where they stood is the B-822 from Thornhill. This will be the way we will approach on this occasion, but only after I have mentioned another option.

That alternative is to take the quieter back roads from Blane Smithy that run you through Killearn and Balfron, before taking you high over to Kippen. I've used these roads on the Cree on many occasions, and this route also does the job very well. This is one of those times when having the relevant O'S map – in this case number 57 –

You could be forgiven for thinking you are riding through the Belgian Ardennes region here, as the shape of the buildings with their red roof tiles certainly give the appearance of that famous area. But it's only just a bit further along the A-811, at lovely little Arnprior

really helps with the planning, though a good road atlas will suffice. This way does involve a lot more meandering and climbing, and perhaps some will feel it takes away too much momentum when doing such a long run, especially early on. So, for that reason, I won't use this way this time. And because I took the direct A-81 route when describing the Callander loop in the Trossachs run, and it's straightforward to use that way anyway, I won't take that route this time either.

Instead, I'm going to split everything right down the middle, in direction, distance, and difficulty. To do this will entail riding up the A-81 again, but this time only as far as the Ballot junction, before breaking off right onto the A-811 and using that as the main approach artery.

Great views north can be had from the A-811 before and after it drops down to the flat of Flanders Moss, as can be seen here with the rounded dome of Ben Lomond (left) and the sharp-peaked Ben Ledi (right) looking superb and inviting across the low-lying crop fields.

Right, away on the 81 we go. Not for the first time, we sweep long and low to get us going and settling in for the 4 miles to the Ballot. On the way, we fly between those rough, and in places not so rough, fields and meadows, always having the Campsies for company on our right flank. They have been showing a surprisingly striking silhouette ever since we turned down off the Stockiemuir Road. All our old mates are crossed or passed on the way to the Ballot – the Endrick Water, the Balfron station houses, the now defunct rail bridge – before that straggly big junction rears its messy head, and we amble towards it. This time, break right and join the A-811 east-bound.

At last we're onto more new territory, and what territory it is. The 811 and its associates will prove as pleasurable a ride as you could wish for, as we go from the edge of the Flanders Moss right into its centre. So prepare to be thrilled.

Right from the start there is a blessing in disguise, because we have a little bit of climbing to do as we are on the very edge of the foothills that radiate northwards from the Campsies. This is nothing too terrible, as we meander gently upwards through the trees at first, before things start to straighten and open out as you begin to flatten out. What this does is to give a glorious look across the valley north and westwards, and distant peaks make an excellent backdrop to ripened fields. A setting to reward for all the miles we've ridden so far.

This time, it is the elegant shape of Ben Ledi (the first mountain I ever climbed) that will steal the show from now on, as it holds the eye, with its long, whale-backed silhouette sitting behind and towering over the Menteith Hills. You can't help but become aware of a real richness in the agricultural landscape below on the slope that takes your eye away north. Already, a couple of miles have passed since you joined the 811, and there's still another 2 to go to the first village –Buchlyvie. The arable fields holding high crops, if its harvest time, with the field edges dotted by older deciduous trees, make for a most pleasing canvas, I must say. These are no rough grazing fields, far from it. And if not holding crops, then the farmland of hereabouts is supporting dairy herds. It feels so rich and soft to ride through this patchwork of green and yellow squares.

The road does its bit to help the cause here, being very easy-going on the old legs and all, by only rising slightly in places as it rolls along in front of you. Sometimes tree-lined and leafy, other times open and view-filled. Never seeming too busy for an A-road, and well surfaced the whole way, it delights as much as the scenery. The large herd-holding Lower Ballaird Farm that you pass on the right, is typical of the big-hitting farmsteads to be found along this road. And so, feeling uplifted and joyous, the red painted stripes on the road are crossed over as you begin the countdown into Buchlyvie. Its grey, round-topped church spire is prominent as you come in, and is passed almost immediately on the left, as you enter into the prettiness of the place.

The Main Street is lined either side by very tight-knit houses, and the ones on the left in particular are reminiscent of Lilliput. This might be due to the fact that Buchlyvie was once a mining village, though this was

THE CREE RUN

From in amongst the fertile fields of the Carse of Forth, you will find that centre stage is almost always held by the unmistakable pointed peak of Ben Ledi. It does look very dramatic from here, and as you are so low down it can make the approaching mountains look a bit intimidating. No need to worry, though, as you will handle any climbing to come more easily than you think.

way back in the 1700s. It does have a certain miners' row look to it in places, and the left-hand row ends with the quaint, white shape of the inviting-looking Buchlyvie Inn. To balance things up, the right-hand side starts with the quaint, white shape of the Rob Roy Inn. This small village is soon exited, and it's on towards the next one, which is Arnprior; it is even tinier. In fact, it's one of the smallest settlements in the whole of Stirling District.

The road to there is in similar style to the one just ridden, though there is a great descent through a long, tree-lined section. Only a solitary single bend leads onto another great-looking, hedge-lined straight, which guides you along this old military road. The loss of height does take away the great views we have enjoyed from the start of this road, but it is more than made up for by these great, long straights under a magnificent leafy canopy in places. A rise in the road, up to the village of Arnprior, does restore the view somewhat, where those fields – rich and with tree-dotted borders – reappear again and delight.

Arnprior is a village that is made up quite differently from Buchlyvie. For a start, the houses are for the most part quite different from one another, and really only occupy the left side. The right is open fields. Halfway through the village at a very bright barn, made up of cream walls and bright orange Belgian roof tiles, there is a cut-off for the Port of Menteith. This is an option to take for Callander, if you wish, or to loop back home on the A-81 for a shorter day. If this (the B-8034) is taken for Callander, it will mean the climb up to Loch Rusky must still be taken. But our intended route takes us straight on, and will continue to do so till we hit a prominent roundabout where the A-811 meets the B-822. This will be another 4 miles away, and will make it approximately 10 miles of riding since the Ballot junction.

The Highlands show a uniform united front from the Carse of Forth wheat fields. The Carse itself is a magical, flat, flying carpet to swerve through on the B-822, only rising to pull you up into tiny Thornhill, whereafter things get a bit more interesting and undulating.

Although the next mile involves a little bit of leaf-lined rising, once the cut-off for Kippen is passed, the road then drops down onto the true flat plain that is the Flanders Moss in all its glory. And what a sight it is – the big easy itself, awe-inspiring, vast and flat, vast and broad, and vast… and vast. The surrounding wheat fields add to the flatness as you meander through. Not that you meander at first, because you continue bolt-straight to the roundabout.

But once you turn left onto the B-822, that is when the bends start. Bring them on, because they do please, in a single-track, curving sort of way. A large modern café block sits on the right, if you require some caffeine; a bit too early in the ride for me yet, so on we go over the River Forth. This area is known as the Carse of Forth, I believe.

Before you cross the river, you first cross the course of the long-gone and dismantled Forth and Clyde railway line, which joined the Strathendrick and Aberfoyle line back at Buchlyvie and thus formed a major junction at that point. Once the initial bends on the B-822 are negotiated, there is nothing to stop the road from straightening out as it crosses Flanders Moss. This gives you a worm's eye view of the surrounding countryside,

The sharp-pointed Ledi appears again as the higher ground between Thornhill and Callander is gained. Rougher ground than what has just gone before, but as the road isn't too taxing it is most enjoyable.

and provides further status to the high ground ahead, in particular again Ben Ledi. The long straights are ended by dramatic bends before you run in, between the hay bales, towards Thornhill. After crossing a burn – the Goodie Water – by a stone bridge, the next rise takes you into the village, and the climbing only stops when you hit the village centre crossroads.

A white, ornate masonic hall stands on the right, and the war memorial on the left, as low cottage roofs run away from you down both roads, to your left and right. Ahead, the B-822 makes a pretty sight as it meanders up through more really rich farmland, in the shape of wheat and dairy fields, which we follow on our way up onto the high ground between Thornhill and Callander. The sign

From the centre of Thornhill at the crossroads, the B-822 dances away and is still the road that continues to carry us on towards Callander. A fairly gentle bending rise is just about to follow, taking us up into rougher country.

THE CREE RUN

The long straight down into Callander starts once we rejoin our old great mate the A-81, and we get a bit of a breather here. On this run, Callander acts as the gateway to the Highlands, so soon it's all change with regards the scenery.

at the start says 5 miles to that town, and a great 5 miles it is. It starts off very gently as it makes its way through the fields, fairly straight at first, but then climbing round quite marked bends.

These allow great views back the way you came, too, to the now distant Campsies. However, after a little bit of enclosed wooded stretch is passed through, you emerge onto higher, more heath-like ground, as you make your way up into the conifer plantations above. Once more, Ben Ledi makes for a dramatic pointed jag in the sky, and looks a lot like Canisp, its more northerly cousin in Assynt. Gain the top of the road without too much effort, and enjoy the slightly undulating plateau that carries you forward. In the distance, the mountain ranges let you know what is to come, as the height gained up among the scatty scrub has uninterrupted views of the hills beyond Callander.

Similarly, enjoy the more profound, undulating drop down to the junction with the A-81. This descent is an absolute cracker and sees you speeding down and down, till the big conifers on the left are reached. This is done by cutting with delight through every curve and dip in this view-filled drop. You emerge at the big sweeping bend

The River Teith always looks really scenic as you cross over it on Bridge Street, just as you enter the village of Callander. The mountains are in cloud this time but that is par for the course, and there is always a danger of rain round about Loch Lubnaig even on the best of days.

Callander Main Street on what appears to be a fairly quiet day. But on a sunny summer's Saturday, expect the world and his weans to be in close proximity as you gallantly do your best to negotiate your way north. Good luck to you! The road you are now on is the A-84 (T), and being a trunk road means that will also up the ante with traffic.

that signals the end of the long straight out of Callander, and this is where you meet the route that you could have taken on the A-81, past Loch Rusky. The last of the real rough terrain is passed as you descend the short hill that carries you onto the almost mile-long flat straight, where the fields either side slowly but surely become a bit more cultivated as you approach the town.

The large stone wall on your right, leading down to the small mini-roundabout, signals your arrival in the old part, after passing all the white modern homes on the left on the run-in. And what a sight greets you when you turn right. Victorian quaintness is in its element as you roll along and over the River Teith on the old brown stone bridge that gives Bridge Street its name. This one dates from 1908. To the northwest, the imposing face of Ledi sits beyond the still and gentle strip that is the Teith at this point. Being Victorian, of course, you expect quality in the buildings, and there's no disappointment here, as you roll up to the lights on Main Street.

The Bridge Street buildings pale into insignificance when the left turn onto Main Street is made, because suddenly everything hits you at once the moment you do. You've just jumped into touristville. This is especially true if it's a summer weekend, when you will bloody know all about it. Mayhem and chaos aplenty is waiting round this corner. There are great turreted buildings, hotels, shops, and stores, between them selling all the tartan, tourist-trap trivia that the country can manufacture and throw at the poor souls. Those poor souls can be heard as well as seen, with accents as diverse as Geordie, Cockney, American, European, you name it.

There's the Taste of the Trossachs tea room; the Edinburgh Woollen Mill Shop; the Whisky Shop, of course; a Sweetie shop. A fairly comprehensive list, and one to tempt me on occasion, if I'm honest. Usually, however, I can't get out the place quickly enough, and batter right up the Leny Road (the A-84). This is a pleasant enough get-out, with the river sitting down on the left and lots of very eye-pleasing stone villas to admire as you go. I assume the town came to grow like a lot of others in the Victorian period when the railway arrived. For Callander, this would have been in 1858, when a station was opened; it was to be the terminus of a branch line from Dunblane.

To further add to the town's prominence, a second station was opened in 1870, half a mile to the west of the first, and this went all the way to Oban via Lochearnhead. So, no surprise to still find exquisite Victorian houses – all, without exception, in very good nick, I must say. The scenery will also be much to your liking, I guarantee, as now the 84 is being canopied by the trees as we head into the sheep fields between Callander and Kilmahog. The distant high ground is starting to close in, and it will arrive much sooner than expected.

It begins even before you have left the confines of the Kilmahog boundary, and you find the road becoming a lot more enclosed as it heads into a gorge that contains the Garbh Uisge (the Rough Water). It flows and sweeps

THE CREE RUN

over the rocks that inhabit its bed, which sits below on your left. The road is forced to twist and turn and rise and fall fairly sharply, as it negotiates the strip of land between the river and the intruding, high, wooded ground of Creag Bheithe, forcing itself in on the right. Rough Water is a most apt name for this typical Highland stream. It is at its roughest when it goes over the Falls of Leny, which you shortly pass, and the river is often referred to as the Leny Water.

a very classy-looking Highland ensemble. Loch Lubnaig is another of those slender, bending Highland lochs that provide such a thrilling roadside experience, very similar in looks and style to the great Loch Eck in Cowal.

The road here, it has to be said, is unfortunately just a little bit busier at times than the Eck road, but it is still a thrill to follow the line round the water's edge. It starts off with stone-walled curves, which is no bad thing, and for the length of the entire loch – about 3 miles – the road

Just approaching the start of Loch Lubnaig, and now is the time you switch over from Lowland to Highland. Here the scenery becomes much more mountainous and serious, and the high peaks and deep lochs will be your constant companions all the way round to Arden at the bottom of Loch Lomond.

The road only straightens and opens out when you begin the run up to the start of Loch Lubnaig, which introduces itself very serenely indeed. Here, the Garbh Uisge doesn't even come close to living up to its name, as it flows most gently out of the Lubnaig and begins its journey towards the Teith. Behind and above sits the rugged bulk of Ardnandave Hill, its craggy, fir-filled east face dropping directly down to the loch and making for

follows a pattern of flat straights, running in and out of slalom-type, bending stretches. Now, *lubnaig* actually means crooked in Gaelic, and that is exactly what this loch is, as it dog legs its way below and round Ardnandave, which gives a more dramatic view of its front face the further up the loch you get. Also, the distinctive bulky top of Meall Mor is seen early on, and you ride right below it as you near the top of the loch.

Looking across Loch Lubnaig to Ben Ledi from the A-84 (T), and it is a magnificent upping and downing, dipping and diving road to ride. It is just a pity it is so busy at times, which does take away a bit of the pleasure of riding this stretch, which I would otherwise rate as being as good as riding the Loch Eck road. The Lubnaig is similar in style to the Eck, and so, too, are the surrounding hills

So, we find ourselves in a very mountainous setting all of a sudden, and the low-lying Flanders Moss seems so much of a memory now that it might as well have been done on a different run on a different day. Right on the lochside you are, straightening out, then dipping and swooping between crash barriers, conifers, oaks, and birches, as the 84 keeps it interesting all the way along. It seems that as part of the Loch Lomond National Park set-up, they are putting in touristy-type facilities right on the loch. I must be honest and say that I am sorry they are, for it will take away the area's really wild feel.

On clearing the Lubnaig, the road straightens again as you make your way into Strathyre. Now strath comes from the Gaelic *srath*, meaning wide valley – usually with a river – and will indicate a broader and shallower valley than the narrower and steeper glen. And that is exactly what you are riding into now as you approach Strathyre Village itself. The road surface at this point becomes bloody awful as you teeth-chatteringly make your way forward. But salvation is close at hand, and colourfully at that, because the tarmac now turns red and becomes smooth as silk as you enter the confines of the village and find yourself back in the Victorian era again.

Strathyre, like many places, only came into being – or shall we say, grew significantly – with the arrival of the railway, in this case in 1870. For such a small place, there are quite a few facilities, most notably a toilet and café down on the left. There seems to be quite a lot going on on that side, though quite indiscernible at times. The right-hand side is a totally different kettle of fish, and is made up of buildings, some homes, hotels, B&Bs and the like, that have a distinctive Victorian flavour. They're all neatly lined up in a row, seemingly applauding your effort as you pedal by. You pick up a real lengthy, solid stone wall on the left, as you start to run out of the place and then find yourself back in the broad strath.

From time to time, you will either see signs for the cycle track or see the track itself, as it comes close to the road on the left-hand side. But unfortunately it isn't tarmacked the whole way, or I might possibly recommend it. This would be especially true when climbing up through Glen Ogle, and I will come back to the track when we reach there.

For the moment, we are making our way towards the Balquidder cut-off, going along long, tree-lined straights. And with about 50 odd miles on the clock, it gets to that point in any long run when you realise just what you've bitten off. This will depend a lot on how fit you are and numerous other factors, but the feeling normally hits you when you are nearing the halfway point. In this case, you still have about 10 miles and the major climb of the day to go before you get to that. So, dig in and steel yourself, for there's many more miles to come.

The Braes of Balquidder start to draw near, and down its broad strath you start to get a view on the left. This itself is a rugged wide valley, running west and lined with tough Corbetts either side. You will shortly pass under the east side of one of them, Meall an t-Seallaidh, sitting on the north side of that glen. The start of the climb for that hill begins next to a small churchyard in Balquidder, wherein lies Rob Roy McGregor. You can almost touch his grave as you pass.

Despite this all being on your left side, to access Balquidder you must turn right off the main road and double back under it to reach there. This takes place when you draw level with the former Kingshouse Hotel, now the Mhor 84, whose sprawling white base covers quite an area of ground.

Ahead, the road snakes away through the trees and shortly lifts you up into the former site of, and what is still known as, Balquidder Station. There are a handful of houses and a hotel here now, the Golden Larches, which sits across the road from the old station wall. This itself is a large affair, comprising of white brickwork, stairs, and a tunnel (now blocked off), to access different platforms. I finally got round to going up the stairs to take a look at what was there, fully expecting to see the remnants of some classic old station. And what did I find? The Braes of Balquidder Caravan Park! (No comment).

The station itself was originally known as Lochearnhead, before they changed its name to Balquidder in 1904, and gives you some idea of just how close you are to Lochearnhead itself. The rail line, for the record, was due to close on the 5th of November, 1965, courtesy of Mr Beeching, but in fact it closed six weeks early, courtesy of a landslide in Glen Ogle.

It's just over a mile or so to Lochearnhead, and is a great ride if you're going north. That's because you sweep down and enter the place at quite a speed. Even if you are only being assisted by a slight breeze, it can allow speeds of over 30 miles an hour fairly easily.

However, if heading south, it can be purgatory, because the road surface is so bumpy that heading uphill into a wind on this stretch is nothing short of murder. Lochearnhead and its surrounding area is a pleasant pitch, I do declare. The loch sits away to the right across long flat fields, where a view down its length is possible between passing the village sign and reaching the village centre. This is quite a considerable distance. Lochearnhead is almost strictly one-sided, with all the houses on the left and bare fields opposite.

Again, it was the coming of the railway that transformed the place from just a few cottages on the old military road – from Stirling to Fort William, and built in 1750[5] – to a much more vibrant community, with hotels, guesthouses, and the like. Keep your eye open for some great old relics from yesteryear, one of which stands outside the village store, which looks like a relic in its own right. I'm referring to an old, very old, tyre pressure gauge standing behind a sort of billboard[6] just outside the shop door. This grand old fellow was made by a company called Laycock, and despite rust getting the better of its main body, the gauge face is still in good nick.

Further up the road sits the ghost of a resplendent old workshop-type garage. It has five folding wooden doors to allow vehicles access, but now they are all redundant, with their paint peeling and windows smashed. Above the doors on the concrete fascia, the large painted word GARAGE is still visible. And despite its derelict state, it still oozes solid quality.

But back to the business side of things, because ahead lies the main event of the day in my book – the climb up

I love the look of this old disused garage. It lines the right-hand side of the road in Lochearnhead, just as you are about to leave the village and start the major climb of the day up through Glen Ogle.

through Glen Ogle. I absolutely love this climb, and this is the very reason I prefer to do the run in this direction. No matter which way you do the Cree, you will be faced with a very long, though none too steep climb at some point.

If going anticlock, it will be Glen Ogle; clockwise it will be the pull-up after the Drovers Inn at Inverarnan on Loch Lomondside. That one goes on for about 4 miles (though not sustained), whereas the Glen Ogle one goes for about 3 miles and is fairly sustained, though not overly steep. The Ogle itself is a really rugged beautiful place and this certainly adds to the feeling of enjoyment

---

5 - The military road not the railway that is.

6 - It advertises the local kirk would you believe.

Dig in and get ready to enjoy the outstandingly atmospheric climb up through great Glen Ogle on the A-85 (T). The beautiful old railway viaduct can be seen sitting high up on the left, and it helps to give this place the feel more of a Welsh slate-producing valley than a Scottish glen. The dampness never seems to be far away either, which helps add to the atmosphere. This climb alone is the reason I prefer to do the Cree run anticlockwise.

as you become part of it. The action starts immediately when you leave the village and make your way through what was another old rail bridge, now gone, that took its track eastwards along the north side of Loch Earn.

Sit down and get ready to make your way up through this sustained wilderness, where a good judgement of effort will be required; this will be no quick charge. That's not a problem, of course, because of the sheer situation, and you've just jumped onto the A-85 from the A-84, though you probably won't have noticed. It has a very dramatic look from the word go, or even before the word go, as the Ogle was actually showing, just a little anyway, on the approach to Lochearnhead. It is the real steep crags of Meall Buidhe sitting high above on the right that give the glen some real early impact, where the lower glen finds you making your way through the trees on long, rising straights that give it a little bit of a softer feel.

These long straights are occasionally broken by double bends that keep it all interesting, before more rising takes

A much closer look at the Glen Ogle viaduct, and she is a magnificent sight. The cycle track runs along it now and it looks so inviting to ride that I did it on one occasion. But to my dismay, I only found the top section to be tarmacked. This is a real pity, because the view you get of the Ogle from the viaduct is absolutely fantastic.

place on long, slightly kinking straights, which eventually brings you out onto the fern-clad hillside, as you steadily draw closer to the high crags. The glen itself opens up especially on your left-hand side now, and the wonderful old railway viaduct shows its splendid elegant flank – an elegant flank that now carries the modern cycle track. The Ogle at this point always reminds me of some wee Welsh mountainside, what with its dampness and its slabs and rocks. Talking of which, just down from the main viaduct, there is a single bridge on the old rail line, and very pleasing it is to the eye, too,. Below it, on the hillside, can be seen a very large boulder field.

Now I read somewhere that you can still see the remnants of the 1965 landslide which closed the railway six weeks prematurely. I don't know for certain if this is the site of the landslide, but if it is, it's no wonder the rail closed when you see the size of the boulders. To your right at this point is a small burn coming off the hillside, sort of in-line with the solo railway bridge, and this can be used to fill the water bottles if you so wish. Despite being wild water, it is perfectly safe to drink and I have used it on many occasions. So now refuelled if needed, we continue our way up, feeling good and moving well into the wilder top half of the glen.

The cycle track that follows the rail track on the left looks very inviting from here. So much so that I eventually got round to using it on one occasion, on the descent of the Ogle, I might add. The road and the track come together at the top of the glen, where at first I thought the track looked totally tarmacked, so that is the reason I took it. Not so, I'm afraid. If it were, I would certainly recommend it for descending Glen Ogle at least, as it holds its height much longer than the road does and therefore affords great views of Loch Earn on the way down.

As it's not totally tarmacked, it's better to stick to the road. But that is not a problem. When you reach the top of the glen, it is a wonderful finish the way everything draws together, both sides narrowing dramatically as you reach the end.

Before you do, you are treated to the steep, untamed sides on both sides. Tree-clad, boulder-clad and crag-ridden, for the most part. The arches on the stone viaduct provide the icing on the cake to this wonderful wilderness, and not for the first time I take my hat off to the men who toiled hard to put it all in place. The drawing close of the rail line allows you to admire more of the railway workings, which were also impressively built. The road straightens and lies back on the final approach to the summit, which gives you extra time with easier effort to enjoy it all the more.

And so finally, we reach the top of Glen Ogle, where once there was a station named Glenoglehead, would you believe? It was originally named Killin when the railway opened in 1870, but the name got changed in 1886 – on the 1st of April, to be exact. Its lifespan was very short, because it closed exactly three years later, to the day. The stationmaster's house is now a private residence, and old sleepers still lie around in the vicinity. At this point, on the right you pass a car park that is sign posted Glen Ogle, and the reason I mention it is because on certain days it has a snack bar which can come in handy on occasion (or at least it did).

Going under one of the great-looking bridges that sits at the top end of the Glen Ogle cycle track above the viaduct stretch. Unfortunately, only this part is tarmacked, and to gain access to it from the bottom half of the glen is very steep and awkward, which would rule it out for young children.

This is the beginning of the descent of Glen Ogle when doing the Cree run clockwise. Although I normally do it anti, on occasion I will go this way – and what a sensational sweep down the old Ogle is. Ahead in the distance, the mountain you can see is Ben Vorlich.

The glen is finished off quite fittingly with a series of crash barrier bends, all very in keeping with the surrounds. And although I love to ascend the Ogle, the descent is just as rewarding, especially the way those two big Munros, Ben Vorlich and Stuc a Chroin, come into view to entertain on your sweeping speedy swoop. Talking of speedy swoops, another lies in store at the top of the Ogle to take you further north then west, down into Glen Dochart. This drop comes as quite a surprise, as you won't have realised at first just how much height you've gained till you are actually firing on down. Unlike the other side of the Ogle, despite being a great descent, it has to be said this is done on a more modern, charmless road, down through fairly heavily forested terrain.

On this side of the hill it will be the Lawers group which provides the mountain drama, and in particular the most westward lying of them –Meall nan Tarmachan. This

It's only when you flip over to the other side, after rising to the head of Glen Ogle, that you realise just how much height you've gained, as there then follows a monumental fall down into Glen Dochart which ends when you arrive in Lix Toll. On this descent, it is the hills belonging to the Lawers group that will steal the show and dominate the skyline.

is a most striking fellow with his famous Tarmachan Ridge, one of the best walks in the whole of the Southern Highlands. The road falls broad and fast here, through high conifer trees and by a long left-hand bend. When it emerges from the trees, the view along Glen Dochart lets you know what is to come. The early view of Ben More and Stobinian, both lying on the south side of the glen, totally dominate the scene ahead. This is hardly surprising, as the pair make a most striking silhouette with their twin jagged peaks and elegant dipping ridge between them.

The drop is not over yet, though, as down you go again, this time through another lunar landscape of cut-down conifers, till you reach the Killin cut-off at Lix Toll. This contains what appears to be no more than a large white house and an even larger filling station/garage. This garage includes a Land Rover sales section, and does have a real masculine feel to it. There are some who claim that the name Lix comes from some lost Roman legion, the 59th they say, as LIX is Roman numerals for 59. The legion apparently went missing, never to be seen or heard of again, after pushing their way into the high ground.

Now, there was a Roman camp based down in Callander, so of course it is perfectly possible that they came this way. But the story goes that the legion was 40,000 strong, so that is a helluva lot of men for the mighty Roman army to lose.

The toll part of the name dates from much later. But our immediate concern is that we are now 11 miles from Crianlarich, which sits due west of our present position. There is just one final rather dramatic section of fir trees to clear before we emerge into the broad expanse of the Glen Dochart valley floor. It is much more a strath than a glen, the Dochart, being very wide, especially here at its eastern end.

Throughout its length, it will remain almost constantly flat and therefore fairly fast – or it would be if the road surface was not so rotten in a lot of places. But mark my words here: there has actually been a lot of good resurfacing work done, especially at the Lix Toll side of the glen, which makes our job a helluva lot easier from time to time. On the right-hand side of the glen sits the Mamlorn range of hills, and although less obvious than Ben More and Stobinian, there is the rather striking Sgiath Chuil in among them, showing off its craggy summit on the descent into the glen from the Ogle.

So, off westward we make a start, and with that we have the knowledge that we are more than halfway through the run. This is always a good psychological boost, though I personally don't feel I've turned for home till I've left Crianlarich. Also, I have found that depending on wind direction, you can get a tail wind to follow you all the way along the Dochart as you head west, even if you were wind-assisted on the road up from Glasgow as you headed northeast. I assume that this is all to do with the way the wind negotiates its way round the mountains and through the valleys, but whatever the reason, it makes for a very welcome companion for the first 70-odd miles of the run.

There is a much of a muchness about the Dochart nowadays, due to the way that the old road was replaced by a newer, straighter version. You tend to find this takes out a lot of the bends, dips, and curves, along with the

On heading west along Glen Dochart, it will be Stob Binnein and big Ben More that will stand out boldly and pull you along. Admittedly, a lot of the road in this glen has seen a modern upgrade and so isn't the charmer of old, but it gets you along to Crianlarich quick and slick.

old quaint charm, but has certainly left a faster, straighter road. It suits the modern automobile, but not so us guys. With a lot of the old gone, we're left with a charmless, monotonous stretch of tarmac that simply has to be ridden to get us to where we want to go.

This, unfortunately, is the case I feel with the Dochart now, but only with regard to the road, and I say that with some authority. That's because this road was the one I had my heart set on driving when I was learning to drive back in the mid-eighties, and true to my word, the first thing I did when I passed my test and bought a van was to come up and drive Glen Dochart. I truly enjoyed all the thrills and spills as I cut through its precarious bends and the like.

They have all gone for the most part now, and you'll find yourself on a straighter, more sanitised road nowadays, though the ruggedness of the glen and its great mountain scenery thankfully haven't changed. Due to the roughness and the wilder high peaks surrounding you, you will still find enjoyment as you travel the valley floor. And as for any suffering at this point? Think Geraint Thomas (read: soldier on regardless).

The mighty Ben More, the highest hill in the whole of the Southern Highlands, will keep your gaze focused early on, before it becomes obscured by a lower-lying ridge. It's still an imposing bulk of a mountain you'll find, as you make your way past isolated farms and hotels on the A-85. The River Dochart, sitting in the valley floor to your right, is unseen in amongst the very rough reeds and meadows that conceal it. Some cultivation goes on in there, but for the most part the farms here are hill/sheep farms, as that's about all this rough glen can support. That suits us, of course, as it gives a great spectacle to our fast-moving eyes. And with the whole setting being so far from urbanisation, it also gives a feeling of space, freedom, and achievement.

You do truly appreciate just how far you've come as you traverse the Dochart's lengthy line. This distance from home is usually reached only by car by the majority of people. However, it's well within the range of us endurance boys and girls, and it's nice to know it and to soak up the reward as you go along. Along, that is, a fast, low, tree-lined, flowing, enclosed road sometimes; other times, much more open.

You're soon passing the isolated Luib Hotel, standing qhite alone, with its flags fluttering bright. These flags are useful in confirming wind direction, as always, and it was with their aid I became aware of how the wind can swirl so much in the glens. Just after you pass the entry to Auchessan Farm (the start for the Mamlorn Hills), you hit one of the few remaining parts of the old road.

You find yourself down beside lovely Loch Luibhair, but as pretty as the setting is, the state of the road totally takes away any pleasure. It soon returns to its modern equivalent, however, as you rather bumpily trundle on towards the vicinity of Ben More Farm. Across the Luibhair, the steep line of crags above the water that constitute Creag Liaragan makes for grand drama. So, too, does the long, brutal northwest ridge of Ben More that sits directly above its namesake farmstead, and is often the way that people will ascend this hill. If you ever

Just before Crianlarich is reached, you hit an old stretch of road whose surface is so rotten that you wish you hadn't, but through the trees you get a fantastic view of Creag Liaragan across Loch Lubhair. This will give you some idea of what the road was like in the old days.

The centre of Crianlarich is dominated by the railway bridge that carries the famous West Highland line, and the place is great because it always feels that something is happening or is about to change. In our case, it's our direction. We are about to turn left under the bridge and start to make our way home down the A-82.

do get round to trying it from this end, don't forget that the gradient doesn't relent till you reach the summit cairn.

You will soon start to pick up one or two houses as the run-in to Crianlarich begins, and with it, Loch Dochart also. This is another pretty, small water that has a most pleasant feel to it, as does the whole ride along from Lix Toll, especially if wind-assisted. Behind Loch Dochart, smaller hills lie close by, their appearance aided by their wooded coat and giving a miniature Highland welcome to a most strategically placed village. That village being Crianlarich, of course, as by now we find ourselves at long last inside the welcome sign, and perhaps heading for the local village store for a coffee.

This lady is indeed strategic, because Crianlarich has signposts pointing to it from more than 40 miles away, and I read somewhere that it has more signs pointing

THE CREE RUN

Crianlarich station at the top of the Loch Lomond road. I've got 70 miles on the clock at this point, and I know there is exactly another 52 to go. The old Morris Minor car in the photo belonged to a Swiss tourist who had stopped for a break, which included him enjoying a malt whisky. You can actually see the bottle sitting on top of the wall. The old car makes the photo look like one from yesteryear.

This is the view you get of Ben More at the start of Glen Dochart when leaving Crianlarich heading east, going clockwise on the Cree run. I've never climbed the mountain from this side, but that big ridge looks brutal.

to it than anywhere else in the country. I don't know if that's true or not, but it has been a major crossroads since medieval times and actually means the withered site in Gaelic. No doubt many of the old drovers came this way when taking their cattle to the southern markets.

In the 1700s, two military roads met here. In the 1800s, the railways came, with two main lines joining together here. In the 1900s, it was the turn of the A-roads, the 82 and 85. I'm talking major junction here, and picturesque charm with it. The show-stealer just has to be that magnificent rail bridge that holds high and elegant court, right in the village centre.

Thankfully, that British Rail bogeyman Richard Beeching didn't get his grubby paws on our West Highland line and all its trimmings, or we would be a lot worse off.

If you fancy it, there is a great wee cafe to be found on the platform of Crianlarich station, although the local store does have a good coffee and tea machine as well. Of course, if you are totally canned at this point, it is possible to jump on the train here and let Scotrail carry you all the way back to Queen Street. However, trains on the West Highland line are so few and far between that it might actually be quicker to ride home.

Especially here, where the white painted iron work sits atop beautiful, tall stone columns, and gives the village focus and purpose. It appears that the bulk of the village, what there is of it, sits on this side of the bridge and you ride past most of it to get to the store. The last census recorded a population of only 185, so the police station is small, the fire station is small, and there's a small row of cottages on the left – all in keeping with the location.

Follow signs for the famous station to access the shop, if you need it. You'll find it well stocked, if you do. There's a table-type bench outside to sit at and enjoy a snack before needs must and you remount the old steed. The station platform has a café as well, though it's closed on Sundays, unfortunately.

It's time to turn for home now, and that means 50 miles exactly for your old mate Liam here. So, after turning left under the rail bridge, you immediately pass the war memorial, whose wee Tommy Atkins figure, resplendent in tin hat, does the fallen lads proud. The toilet block comes next on your left, just before passing under the second rail bridge which takes trains west to Oban; the first goes north to Fort William.

It's a great wee snaking climb from the bridge up past the rail station, which just happens to be a most striking fellow, in a most striking location. I think that is because of the way the mighty Cruach Ardrain towers right above it and makes the station look like a model railway, instead of the real thing. This one has old charm in abundance, dating back to 1937, when the platform buildings you see now replaced the originals destroyed by a fire in that year. Even if it's not all Victorian, it's still old and quaint – from the green waiting room, to the brick engine shed with its black and yellow diagonal striped doors, to the railway sidings.

There is a feeling that something is always just about to happen here, even when no train is due for ages. This was one of two stations that inhabited the village at one time, when it was known as Upper Crianlarich. It became simply Crianlarich when the other station closed, thanks to the Beeching boy. Getting the station built in the first place took quite an effort and a compulsory purchase order, as the wealthy Place family who lived in Glen Dochart House refused to sell the land for the building to begin. This was despite the inducement of sweeteners, most notably the promise of all the proceeds from the two station cafes indefinitely. But they felt it would spoil their hunting estate. The station finally opened in 1894, and the Places took the hump and returned to their other stronghold in Yorkshire.

The road leads out now onto the wonderful plateau that is upper Glen Falloch, which is an awesome big bowl in its own right. Yes, the long lowering ridge of Craig Knowe runs ahead and cuts in on the right, with the splendidly isolated Keilator Farm sitting below it, but it is the big bad boys on the left that really make this glen what it is. Quite a line-up is to be found among the crags up there. The already mentioned Cruach Ardrain, with its great Grey Height; An Caisteal, and its equally great Twistin Ridge; with tough wee Beinn a' Choin hiding up the back. The road swings round in a long curving arch,

After leaving Crianlarich and heading south, you will be carried by the A-82 into the broad Glen Falloch. The views are still mountainous and good, and soon there follows a massive fall down to Inverarnan at the head of Loch Lomond.

and away south in the distance the high peaks of lower Loch Lomond will also start to appear.

It's all very wild, mountainous, and exciting, I must say. At the end of the long straight, the beginning of the 4 miles or so of descent to Inverarnan will begin, though only fairly gently at first. The road here is no double bending specimen from yesteryear, but a modern bulldozed brute, the making of which has left its scars on the rock faces that line it. This version has been in existence since the time I started driving, and so I know no other. On the way down, however, there are from time to time glimpses of the old road in places, but it's one I never experienced. The modern version falls fairly gradually for quite a time, snaking ahead purposefully.

It is quite an exhilarating descent even in the early stages, despite there not being any serious gradient to go down. The overall surroundings help with that, of course, before the main fall begins, which comes in two stages. Hold onto your hats here, for these are a couple of banshee jobs – but only in speed and length, for they are nothing technical. After flying down the first one, level out a bit and then plummet down the second, with the impressive bulk of Troisgeach sitting dead ahead conducting the orchestra as the violins start to play. That is just an indication of the high you're in as you come off this hill straight into the woodlands and old road at Inverarnan.

For approximately the next 10 miles or so, you will be riding what is left of the old Loch Lomond road, and that is something to savour, for us at least. The old girl suits us better than some motor vehicles, certainly the big stuff. I know there are a lot of lorry drivers who refuse to go up it, and I can't say I blame them. The deciduous trees here are wonderful and what a splendid welcome they give, as does the look of the old Drovers Inn just ahead. Since 1705, it has stood here, and must have been a welcome site to those old hardy cattle men. The outside has a weary look to it when seen across the top of the rough meadows as you approach; I wonder if it has actually changed all that much over the centuries.

Ghost stories abound about the place, and despite what some people say about staying overnight in the inn, it is a great place to spend an evening. On passing it, you leave Stirling District and enter Argyll and Bute. Then it's round the first of countless curves in this stretch of road, which is one I'm always glad to see the back of when driving, but not when riding. Over more rough reed and fern-filled meadows can be seen the hill tops and ridges that sit above Loch Lomond's east bank, and also in the meadows are some very old remnants of shielings. Flat and flighty follows next, through the trees, along straights and over bridges, till one comes to the place where you would rendezvous with Hugh (*meet me in Ardlui, Shooey*). There's not much to the place, but I like Ardlui.

The Drovers Inn at Inverarnan is an iconic and authentic bit of Highland history, which is met as the winding section of the Loch Lomond road begins from here down to Tarbet. The next 10 miles or so of road is scenically stunning, and is much more enjoyable to ride than to drive, I always think.

The hotel is the mainstay of the hamlet – a good-looking building, with full leaf-clad walls, it has a wee shop attached to it, where a cone can be purchased on a really hot day. I don't eat ice cream *per se*, but a lot of the pros like to, as it keeps them sane, giving them a break from all that starvation and dieting. I don't usually equate Ardlui with sunshine, though, more with dampness and wet. This place just oozes aquatic, what with its position right beside the loch and the way it sits below the magnificent Ben Vorlich (one of my favourite hills), with its tumbling burns.

Big rhododendrons line the road here, and the red phone box and red rail station signs add a splash of colour to the green drab damp. Just under the rail bridge along the road is the best place to start for Ben Vorlich, in my experience, and I still have fond memories of my first ascent of that hill, in the spring of 1989. I always think of that as I ride past the station on the world-famous West Highland line, which quite rightly is regarded as up there with the best train journeys on the entire planet. After this, a slight rise brings you out onto a rare section of newer road, which was only possible to construct here because there was a bit of room to build on.

and come to a traffic light. Vehicles are only allowed round this rocky bend in one direction at a time here. Now, this has been going on since I started driving back in '86, and the first time I came to these lights I thought they were just temporary. Not so. They have been there regulating traffic ever since.

Having said that, at long last there appears to be a major bit of civil engineering work going on now, where they seem to be filling in the loch to allow more width in the road and once again make it two-way. Cyclists could press a button on the old set-up to get the lights to change in their favour. This place is known as Pulpit Rock, named after the big boulder you pass on the right just before reaching the lights. It is an enormous, curved, big block of pale stone, with a chiselled-out section in the middle, purposely done to allow a preacher to do his business from it. This spot was used for summer services for 75 years from the 1820s, and hence the name Pulpit Rock.

It is only recently that you have been able to see it from the road, as it was previously hidden from view by some trees that have now been felled. I only discovered it by accident a few years back, when I went into the woods to answer a call of nature and spotted it then. I must say I was most impressed when I saw it, and realised it must have served some purpose; I thought it looked like an altar at the time.

Once round the Pulpit, enjoy what comes after, as you sweep the shore and small fields that border the mighty one. The freshness of it all is almost tangible at this place. The far bank, so steep, is close enough here for you to truly appreciate its detail and ruggedness (it's the long craggy ridge running off Stob nan Eighrach), and brings home the sheer scale of the Lomond.

Passing the Pulpit Rock just south of Ardlui, which can now be seen clearly from the road; at one time it was hidden behind some woodland. I only discovered it by chance when I just happened to stop there one time when doing the Crianlarich run. The road at Pulpit Rock has for more than 20 years had a traffic light in place which is only now being replaced by a modern upgrade. It looks like it will be good, but it isn't finished as yet.

Just about all the road from Inverarnan down to Tarbet is tightly sandwiched between the loch on one side and high ground on the other. This is what has kept the old road in place for so long. There is quite simply no room to manoeuvre with regards to an upgrade. This point is borne out only too well when you round the next bend

THE CREE RUN

A view down the loch from the A-82 above Tarbet, and all the way down, the mighty loch looks so dramatic and sheer as its steep far bank seems close enough to touch at times. Beautiful bluebell woodlands, stone walls, and scenic swerves make the Drovers Inn to Tarbet stretch a real ride to savour.

The next point of interest will be the Sloy Dam power station. This is reached after going round a great series of walled bends, guiding you up and round high above the loch's bays. Just before you reach it, there is a great toilet and café in the car park by the loch, where the cruise boats like to come in and dock. Now, the power station itself is a big, square, brown block of a building, with four massive pipes running up the hillside behind it. A staircase beside the pipes can actually be used to access the high ridge of Ben Vorlich (another great way up). Despite its size and shape, I don't find it an eyesore, as it has been here since 1950 and now just seems part of the furniture.

It does seem to have an elder statesman-type right-to-be-here look about it. I think so, anyway. It gave the village of Arrochar their first electric lighting in 1950.

The dam itself is found up Glen Inveruglas – the old homeland of the Clan McFarlane – and sits beautifully between Ben Vane and Ben Vorlich. It is one helluva spot, I do declare. You can ride up to the dam on a great wee road, if you fancy it. Work actually started on the Sloy Dam project in 1945 and famously used some German POWs in the construction process. This seemed to benefit all involved, and the Jerries were allowed access to the local villages and the like. After the war, some kept in touch with their former British workmates; many actually feared going home to the Russian sector. Their fears where well grounded, for they wrote back saying things were grim there and that they had nought. Things went well with normal German prisoners, but when they tried to get some Waffen SS men to work on the site, they mostly refused and were sent back to their prison camps (*Sieg Heil*).

So, with some serious national socialist ardour in our bellies now, we soldier on round the crash barrier-lined, water-edged curves that take us towards Tarbet. It is soft and beautiful deciduous woodland that slopes gently up and away from the water side here'; in May, the bluebells provide a stunning carpet of colour on both sides of the loch, I might add. So vast and intense is the blueness, that it can easily be seen on the far bank, almost a mile's width at this point.

The Loch Lomond Cruises fleet is seen sitting quietly berthed as Tarbet is entered, and now the more modern, brutal, big bruiser that is the A-82 from Tarbet to Arden, must be ridden.

The road surface here was once notoriously bad, and therefore spoiled the setting, but not any more. Major works at night over the last two or three years, resulting in road closures between 10pm and 6am, have meant that now it is a pleasure to curve the crash barrier and sensuously squeeze between bay and bluebell, all the way into Tarbet. As you make your final roll in, the small flotilla of Loch Lomond Cruise boats sits in the bay, under the shapely pyramid hill of Ben Reoch.

In you go, shortly arriving at the main junction beside the sprawling grey flank of the Tarbet Hotel. When you turn left, it means you're back on the modern stuff. Traffic volume will pick up noticeably a lot of the time, even before you have cleared the rise out of the village, which isn't far, of course.

Not too far to the clearway signs, though, where again sanctuary can be found in the unofficial cycle lane just outside the white line. And once again we settle in for the long haul back down the lochside, on the fast but fairly charmless modern bulldozed babe. Just think long time trial mode. That is what the lower Loch Lomond road is for us now.

It's a good time to get an energy gel down your throat, which I personally find is much more advantageous than an energy bar. I say that because I can feel a real kick kicking in, about ten minutes after I've gubbed one, so thoroughly recommend them.

As for road choice, there is only one option to take and that is the A-82, which understandably had to be upgraded for the modern volume of traffic. The older, more meandering version would have stayed closer to the loch and been prettier for us to ride, but alas it was put to the sword by so-called progress. Just make the most of the new stuff; it's all you can do. Fortunately, the overall scenery hasn't changed, and is particularly appreciated early on when you gain some height, and there are great views down the loch when the summer foliage allows.

A continuous long avenue of trees is followed on the long, slender, grey snake that will bring you to a very pronounced right-hand bend, whose curve signals the start of the drop down to the lochside again, just before the Inverbeg Inn. The gouged rock here, cut away to make the road, is hardly natural but it does have a certain dramatic look to it, with its steepness and all. It flings you downward, broad and open, and allows you a springboard of a start for the remaining lengthy flat that lies ahead.

As we pass the start of Glen Douglas, there is as near as dammit 30 miles to go for me, which means we've already covered about 92.

It isn't a hard run home, which is just as well, for the old Cree is a lot of miles. But with plenty of training miles under your belt beforehand, it is well doable.

We've been on this stretch a couple of times already, so you know what to expect, and just keep those old cranks turning and you'll get there. The good news is that the going between Inverbeg and Luss (just over 3 miles), will be almost dead flat and therefore real fast. This is a good psychological boost this late in the day, as the old energy gel kicks in and gives you another real good lift. I like the Torq gels, which are easy to swallow and taste good, so I always carry a couple on all my long hauls.

I also carry their energy bars, or other brands of purpose-made energy bars on really long runs, but I don't find them as effective as the gels. Anyway, no matter what your preferred poison is to keep you going, one thing to boost all spirits on the way down to Luss will be the views across the mightiest water in the land. You will get them here, and be in awe of them. It lets you know you're tiny.

After passing the entrance to Luss, be ready for some respite as you dip long and gradual down over the Luss Water, then climb long and gradual back up. No great hardship this, as your cadence and momentum won't be disrupted to any great extent. The new girl is a forgiving miss. She will now lead you on, through her curvaceous lower bends, and take you past Luss's second entrance, keeping you blind from all around by her thick belt.

Underneath the cut-away rock face by the side of the road, you'll now find that some beautiful plants and shrubs have colonised it, free gratis to the local council. These colourful plants are a most welcome addition to any roadside, and again just go to show how nature will creep back and overtake all of man's mis-shapings. Talking of which, the next one is the left-hand bend that brings you to the top of the long stretch leading down to Arden, which also means welcome back to the lowlands. This is characterised by the fertile fields you soon find yourself in, and a lush softness surrounds you. Oh, the nice, oh the lovely. Yes, behind now lies the Highland fault line and all its harshness.

Now we're into the last quarter of the run, and sense the change around us. The approach to the Arden roundabout is a long flat, then slightly rising batter, where a multitude of small stones seem to clutter the

THE CREE RUN

The A-82 Loch Lomond near the new Carrick Golf Club, and the evening sun has come out to welcome our return into the Lowlands. The Highland scenery is now behind us, and we will soon enter the urban sprawl of the Vale of Leven.

road, especially our space by the side. These wee buggers disappear when we pass Arden House and make our way towards the Duck Bay Marina. The last look at the loch on the left is a most fitting one, for it looks its largest and most awesome at this point. The trees have closed in on the right, and we have left the fields on that side behind as well, as we take to the pavement right at the entrance to the Duck Bay.

Then we make our way onto the Old Luss road and therefore gain the cycle track. Ssssh, or you'll wake the baby! For it's all gone quiet again. Quiet, peaceful, and pleasant, that's the Old Luss girl for you. And what a welcome respite from all that bloody traffic she is. Here, for all the young team, is a blast from the past. Though not the only one, I might add. Had you been eagle-eyed, you would have noticed the old road bridge and old road layby, as you came down past the new Carrick golf course a mile or two back. This stretch is quite sustained, though, and is a fast downhill with it.

You fly and flow between the walls on the way into Balloch. Stone walls that are tree-lined and field-lined and make for a fond farewell to the greenery, till the next time. Those well-to-do looking homes that sit at the end of the road mean it's welcome to Balloch, as do the couple of roundabouts that you must negotiate shortly after. No sooner are you in Balloch than you're back out of it, and the second roundabout means hello Alexandria. This again is familiar territory to us, and we purr past the old Argyll Motor Co façade, resplendent with its sort of pineapple finish on top, and turn left at the ornate fountain ahead.

This is equally resplendent, with its sunbathing Cormorant on top, and should perhaps be given some sort of national heritage status, as it's refused to work for so long. Talking of which, another structure that could also qualify for some sort of distinction is our old mate the Bonhill Bridge.

A sunburst evening view of the River Clyde from the Erskine Bridge, as once more the river is crossed back to its south bank. Soon, I'm on the home straight, which is always welcome, but more so on this run as it's the longest one in the book.

Now, I could have been in the wrong all along here, because not long ago I just happened to have a gentleman from The Renton in my cab. He informed me that the Bonhill Bridge is known locally as the "Rainbow Bridge", and was quite a pleasant site when first painted. He was quite a first-class individual, I must say, and so I'm prepared to take his word for it. I've been highly critical of its appearance in previous runs, but perhaps I was well wide of the mark this time (nothing new).

Turning left at the fountain brings us down and over the bridge, where the tough wee pull-up takes us under Bonhill greyness and through the bonnie Vale of Leven Industrial Estate.

Now, when I hit the A-82 again at Dumbarton, I will take the quickest way home on the Cree run, and that means battering right along the big girl herself. No messing around here, as it's a long enough run even by the shortest course. So regardless of danger, I make my way, as fast as I can, towards the Dumbuck Quarry, risking life and limb – without any insurance cover whatsoever, I might add. Once through the Dumbuck lights, it's only a mile or so left of the madness till the big Dunglass roundabout is reached, and it's Bowling here we come. Don't forget that the BP filling station you pass on the way has a good store and a cludgy, if you require it.

Bonnie Bowling looks even better when you've just escaped the hustle and bustle of the A-82 in one piece. Pretty as a picture, and all the more so when the big Erskine Bridge comes into view for the first time in about six hours. It's the last major hurdle between me and home, and must be taken, of course. Ride past the old tenements and under the long-gone railway, before the snaking slant uphill into the top of Old Kilpatrick means you're drawing close. Dive into the village and admire the old blue clockface on the church tower, as always, then begin the wee churn up and under the bridge, which starts on Station Road.

If it's late in the day, you may well be treated to a most magnificent view westwards as the sun shimmers on the water and sandbars of the lower Clyde. So, it is a good idea to ride the downstream/right-hand side cycle lane on the way back over, as it will give you a much better view of the sunset. It's just a case of dig in and get in rhythm for this pull-up, which is felt a bit in the knees at times, being so late in the day on such a long day. The view does keep your spirits up, as does the knowledge of the welcome descent on the other side. It's always done in screaming down, recovery mode.

Once you extract yourself from the bridge, which is always a bit higgeldy-piggeldy when coming down the steep, twisting access ramps, freewheel gently down the A-726 into Erskine. They've found a bit of space to build some new buildings at the Bargarren roundabout, would you believe? Where there's a will, as they say!

We are soldiering on and getting in the mode for the gentle, but long pull-up towards the Southolm roundabout, which then allows a nice easy glide down towards the Red Smiddy. The Barnsford Road at the back of the airport, being long and flat, can be used as a bit of a wind-down road, especially if the old wind sock shows the blow to be in your favour.

It's nice when it is, of course, and only a little bit of effort is required – usually out of the saddle – to lift one up to St James's interchange. And then back into the streets of the old home town we go. The Carlton Die Cast building and all the industrial stuff that you meet early on down the bottom of Greenhill Road is hardly going to win us any awards in a prettiest village competition, but as we're too big for that anyway, what the hell. There's not much left of our industrial past as it is; not that I'm really complaining, I never fancied working in a factory anyway.

So, in no time we're up through Maxwellton, where I must make my way, and my climbing doesn't stop till I'm well past the Royal Alexandra Hospital (RAH) on Corsebar Road, then shortly home.

Another view of Dumbarton Rock, the Clyde, and Mar Hall golf course from the Erskine Bridge in the late evening sunshine. Expect a few places to hurt when doing the Cree run, as it's so bloody long. The old front door will be well looked forward to, let me assure you.

Phew!! That was the Cree run for you and, boy, am I glad when it's over. Thanks for coming with me once more; we'll have a few days' recovery before we venture out again. See you then…

THE CRIANLARICH RUN

> **102 MILES**
> **6.11 HOURS**
> **ASCENT 2600 FEET**
> **CALORIES BURNED 4050**
> **O'S MAPS 64, 63, 56, 50.**

Now, I mentioned earlier in the book that a lot of the runs I cover will be long ones, and also the main skeleton of any given area. Therefore, numerous other smaller runs will be contained within the ones covered. For the most part, I have left you to your own devices to come up with your own permutations, suiting yourself in length and difficulty when choosing a shorter run.

In this case, however, I will mention the Crianlarich run, which is completely contained within the Cree, and is a great outing in its own right. It comes in at just over the hundred mark for me, and I rate it very highly. I specifically mention it because of the joy and pleasure to be had when riding the top half of Loch Lomond, either when the bluebells are out in May or the leaves are turning in Autumn.

After a short coffee break in the Crianlarich Station Café – if it's open; or at the local store if it's not – then you can return joyfully down the lochside for a great day's riding. You'll find yourself on a classic within a classic, promise.

Liam Boy

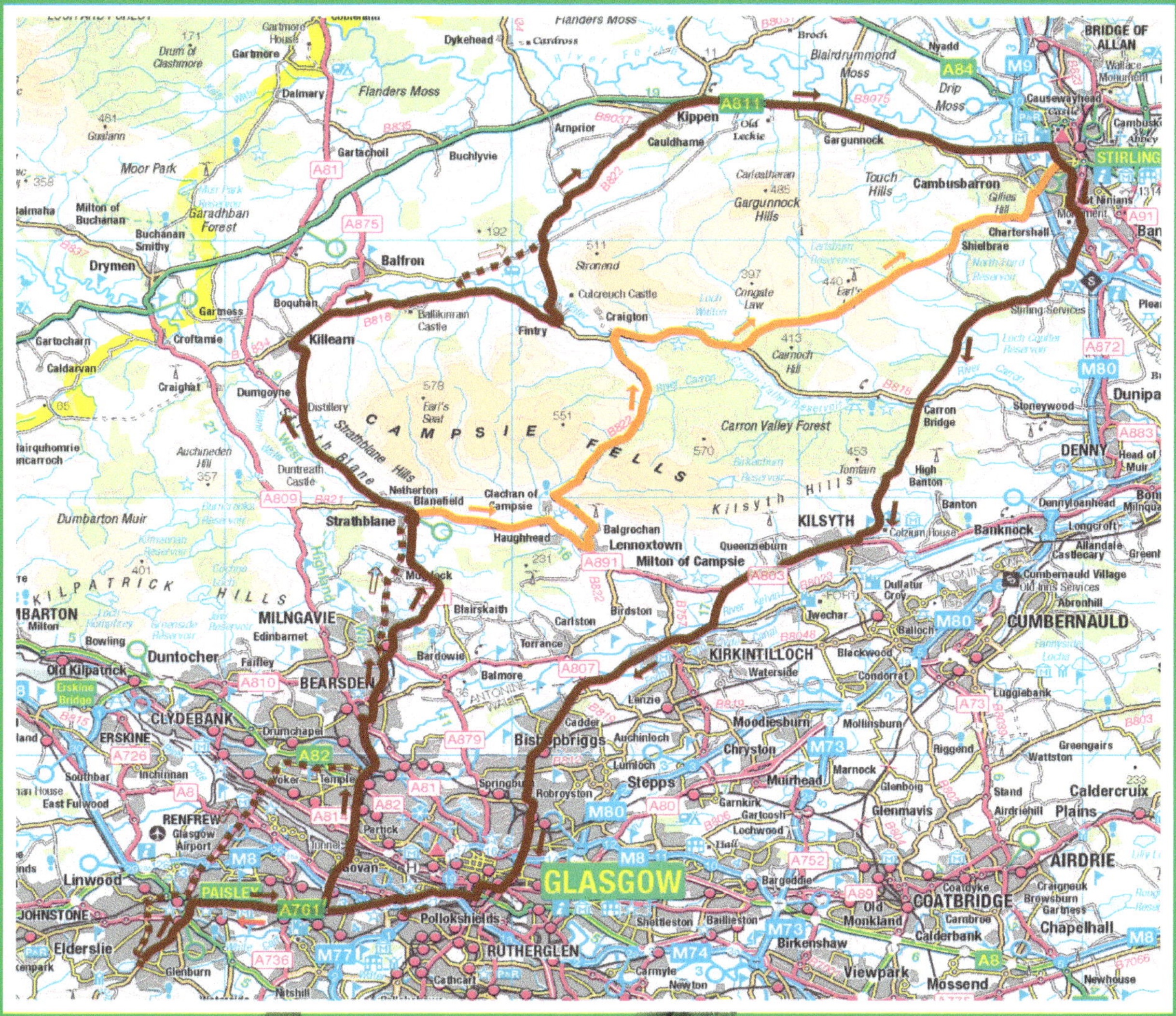

STIRLING CASTLE RUN

VIA KIPPEN
81.6 MILES
5.47 HOURS
ASCENT 3620 FEET
3209 CALORIES BURNED

VIA CARRON VALLEY
75 MILES
5.36 HOURS
ASCENT 4660 FEET
3669 CALORIES BURNED

OS Landrangers 64, 57

ROUTE SUMMARY

OUTWARD ROUTE

Renfrew
Shieldhall Rd
Clyde Tunnel
Crow Rd
Anniesland Cross
Milngavie

Mugdock Or A-81
Strathblane
Killearn
Fintry
Kippen
A-811
Stirling Castle

RETURN ROUTE

Stirling Town
Bannockburn Centre
Carron Bridge
Tak Ma Doon Road
Kilsyth
Kirkintilloch
Bishopbriggs
High St (Glasgow)
Albert Bridge
Paisley Road West
Paisley

ALTERNATIVE START

Renfrew Ferry
Yoker's Kelso St
Knightswood's
Alderman Rd & Anniesland Rd
Anniesland Cross

ALTERNATIVE ROUTE

Lennoxtown
Crow Rd B-822
B-818
Carron Valley Reservoir (North West Edge)
Minor Rd (Running North East)
Stirling Castle

STIRLING CASTLE

SCOTLAND'S HISTORIC HEART

Now, I think in the intro I mentioned that on one occasion I cycled through to Edinburgh and they refused me access to the castle with my bike – rather haughtily, I might add. As luck would have it, about a month after that, I was looking at the old O'S map and spotted what looked like a great wild run over the high ground to Stirling, and so I thought I'd give it a try. I visited the castle there, and the reception I got could not have been more different. They took the bike off me, put it somewhere safe, and said, "Just let us know when you're leaving, mate." The people in Stirling are very similar to the people in Glasgow. No standoffishness here, it's "Hello rerr." Add to that the history, the setting, and the scenery, and it's no wonder I like Stirling.

On this outing, we are going into some great scenery and wildness right on good old Glasgow's doorstep, as we make our way round the back of the Campsie Fells and get in and about the Fintry hills. Through these, I will suggest a couple of different options to get us to Stirling. One will be by the B-822 from Fintry over to Kippen, before joining the A-811 and going in via that way. The second will be by Crow Road from Lennoxtown, and then taking the minor road from the start of Carron Valley Reservoir to Stirling by that way. To make it an all-out round trip, the return will be via Kilsyth on the famous Tak Ma Doon Road. This gives a great day out and a run coming in about the 70 to 80-mile mark, which isn't overly long for an experienced endurance rider.

It can be tough-going on the Carron Valley route, and can make it feel like a longer day than it really is. However, going that way on a warm, glorious summer's day is an unforgettable experience, and I do recommend trying that route at least once. It does involve a fair bit of climbing, yes, but it affords outrageous views and scenery the whole way through, and so you will be well rewarded for all your efforts. It's best to make for Strathblane, as either route can be accessed fully from there. However, if you find it more convenient to make straight for Killearn instead, then both choices are still available to you, though it means you would miss out the Crow Road climb if you decided to go via Carron Valley Reservoir.

Now, it is possible to reach Killearn by taking the routes we have used previously to reach Blane Smithy when we were doing the Trossachs or Cree runs. Killearn is only a climb, though a fairly long one, up from that roundabout, so if it suits by all means use the Stockiemuir Road to reach it. However, that way isn't so handy for Strathblane, and as we have used the Stockiemuir approach enough already (so I won't go over it again), and bearing in mind that this book is all about learning new and different runs, we will try another approach. This one will involve using our old favourite and great road north, the A-81, but this time picking it up much earlier than Blane Smithy roundabout, instead round about Bearsden in Glasgow. (Did you get the clever word play there?)

This is regardless of whether we go via the Renfrew ferry or the Clyde Tunnel. I've already described the two options I have for getting to the Renfrew ferry, so I won't go over them again either. But if using it, I will usually take the back-of-the-airport option as opposed to the main Renfrew Road option, as it is quieter, safer, and slightly more convenient for me personally. After paying your fare across, ride up Yoker Ferry Road, then cross over Dumbarton Road into Kelso Street, and ride up to the roundabout at the end. Don't turn left this time for Drumchapel, but instead turn right along Alderman Road. This takes us through Knightswood, which is similar to Mosspark on the south side of the city, and was built about the same time, I think.

These have been two of Glasgow's most successful housing schemes. Alderman is a long, straight affair, with a well thought-out cycle lane running beside the road to aid your passage along it (*très bon*). In evidence are the semi-detached houses that were constructed back in the 1920s and 30s, and have stood the test of time, because people liked them and have taken a pride in their appearance and upkeep. This is in contrast to the 1960s solution to our housing problem – the high rise flat, many of which have already been pulled down and weren't so successful. A lot do still stand, however, but that is due to the sheer volume of how many were built in the first place.

So, through the long standing semis of this fine old place we ride, which makes for a fairly quiet and pleasant spin along past the white walls and gardens of Knightswood. When we reach the end of Alderman, we turn left onto Anniesland Road. We now make our way towards the mega-busy and important junction of Anniesland Cross. Standing tall behind it is its striking big high rise flat, with its red stripe running its full length and its white base colour, towering above all the ants below.

Anniesland Cross can also be reached from Paisley or the south side by the Clyde Tunnel. This has the added advantage of being free to use, of course.

Entering the Clyde Tunnel from the Govan side, and just about to descend into the bowels of old Mother Earth. However, things are not as gloomy as they used to be, with a recent white paint makeover and safer door entry system making the old tunnel a lot more user-friendly nowadays.

I will be honest here and say that although I used the tunnel from time to time in the past, I didn't really like it, and was glad when I got through it. Not so nowadays. It is nearly a pleasure now to go down deep below the Clyde and pull up the other side, in what is today a white painted shaft, safe and sound to negotiate and use. Gone is the dark, dank tunnel of old, where any undesirable Tom, Dick, or Harry could be lurking. The new door entry system has seen to that. To access the northbound cycle lane of the tunnel, you turn down Burghead Place off the Govan Road (at the Gazelle Bar), just along from the entrance to the Sou Gen (Southern General Hospital).

From Paisley, there are of course various ways to get to that point, all of which are of about equal length and busyness, as there is a lot going on in this neck of the woods. Not least the massive Braehead shopping complex, the hammer of Paisley retailing. For me, the

STIRLING CASTLE RUN

easiest way to get there is to enter Renfrew and then take first right at the lights and head down Cocklesloan. This, after mucho swerving round speed bumps, leads onto Dean Park Road, containing the King George V playing fields, before it brings you out at the dual carriageway A-8 Glasgow Road. Head along this, eastward, taking you onto Shieldhall Road, but not before you go rather hairily through the big, bad, busy roundabout that feeds Braehead itself, no less.

You also pass through what has now become a stronghold for very upmarket, expensive, and ugly-looking motorcar dealerships, as well as a drive-through Costa Coffee. The drive-through bug seems to be catching on, and you wonder what next.

The Bells Whisky plant has a major presence on the Shieldhall and will be the second whisky installation that I've passed already. The first was Chivas Bros. back on Paisley's Renfrew Road. Long may this continue, for I've just found out that Scotch whisky alone accounts for 25% of all the UK's – not just Scotland's – food and drink exports. Now, if that's not worth blowing your trumpet about, I don't know what is!

At the next roundabout, which comes at the end of the long, straight section you're on, take the second exit onto Renfrew Road, Glasgow. This sees you leave behind the life-blood lane of the city, the M-8, which you were running parallel with on the Shieldhall. The road down to the big right swing at the entrance to the King George V Docks (they seem to have had a soft spot for George V about here) is industrial and colourful. None more so than the large Glasgow Corporation amenities site, with all the Corpy's green wagons in attendance (their colour tells a story). This is in keeping with the rest of the commercial landscape that dominates this area, including – dare I say it – the Govan sewage works, which you are just about to pass shortly.

The big baby on the block here, as previously mentioned, is the Sou Gen, which was due to get a helluva lot bigger with a new super-hospital already under construction as I write (Sept 2013). It certainly isn't an eyesore, that's for sure. And with it being very modern, I'm just wondering if their A&E department will be a drive-through!

Go through the roundabout beside Thales, which makes defence components and the likes, and was formally the Boys' Brigade-loving Barr and Stroud (up periscope!). Take the next right into Burghead Place and swing up to the tunnel door via the footpath, as the cycle lanes start is now locked.

Nowadays, you press a buzzer and the boy in the control tower should oblige by opening it. Then begins a long descent (mind your head, please!) as you start to plummet down into the bowels of old Mother Earth. There is only one slight kink in the whole lane, near the top, before you dive bolt-straight down to the bottom. A barrier separates the cycle lane from the pedestrian lane. You do see the odd soul or two walking through, but it's rare to see anybody else down there. By all means, make some ghosty noises (if you're a big kid) to keep yourself amused on the way down.

As I said earlier, the door entry system does provide a reassuring level of reassurance, because you're not expecting to meet any cutpurses down there nowadays, as entry is closely monitored. There is literally no bottom to speak of, as the moment you do bottom out, you start an almost identical climb back up to Whiteinch. The last overhaul meant that the iron grates have been removed, making for a quieter and smoother descent, and the replacing of the old paintwork by the brighter white removes the former feeling of dankness. Just get into a rhythm and force your way up the long far side, where all the time you will have the sound of the traffic from the road tunnel for company, as it actually goes right above you at this point.

The Clyde Tunnel was cut perfectly circular, and the car deck was built about a third of the way up, allowing the cycle lane to be built below that. The tunnel's services are below us again. Work started in 1957 and saw the northbound side open first in July 1963, with Liz II herself doing the honours. The southbound followed shortly in March '64. For the record, it proved to be quite a difficult tunnelling job, due to the geology of hard rock with soft silt sitting on top. A couple of deaths were recorded, as two of the miners succumbed to some sort of decompression sickness, due to the type of mining involved. So, it's with the sacrifice of these hardy souls that we give thanks for a safe passage under the Clyde, as we exit the tunnel and enter back into daylight onto Dumbarton Road, Whiteinch.

Now we want to make our way north towards Anniesland Cross on Balshagray Avenue (the A-739). This is quite easy to do, though not that obvious. Diagonally across from you will be Glendore Street, so go down to the bottom of it and turn left. This runs you alongside the

The Forth and Clyde Canal looks oh so pretty as we pass over it on the Bearsden Road (the A-739) just up from Anniesland Cross, but don't admire it for too long because the road we're on now is super busy at this point, so keep your wits about you.

Expressway, where you shortly come to an underpass on your left beside Whiteinch Library. This allows you to reach the other side of the Expressway (all rideable) and come out at Victoria Park. Follow the pretty park's green railings round to lead you most conveniently onto Balshagray, just at the junction with Victoria Park Drive North. From there you're able to get going up Balshagray proper.

When you do, it's a slight spin uphill, till you join Crow Road, and then fire straight and flat under the rail bridge at Southbrae Drive, and shortly arrive at Anniesland Cross. This is where you meet up with the other route coming up from Renfrew. Now, it is one busy babe, the road coming from and leading to the tunnel, but it's also dual carriageway and 30mph, so you shouldn't find it too scary. It will also be busy and dual carriageway after you pass through the cross and start to head up the Bearsden Road. This is you making for the very north end of the town, and in Bearsden and Milngavie you have two of the city's most upmarket areas. The Forth and Clyde Canal will be crossed over shortly, once the slight rise from the cross has levelled out.

It is, in fact, very straightforward to reach this point from the Renfrew ferry by using the canal towpath, and is safe and scenic, too. However, as it isn't tarmacked a lot of the way, I never use it when I'm on my road bike. I do recommend it if you're using a hybrid or mountain bike, and it is great to go its full length all the way to Falkirk. By all means take the kids along it any time you wish for an easy day out with the little ones, and don't forget to bring some bread to feed the swans and ducks as you go along; most enjoyable.

STIRLING CASTLE RUN

only gentle rises and dips to be taken before you reach the Burnbrae roundabout.

MUGDOCK ROUTE

There now presents itself an alternative route to reach Strathblane from Milngavie. This one avoids the busier A-81 and takes us up through the pretty place of Mugdock by a route that is in itself as picturesque as it is tough. This is no easy way to reach our intended village, but rather condenses all the drawn-out climbing that you would do on the main A-road into a much shorter and dramatic pull-up. If you wish to use this option, and it is well recommended, then continue straight on at the Burnbrae by a convenient cycle lane and carry on to the second set of lights. Turn left here (it is signposted for Mugdock) and make your way through some early houses till you run up beside the most beautiful of walls that separates you from Mugdock Reservoir itself.

It is a most impressive setting all around, I must say, what with the greenery and the agedness of the waterworks paraphernalia, the country park on the left, and the Scots pines lining the dam side. At the end of the dam wall, be prepared for a very tough ramp-like pull-up that ends when the road turns hard right, and I do mean hard. Sudden relief is felt the moment you make the turn, as the road levels out quite markedly and the payback for all your effort is a glorious view back down to the reservoir, sitting behind another line of Scots pine. Soon you're running beside more old walls and the gardens that belong to the very good homes of this highly perched place.

Looking back along the Switchback (still the A-739) from the entrance to the old Canniesburn Hospital, and soon we're off the real busy stuff and onto the great A-81 the moment we get through Canniesburn Toll. I'm always glad when I get through this section because it is so heavy with traffic, but it allows us fast access to the north end of town.

The following curving wee rise means you've just joined the Switchback Road, and it will undulate continually on the other side as it takes you up to the next major roundabout at Canniesburn Toll. On the way there, you will pass the famous Glasgow Vets' School on the right (they come from the world over to attend it) and on the left the first batch of salubrious bungalows, heralding your arrival in suburbia and East Dunbartonshire. You can't help but notice the total change in social landscape from the tenements of Anniesland only a short distance down the road. A short wee drop deposits you at the toll, and taking the second exit means you're on the A-81 again, and who's complaining?

As always, things just seem to get better the moment you roll onto the tar of the 81; well, that's how it feels for me, anyway. The Bearsden/Milngavie stretch is no exception. For a start, the dual carriageway is left behind and things settle down a bit, as up between the bungalows you flow. Steeped in history is this area, with the remains of the Roman Bath House sitting just up the Roman Road on the left. This great historical site is counterbalanced somewhat by the slightly more modern architecture sitting on your right, in the shape of an Asda. The Milngavie Road starts to broadly sweep and bend as you pass Hillfoot Station and a red cycle lane appears in the road.

It runs out from the pavement at times, allowing cars to be parked inside of it and thus avoiding any conflict between bikes and stationary vehicles. So, with only single lane traffic, wide roads, and a cycle lane, you feel pretty safe negotiating this stretch as the old A-81 comfort factor kicks in. The going too is easy-ozey, with

After leaving Strathblane; we're battering along the A-81 enroute to Killearn; which will run us past Glengoyne Distillery; and a brilliant flying fall through the trees is about to follow. Wee Dumgoyne Hill always looks great and stands out well from quite some distance away; it lets you know you're on the right road.

Just approaching Glengoyne Distillery and; like all whisky distilleries; it is a fine-looking; whitewashed building. Shortly after we pass it; the cut-off for Killearn is taken; and alas we have to leave the great A-81 behind.

You just skirt the edge of the village till you come over a rise, and a stunning view of Dumgoyne hits you full in the face. There is also a quaint wee junction in the road at this point, and the second turning for Strathblane is ours. It will run you rather spectacularly down into the village by a series of dips and turns, which run past some seriously expensive-looking pads, whilst giving stunning views across the muir to the Campsies beyond. The finale is a real steep drop down the Old Mugdock Road, Strathblane, in amongst this village's older council-style homes, finally emerging at the mini roundabout beside the Kirkhouse Inn. This is where you would also arrive if coming via the main A-81.

MAIN A-81 ROUTE

The Campsies have already been spotted by now, as you take the second exit at the Burnbrae roundabout to keep you on the 81. Now we roll under the rail bridge and climb lightly up towards the cross, where we sample the brown stone homes of Milngavie. There is something of old money about Milngavie, especially the part round about Mugdock Reservoir, which is the area that we are heading into. The feeling starts once you pass through the crossroads and run past a row of terraced houses on the left, which seem to date from an earlier time. So do the houses on the left up ahead that you pass as you swing up and onto the Strathblane Road, which you have now just joined.

A very impressive row of des-res's, I must say, line this stretch of road – all old stone cottages or houses of similar age, and some with lovely, long gardens to finish off the look. We're almost out of the city now, which ends very beautifully indeed. After passing the last of the bungalows and tall hedges, the road swings again, left this time, and draws you up the avenue de delight. This is you running right alongside the reservoir now, Craigmaddie to be exact. The typical stone walls built by the water work companies of old would do the boundary of any rich man's estate proud, and the one on your left is no exception.

The branches of aged deciduous trees, which line both sides, almost touch above and form a leafy canopy to guide you up this most gentle of climbs. This one goes on for quite a while, with only a slight bend in the middle of it all. It continues in a similar vein till you pass what must have been the house of the water worker in charge of the place in days gone by. This house is in keeping with the surrounds, with its iron gates and slate roof, its stone walls, crimson, ivy-covered, and solid, of course. Very impressive it is. We've not got too much time to admire it, because we're off out into the countryside now and will soon be climbing on the great bends of the Strathblane Road, which pull us up through the trees and fields on either side.

Double white lines run the centre of the road here, and you swish fairly quickly up through them and straighten out as it all opens up. You enter Stirling District as you do, and quickly Dumgoyne appears rather grandly ahead. So, too, does the craggy, steep flank of the Campsies,

STIRLING CASTLE RUN

and to me they are very impressive from this angle. They become even more so as you bank right and pass the Strathblane sign, where you're still high at this point, but about to plummet down some real steep, tight bends to the village below. Just beyond the village name post is a small, brick bus shelter, the sort of thing that is so rurally quaint and doesn't exist in the larger towns, of course.

At this point also, Dumgoyne is seen across high, rough meadows, and takes on a very rugged appearance indeed. Full attention on these bends, please! They do require care, and at the bottom you meet a wee mini roundabout. Now it's make your mind up time, because this is the point where you have a choice of routes. You can turn right here and go a slightly more direct way over the Campsie Glen, which involves more climbing, but is approximately 5 miles shorter, or you can carry straight on and head for Killearn, then access Stirling by another great hill road – the B-822 over to Kippen from Fintry. This makes for a more circular route.

THE FINTRY ROUTE

If going via Fintry, then head straight through the roundabout and enter the village. Perhaps I should have said villages, for Strathblane almost immediately becomes Blanefield. They are both of similar character, hardly surprisingly, and both very, very pretty. A few years back, I think I'm right in saying, they were always winning the best looking village competition or something of that ilk. It's flower baskets aplenty, and colourful hereabouts and delightful, as are some very ye olde-looking buildings that you'll shortly pass. The village club with its wonderful high chimneys, and another hall opposite, showing 1926 as its year of construction, are especially so. Then a bit of a surprise, when you find yourself descending and descending down through the rest of the village.

It's only then that you realise just how high it sits. For after the first drop, the road steadies a little and then drops again. The first part is through middle-class bungalows, which stamps the place as a commuter town for Glasgow. But near the bottom of the second drop, older sort of working class houses exist, white-walled in semis and in rows. These perhaps indicate that this was once a weaving village at one time, though no remains of the works themselves have survived as far as I know. A road sign makes you aware that the B-821 is coming in from the left. It is a great road taking you over to the Carbeth Inn and can be climbed Alpine-like, over to the Stockiemuir Road, if you want to make a short circuit that way. The descent down at this point is quite a steepy, so what's left of Blanefield passes by as a blur. The sanctuary of level road only appears as you leave the village and roll out into the countryside once more.

We are now heading in the general direction of the Glengoyne Distillery, which is most picturesquely positioned right at the bottom of Dumgoyne Hill. This can only be described as a most striking volcanic plug, instantly recognisable from a great distance and one that hasn't erupted in quite a while. If it ever does, avoid the area for a while, as molten lava can seriously damage your tyres.

On the road between Killearn and Fintry; the back end of the Campsie Fells holds the entire right flank in very impressive style; and the finest feature is the massive scoop of the Corrie of Balglass. Here it can be seen behind a line of deciduous trees.

The road from Blanefield to there is a bit of a delight (apart from the road surface), for there are great sweeps through the green, along with another unexpected descent which makes for enjoyable riding. This deposits you in the strath of the Blane itself – a fairly broad, flat, valley floor that has a similar, Dumgoyne-looking, volcanic plug in its midst that carries you along till the white walls of the distillery are reached.

Regardless of whether you enjoy a glass of bold John or not, there is something a bit special about the whiteness of a whisky distillery. They do have picture postcard prettiness about them and that is pleasing, but I also suspect it's down to the quality of the product they produce. No doubt about it, it has a draw on people and they come by the coachload to visit. This one's no different, and I always have an admiring glance as I ride by. It has the advantage of being a rare breed, the

49

Glengoyne, for there are few Lowland distilleries left compared to their Highland counterparts. This wasn't always the case, by any means, for the hills around here and many other parts of the country contained numerous illegal stills producing hooch.

This was because of the heavy taxes imposed on whisky at the time, to help pay for the war against Napoleon, which meant it simply wasn't viable to produce whisky legally. However, that changed in 1820, when the rate of taxation was greatly reduced and there was a rush for licences, including one for Glengoyne. It is the only one remaining in the entire area.

The high ground across the strath rises quite abruptly onto Quinloch Moor and gives a great, wild feel, even to this Lowland glen. Now, alas, we must part company in a short while from our beloved A-81, because just up ahead comes a fork in the road and we branch off right (on the A-875) to get to Killearn. There now follows a long slope, ever rising and undulating, through the fields at first and passing Westerton Farm that has a silo shaped like a castle turret.

All very pastoral, I must say, and then the countdown markers begin for the village. There seems a bit of a false start to Killearn, because you hit as many trees as you do houses, as you come in. This continues for a short while, till the buildings take over and you come into the village centre. In keeping with the area, this is another picture postcard place, and the quaint wooden village sign tells you one George Buchanan was born here. There's stores and mores here, too, so if you need ought you're in with a shout. These come in the early part, before you climb again up to the top half of Main Street. To a council house boy like myself, some of the homes here really look delicious, especially a house called Camelot. This sits just to the left of the local family butchers, McDonalds, and is not a big house by any means, but looks like it was designed by Charles Rennie MacKintosh.

I stopped dead in my tracks the first time I saw it, what with its white curves, dark slated turreted roof, elongated chimney, and stone plaques on the wall. One bears the house name, the other an arm and scroll. A classic-looking house if ever there was one. In fact, even the solid stone butcher's shop right next door is impressive. The owner has a fair bit of competition nowadays, though, as just along the road sits a Co-op and Spar.

The gentle climb up the Main Street is pretty and flowery. More baskets and tubs hereabouts, spilling their sweet colours forth onto the pavement. Tight-knit, white cottages all sport red doors to add an extra bright splash of colour, along with the double yellow lines that run Main Street's length.

On the left at the top sits what they call the village square, and inside some railings is a massive, grey, towering stone monument to Killearn's most famous son. George Buchanan was a writer and scholar who eventually achieved high office as the Moderator of the Church of Scotland. He was imprisoned, but escaped and fled to Europe after criticising the corruption within

Fintry itself is a most pleasant-looking village, and always a delight to ride through. Here we are just entering it from the Killearn side on the B-818. Unfortunately, it doesn't last too long, for soon we take a left turn at its ornate central junction and head out for a climb-and-a-half on the B-822 up onto Kippen Muir.

STIRLING CASTLE RUN

the Catholic Church in the time of James V. He was renowned on the continent for his wit and poetry, before returning to Scotland to become Mary Queen of Scots' classical tutor.

At first he was fiercely loyal to the young Catholic Queen, but became increasingly hostile to her when he suspected she was involved in the murder of her husband, Lord Darnley (a bloody no-user). Mary ended up being executed in England on the strength of trumped-up charges of treason by her cousin Elizabeth I. George Buchanan went as far as giving evidence against her at her trial (I can't say I'm one of his fans).

Perhaps it was his religious high office that led to so many churches being built in the village. As you roll out along the A-875 towards Balfron, you pass the impressive Killearn Kirk. Its bright blue door contrasts well with its superb grey stone ornateness, and its skyward steeple with black clock face is of equal quality.

The road to Blane Smithy runs long and hedge-lined off to the left, as past another couple of former churches you go. One is all big, white, and appears to be the local village hall, and the second is now the pharmacy. So, we leave behind the charm of Killearn, which includes a pink cottage as we gamely throw ourselves into the fields beyond.

A bit of twisting and dipping leads us to a junction. It's the right fork for Fintry. Ahead would take us to Balfron, but that's not the best option. By taking the right fork, we're on the B-818 and we're up for the cup. That's because this is a beautiful bit of countryside we now find ourselves in, and even the junction itself is a delight. Big, bold old trees line the fields along this stretch, as the green shallow valley to the left rolls down then up and away gently, showing Balfron in its midst. Our attention is straight ahead, of course, as we plough on towards pretty Fintry. No great hardship this, especially at first, as the road is kind to us with its easy flow and charm. Stone walls and big old trees give the game away that we are running along beside some great former estate or other, and a rather ostentatious grand gatehouse informs you that this is the entrance to Ballikinrain Castle.

It is a baronial-style castle, built in 1868 for Sir Archibald Orr-Ewing, who was the Conservative Member of Parliament for Dunbartonshire. Clearly a man of means Sir Archibald, as his baronial pile sat in his 4500 acre estate. It's along past his estate grounds we now ride, of course, and there was no expense spared by his Lordship on the walls marking his boundary, I'm glad to say. Long after his death, Ballikinrain was badly damaged by fire in 1913, in what was believed to have been an arson attack by those most determined of ladies, the Suffragettes. Perhaps they saw the house as a symbol of the establishment. The place was restored in 1916, but that took 100 grand. It is now a residential school indirectly run by the kirk, but has had many guises over the years, including being a hotel, girls' school, and even a camping and caravanning site. No doubt Sir Archie must have turned in his grave.

We are out in the fields briefly as we fly along, but shortly find ourselves bending and undulating back through the trees again, following mossy-lined walls as we go. We then pass what appear to have been the workers' houses for the estate, which are fairly showy

Taking a quick look back at the lovely old stone brig that carries us over the Endrick Water as we leave Fintry. We're now on the B-822, and are in for a treat on the great old climb up and over to Kippen.

in themselves. We finally clear the estate's woodlands as we run up to Ballikinrain Farm, where we start to draw level with the massive Corrie of Balglass – one of the Campsies' finest features. It is an enormous cavity sitting high away to the right, impressing all who view it, for it is an elegant, brazen, big scoop. The whole broad mouth of early Glen Carron (ahead) is starting to make its prescence felt, and in particular the shapely nose of Stronend, jutting out above the left lying Fintry Hills, gives a real impression of upland.

Now, the plan here is to continue along the B-818 all the way to Fintry, only a couple of miles up the road, and to turn left onto the B-822 to take us over to Kippen. You can actually see the lie of the land and the way to go from Ballikinrain Farm, and it looks nothing too

On the climb up onto Kippen Muir from Fintry, pleasant and at the same time quite dramatic views can be had back towards the Campsie Fells, once a little bit of height has been gained. This will take some time, as it is a fairly elongated and meandering pull-up.

intimidating. There is a bit of a shortcut available to you from here, though, because you will see a blue sign pointing left for Balfron. You can follow this road down through the fields and then delightfully over the Endrick Water. The Endrick, incidentally, runs down from Glen Carron but does not originate from the reservoir, as one would imagine. Once over the water, turn right onto a small minor road, which will take you past the farms till it meets with the B-822 itself. In fact, it is possible to pick up this road in Balfron and take it from there.

Now, this road climbs a bit higher than the main road to Fintry, and therefore provides some very nice views indeed. But being a minor road, it does have steeper inclines and a poorer surface in places, so it takes away a fair bit of your momentum. For that reason alone, I tend to prefer the B-818, though at times its road surface is anything but smooth. By all means try the minor road out for yourself at least once, for it puts you in a great position to appreciate Stronend, Corrie of Balglass, and the Earl's Seat. Believe it or not, for years this was the way I used to come when doing the mighty Cree run.

Once the top of the B-822 is finally reached, then behold the Highlands proper. Ben Lomond and Ben Ledi will be the dominant hills in view, but there are plenty more behind them to fill in the rest of the scene.

STIRLING CASTLE RUN

Pleasant wooded stretches of road are to be found high on Kippen Muir, which contrasts nicely with the more open views of the northern hills and Carse of Forth that are still to come. This photo is actually taken whilst looking south, back to Fintry.

So, if we don't take the minor road option, we will continue quite merrily along the B-818, running fairly straight at first, with Stronend's craggy point dead ahead. This comes before the road turns southeast just at Cockburn, where now it is the former fort-holding Dunmore Hill in the Campsies that dominates the skyline. This is another steep-sided volcanic plug, by the looks of things.

The road starts to undulate a bit more as it slowly rises above the valley floor, and below, one of the farms has another one of those castle turreted-looking silos, just like the one back at Killearn. They must have been all the rage at one time. Soon you pass the wonderful looking and equally wonderfully situated Kilewnan Cottage, a beautiful, white-walled, grey-slated property, sitting right below the crags of steep Dunmore. I cannot remember seeing a more idyllic-looking and positioned property ever. You make up your own mind.

The final straight run in to Fintry now begins, and as for the place itself… well, it's helluva nice, so it is. Yes, helluva. You sort of bobble down into its whiteness and expect to come under its spell right away. It's just a pity it is such a short experience. Small, that's Fintry. Small and cute would best sum up this village of white and black stone homes. The main street is a corridor of such houses, with only the red of the old-style phone box – obligatory in these sorts of places – giving any real splash of colour. The only exception to the white houses, as far as I can see, is the brown stone ones you encounter at the junction of the turn-off for Kippen. This is right in the centre of the village, and is unmissable due to a very ornate traffic island, containing a really old street lamp.

Just after turning left, you cross the Endrick Water by a lovely stone bridge, and now begins your journey on the B-822 over to Kippen. I would say that this road is the best excuse for coming this way. Now it is a climb up to Kippen most definitely, but not so as you'd notice. In fact, it is only when you are screaming out of Kippen in the other direction that you are aware of just how high up you are. Well, ok, some of the earlier views you get give the game away as well. That's because it is a very long, meandering, gently rising road, all the way from Fintry up onto the high of Kippen Muir.

Now, even before you leave the village, you pass the entrance to Culcreuch Castle, which is a hot spot for wedding receptions nowadays. This rather splendid tower house was built way back in 1296, and was originally the seat of the Clan Galbraith. It has changed hands many times, and is a hotel in this era. In 1654 it was a garrison for Cromwell's troops, though I don't think they were paying guests. Like all old castles, it has a resident ghost or two – one is a phantom harpist, and another likes to turn up the sound on the hi-fi. Perhaps it's just the same spook who's into their music.

So we roll out of Fintry, and now begins what I consider to be the best part of the run and the main reason I take

Heading down Main Street, Kippen, and it really is very old and very fine. It's a good idea to either slow down or even stop a while, just to enjoy it more. On leaving the village, the plummet continues all the way down to the A-811 on the Flanders Moss far below.

53

this route. It is a fine and most enjoyable climb from here over to Kippen, though I use the term climb quite loosely. That's because it doesn't start climbing right away this road, and even when it does, it is a big easy. It's only gentle rising at first, if at all, and this even includes a little bit of equally gentle downhill as you follow the hedges and trees through the remainder of this pastoral plain. All delightful riding, I must say, as the beech hedges guide and protect you from any easterly wind blowing your way. It's on past the cottages and farms, as the craggy and stunning Stronend sits above, poking its neb out and pointing the way.

Eventually, you approach a minor crossroads, and the road you meet is the back road from Balfron, which is the one you could have taken after passing Ballikinrain Farm. Once past this, the terrain changes noticeably from rich dairy fields to upland sheep fields. Gone are the green pastures and black and white heifers, it's now rough pastures and small woolly bundles that keep you company. All fine and well, and as you rise, it won't be beyond any competent rider to keep up a fair old cadence on this climb, as a lot of it will be of a gradient in low single figures. The Fintry Hills to the right and Campsie Fells behind, add a fair amount of handsome drama, as up onto the muir the B-road bends. Rusty, old, red barn roofs appear on the horizon, as up towards and past the high, isolated Balafark Farm you go.

A long, slanting rise takes you up there, before the road rests a little, then begins another series of rising bends to take you as near as dammit onto the top of the muir. Here, as you'd expect, you find small lochans, conifer plantations, and really rough pastures all around. A fair old size is Kippen Muir, and it takes on American prairie proportions in its featureless flatness at this point. An interesting wee side road heads off at an angle down towards Arnprior at what is an official scenic spot here, but we continue quite enjoyably along the 822, past some woodland that hides small Loch Laggan on the left. When you clear the small rise at the end of the straight you're now on, that's it, there is no more climbing. You're sure to enjoy the muir's high offering of curving tarmac through the remainder of its roughness.

If it's a clear day, then it's a spectacular scene away to the north, with the flat land of the famous Flanders Moss way below being the tablecloth in the Carse of Forth. This billiard table brilliance makes a sensational contrast with that fine-looking fellow, Ben Ledi, whose imposing bulk steals the show again. As the road starts to descend, then the fields on the left become softer before the woods are entered on the final, great slither downhill into Kippen. Fire down into it with a wish, a whoosh, a pump, and a push. Magic is the road leading in, and it keeps falling all the way through the fine old Main Street of this fine old village. Old, incidentally, doesn't do the age of this place justice, not by a long chalk.

One James Lauder was recorded as the local vicar in 1454, but there was a church recorded here in 1238 and most likely a settlement to go with it. The splendid looking Cross Keys Inn (1703) is the oldest inn in Stirlingshire. Even the garage which you pass on the way down, the Glengyle, has charm aplenty with its white-painted, tractor-tyre flower beds. From its start to its finish, Kippen village falls fast downhill, but hit the brakes a bit and marvel at the age of some of the properties that lie within it. Better still, stop at the wee café on the left – called the Sublime, I think – and admire the homes and buildings all around you as you enjoy your latte. Small, in fact very small, windows give away the age of the cottages hereabouts, which look like they come from the Robert Burns' era. They still look super solid and it goes without saying, "They don't make them like that any more." Well, they don't, do they?

Continue falling towards the north, when you get going again, where things seriously speed up as you leave behind ye olde, and plummet, slalom-like, down through some thick vegetation. It's hard to tell exactly what it is as you are flying down through, as you take the bends so fast, gamely riding out the twists and turns without slamming on the anchors if you can help it. And then PHEW! Relief comes quickly as you bottom out and find Kippen station roundabout on the A-811. What a contrast in such a short distance. Coming from the upland of Kippen Muir to the swath of Flanders Moss, all done in seconds, more or less. This roundabout was the one we turned left at when doing the Cree run, and this time we turn right for Stirling.

The roundabout takes its name from the former station which stood nearby on the old Forth and Clyde rail line which ran from Balloch to Stirling. This line closed well early in 1934, having opened in 1856, which is hardly surprising. Not only did it run through a sparsely populated area with no major settlement to support, but most of the stations were a good bit away from the places they were meant to serve. This included Drymen,

STIRLING CASTLE RUN

Balfron, and here at Kippen. It would be a steep, fair old walk up to the village from the station, to say the least.

Anyway, that is all in the past and we are concerned with right now, of course, but nothing too much to get concerned about, for the next 10 miles of road will be dead flat, dead straight, and dead right through the Flanders Moss. It will take us to right below the cliffs that hold the majestic Stirling Castle. It is quite a rarity to ride 10 miles of flat in Scotland, and I can think of nowhere else that it is possible to do so, for me at least.

Right away, it feels very strange as you suddenly find that from having a bird's eye view, you've now got a worm's eye view, as the Gargunnock Hills tower above the plain on the right. Also, we've just gone from a quiet back road onto a busier A-road, so there is a fair bit of adjustment to get used to. But the A-811 isn't too bad traffic-wise. So off we go with a bit of a charge and settle into a time trial frame of mind for this stretch. This road and one or two others in the area are just made for time trialling, and I used to come up and do the odd one myself. This ride, however, is for sightseeing and pleasure, and the run in to the castle will provide both.

Expect to be met with a view like this the moment you drop onto the A-811 and begin to head east towards Stirling. It really is as straight and as flat as this all the way in, and the castle and Wallace Monument will slowly come into view after a while. The castle is just about visible in this photo.

Almost straight away, you pass the massive Boquhan Home Farm, sitting to the right, with its enormous, red-roofed sheds. Look ahead and all you will see is straight road. No deviations, bends, corners, climbs, dips, or anything else for a while a least, and quite a while at that. The left side is totally flat. A flat calm of wheat fields that lie low and long towards the distant Ochils. There's a fair bit of valley space still on the right, before it slopes up onto the fine-looking Gargunnock Hills. These are anything but bland boys, as the exceptionally long and striking Standmilane Craig and Black Craig, amongst others, run just about the full length of their flank, and provide a rugged appearance. Now, it is better if we have an east wind blowing in our face at this point, because it means a tail wind on the way home. But if we have a gentle westerly behind, we can purr along at 20 mph no problem here.

After about 2 miles, the Wallace Monument will come into view – a most striking needle which has the Ochils for a backdrop, and is a most fitting tribute to that great, great man. Had it not been for this man and Robert Bruce, Scotland would have most likely been swallowed up into greater England. Wallace was not from a high noble family, and was therefore looked down upon by the Scottish nobles of the time, despite what he did for them. It was one of them – the keeper of Dumbarton Castle, John de Menteith – who finally betrayed and captured him at Robroyston, just to the north of Glasgow. Unlike Bruce, there was no personal interest in what Wallace was doing; he was just a true Scottish patriot. The death the English gave him, starting by being dragged behind a horse, was barbaric, even by their standards.

Stirling Castle will also come into view shortly after the Wallace Monument, and will then dominate the horizon on the run in. By now you are level with Gargunnock Village itself, which you don't see a lot of as it sits a bit up the hill and away from the road. You do, however, get a close look at the wonderfully named and equally wonderfully dilapidated-looking Dasherburn Farm, which you pass very near to. Now, just after Dasherburn, there is a rare bend in the road as you pass the cut-off for Doune. There, the 811 becomes a bit of a tree-lined avenue for a while, but it's not long till normal service is resumed and you find yourself back out in the open, long straights again. You're on the final approach to Stirling now, but still there's a fair wee bit to go. The Gargunnocks have been replaced by the Touch Hills, and these start to close in on the right.

The castle acts as a real magnet, drawing you closer and closer, and as you do, it becomes more magnificent by the minute. Standing as it does so majestically on top of the cliffs that rise sentinel-like right out of the flat plain below. It is just such a wonderful, wonderful sight, and

Stirling Castle makes for a most magnificent sight as you get closer to the town on the A-811. Expect to see a few local riders out training on their time trial bikes on this road, as it's just made for such a thing.

one to make you forget any suffering you are undergoing at that precise time. The final hurdle is a slight rise taking you over the modern M-9, which really does give a great sense of time contrast between itself and the nearby castle. Turn right at the big roundabout ahead, and reach the park that is known as the King's Knot. This sits right below the castle cliffs, and what can I say? For above the former Royal Gardens is one of the true jewels in Scotland's historic crown.

Everything about it is appealing, from the flat green baize of the King's Knot below, to the trees so strongly rooted to the lower and mid cliffs, to the barren steep upper cliffs, and finally to the magnificent castle walls and buildings above them. Having said that, the King's Knot or Mound as it is known, is worth a quick look as well, for the octagonal shape of it is something quite special. It was created in 1627/8 by William Watts, who was brought up from England to supervise the creation of the Royal Gardens. If you don't have time and want to access the castle instead, continue up this street where you will soon come to the Royal Gardens roundabout

Stirling Castle gets more impressive the closer you get to it, and especially from this direction. Here we are at the end of the A-811, almost right below the cliffs of the castle and just about to enter the town itself. The flat stuff's over for now, as the pull-up to the castle gates will begin shortly. However, there is an alternative approach to this route that involves climbing the Crow Road over from Lennoxtown, and then taking a minor moor road from Carron Valley Reservoir.

at the end of the park. Now, you can also reach this roundabout by the road coming in from the right, by taking a different, shorter, more direct, but tougher and much quieter route from Strathblane or Fintry.

CARRON VALLEY RESERVOIR ROUTE

From the very edge of the western end of Carron Valley Reservoir, a small minor road heads off at an angle and makes directly for Stirling. This slender old road is an absolutely superb approach route to Stirling and takes you very loftily over the high quiet moors to this fine old town. If I decide to go this way and include Mugdock and the Campsies, then it will add over 1000 feet of climbing into the run, and will mean a total ascent of over 4500 feet by the end of the day. However, it means that instead of having to batter along a busy A-road to reach my destination, I will have a fantastic traffic-free freefall all to myself, as my finish into Stirling. I strongly recommend it.

On the road from Strathblane to Lennoxtown (the A-891), a great-looking volcanic plug called Dunglass sits in the right-hand side fields, as you gleefully swerve around the bends coming at you thick flat and fast on this fairly quiet A-road.

So, to access that route from Strathblane, turn right at the mini roundabout beside the Kirkhouse Inn and climb slightly up on the A-891. This will be about the only climbing that you will do on this road, as you now twist and turn and undulate slightly, from time to time, along this most pretty of pastoral parades. Very shortly the dramatic-looking lump of Dunglass volcanic plug will appear in the fields on the right, as you fly into East Dunbartonshire, where shortly the great, craggy flank of the Campsie Fells will show strongly. Soon you curve through tiny Haughhead, and before you can say "Quack, quack" you reach the Lennoxtown duck pond. You can

STIRLING CASTLE RUN

Time to get the old climbing legs on now as you start up the Crow Road (the B-822) from Lennoxtown. This is a fairly long climb, though it's only steep at the start and after the big right-hand bend has been taken up ahead at Jamie Wright's Well. Simply sit down and get into a rhythm beside the crash barrier, and judge your effort accordingly.

either take the first on the left after it, or carry on and take the left at the Black Swan pub to get you on the start of the Crow Road.

After a quick purr through the remaining houses, the Crow starts proper with a bending ramp-like start, before it carries you long and diagonally up and away from the valley floor. A great, slender, elegant rise it is, which follows the crash barriers, right on the side of the broad Campsies' flank. After the initial steepish start, it lies back a fair wee bit, about 4% gradient, which is just as well, for it's a long haul up and it allows you to sit high on the bars and admire the scene below. The scene is rather fieldy and bland, if I'm being honest, which doesn't change till you make the big, steep swing right, when you reach the end of the straight you are on.

Now things get tough again, as the road pulls straight up onto the moors, with an ever-rising, undulating gait. Slowly, and I do mean slowly, the road eventually starts to lie back again, and brilliantly bleakly you rise onto the crest of the Campsies, passing into Stirling District as you do. This is as high as you get this time, over a 1100 feet in height – one of three times that you will be over 1000 feet on this run – and now it's time to enjoy the short plateau. The descent off it starts when you pass a high, isolated cottage called The Neuk. What a descent it is, and after some early, easy, long, shallow bends, things start to get seriously fast, frantic, and flashy.

No more bland scenes now, as into the dale-like drama that is the Fintry Hills you drop. These are only in the near distance, of course, because far away to the

Hitting the second steep section on the Crow Road, just after Jamie Wright's Well. This can be quite a lengthy section, so conserve enough energy early on so you don't suffer too much at this point. Soon you're up onto the top of the muir, though, and then it's simply superb riding to come.

road, as the bends that appear will now become tighter and steeper, requiring the old descending and braking skills to be at their best. One or two really do switch back hard, so be ready for them, but relief is coming quickly when you hit the valley floor just at the small enclave of houses that have the right turn for Denny as company.

12 miles to Denny says the sign, and this is cut-off we want. If you were coming from the Killearn/Fintry direction, it is very simple to reach this point, as you merely continue along the B-818 instead of turning left when you reach Fintry village, and a short, flat, pleasant bumble through the fields and along the valley floor will lead to the same destination. The Denny road is officially still the B-818 and it starts off with a lovely, old bridge over the Endrick Water, and this is followed by a long, pretty, fairly arduous in places – though not sustained – meandering climb that will lead you up to the western

northwest will come into view the Highland hills. Simply too many all appearing at the one time to be able to name them all, and this is despite the fact that I've climbed them all. What a show they put on, and so too does the

On reaching the Carron Valley Reservoir, break left on the minor road that runs northeast from the very edge of the dam, and it's across the high, barren Cringate Muir you go. It's single track all the way, and expect a few potholes and plenty of stones on the road, as the picture above shows. However, on a hot, sunny day, it is a fantastic way to go, and no doubt about it, the best way to get to Stirling.

end of Carron Valley Reservoir. This is where the fun begins, because just running off to the left you will notice a very discreet (unmarked) single track road.

Now, let me say right away that this is more than rideable. The surface is old, especially for the first half (it runs for approximately 9 to 10 miles), but then you hit a much newer surface just when you need it, when the long, great descent down to Stirling begins in earnest. The road for its entire length is narrow, and the early part being old means that if you are riding in a group you will certainly need to spread out. This route, more

On the descent of the Crow Road from Campsie Muir down towards Fintry, though we don't go as far as that village this time. We'll take a right turn onto the B-818 at Gonachan and head uphill in the direction of Carron Valley Reservoir. On the descent of the Crow here, there are fantastic views of the mountains ahead, and just watch out for those wicked S-bends that are just about to follow.

STIRLING CASTLE RUN

Fantastic vast views open up to you after the high point on Cringate Muir is reached and the descent down into the Forth Valley begins. Here the flames from one of the Grangemouth refineries can be made out when we are still quite high up on the muir. With the flatness of the valley floor, and the contrast of the Ochil Hills behind, it makes a most impressive sight.

than most, would be better suited to a solo rider, but as already stated, it is rideable its entire length, even on your best machine. The setting it takes you through more than makes up for any of its imperfections, as it follows a general trend of gently rising continuously through the quiet and, at times, forested muirs.

Not even a fairly recently installed wind farm can take away the feeling of isolation, as you shortly reach and pass the lonely Cairndoch Lodge. The road continues on, rising and undulating continuously, crossing burns and feeling airy, till a short, steep, ramp-like section is taken. Once over, that is the signal for the fantastic, long fall-down to commence, which begins with a crossing of the infant Bannock Burn no less. A much more modern road surface has been laid on this section, though caution must still be exercised constantly, as it's fast, tight, and twisty in numerous places. The full flat Forth Valley opens its heart to your gaze, along with its fiery furnaces belonging to the Grangemouth refineries.

Closer at hand you will find a very scenic and dramatic landscape surrounding the picturesque North Third Reservoir, where your speed here is exceptional and exciting, and this plummeting, punishing road then carries you into an equally dramatic landscape of rocks and conifers as you again fly down through the area around Gillies Hill. This is seriously wild-looking in places, but it only takes a short wooded section of road to transport you into a completely different setting of rich farmland. This in turn, after the unexpected appearance of a right turn over the M-9, leads you almost immediately into the streets of Stirling. Boy, that was some arrival! There's no doubt you will be saying that to yourself.

It isn't difficult to pick up the right road for the castle, as you can see it a mile away and it leads you down to the Royal Gardens roundabout where we join the other route that took us in from Kippen. So now once more, if you fancy it, it's time to get the old climbing legs going again for the pull-up to the castle itself.

STIRLING CASTLE

When you do arrive in Stirling, you obviously do not need to visit the castle or even ride up to it. I usually do, ride up to it that is, and on occasion actually pay the entrance money and have a wee quick look around the place. From the Royal Gardens roundabout, it is a very straightforward procedure to get there. You simply continue on down Albert Place, past its wonderful houses, till the sign pointing the way to the castle appears. When you turn left, you are immediately confronted by the statue of that most famous Highland brigand, Rob Roy McGregor, and up past him you go, into an old world. Now, it will become quite apparent early on that you are faced with a wonderful, narrow, steep climb up into the land that time forgot.

This goes down to single lane as the road swings round left and rears up towards the high, hidden castle ramparts above. The only real bugbear I have found when climbing up to the castle, has been the cobbled road that takes you up and down. It's no problem on the way up, but on the descent it can become a real bone-shaking experience, so I recommend descending on the pavement. Going up the cobbles is anything but a problem, as you pass fantastic buildings from different eras – some still in use, others very old and dilapidated, but all speaking Scottish history. As you slowly grind your way up, it's hard to know where to look, for there are simply just too many beautiful places coming at you all at once.

Simply magnificent are the stepped gable ends belonging to the buildings that line the road to your right, which will be the way you return down the hill. On your left, you pass the large Stirling Highland Hotel, not looking out of place with the surrounds. As the cobbles are met higher up, so the buildings get older and older. This is, if you haven't already guessed it, a real trip into the very old past and the age and dark greyness of all you meet will become more profound in the final furlong. There's the old jail, the ruins, then the Church of the Holy Rude dating back to 1159, making it the second oldest building in Stirling. Holy Rude saw the coronation of James VI in 1567, and it's where John Knox himself preached a sermon on that day. They all lead very picturesquely up into the castle foregrounds, and finally you arrive at the castle walls themselves.

Now, even if you do not enter the castle itself, you will not be disappointed with what you see from all the effort it took to rise up this far, especially the view north from the ramparts beside the statue of Robert Bruce. From there, the Wallace Monument looks absolutely magnificent when seen against the Ochils. Fine views are to be had all around, and a very strategically positioned ice cream van can provide a cone or two on a very warm day, should you require one. Even from the outside, the castle presents a very impressive front, but to get the full benefit of the place it's better to go inside. This will cost you nought if you're a member of Historic Scotland, but that alone costs £48 a year for an adult membership. If not, then the entry fee at the time of writing (Oct-13) was £14 for an adult and £7.50 per bambino.

Now, I know a lot of serious road bike men and women that would never consider any form of sightseeing when they are out for a run, and that is entirely up to them. No

The minor road from Carron Valley, just like the A-811, brings you to a point right below the castle cliffs. And at Albert Place, Stirling, both routes become one again.

STIRLING CASTLE RUN

When doing the Stirling run, going up to the castle is optional, of course, but I like to make the pilgrimage up even if I don't actually go in and visit the castle. The views from the car park make it all worthwhile, but so too do the old buildings that you pass on the way up and down to the castle door. The higher you go, the older the buildings get on the cobbled stone road, and they are nearly as much a trip back in time as the castle itself. Here, we are actually looking across to the old, quaint descent road from the one that carries us up.

Needless to say, it would take several books to write the whole story of Stirling Castle, and I obviously won't even attempt to do that as it is way beyond the scope of me or this book to do the place justice. However, it's good to know a little before you go in, and what was important back then was that whoever controlled Stirling controlled Scotland.

That's because of the town's strategic position. There is only a slim strip of land between the Clyde and the Forth – about 20 miles from Glasgow to Grangemouth – and some old maps I have seen in books, practically showed Stirling Bridge as this strip of land. So, the castle was able to have a great influence and control of

The boy who would be king. Robert the Bruce's statue outside the front door of Stirling Castle.

problem; they're out for a bike run and a bike run only. I usually don't stop myself, even for café breaks, which I know a lot of riders like to make as part of their ritual. So, it is totally personal if you want to take a trip inside this magnificent icon of our past and see it for yourself. I thoroughly recommend that you do, and do so myself on the odd occasion. A warm welcome awaits from the staff, and I was assured on my last visit that a new bike rack would be in place shortly for visiting cyclists.

movement between the Lowlands and the Highlands. In fact, Bonnie Prince Charlie and his men came under fire from the castle's cannons as they moved south in 1745. The siege that the Prince put the castle under (which was unsuccessful) was the last Stirling saw. Now, admittedly, it can be hard to totally relax and enjoy a tour of the place when you know that you have a long way to ride home, and therefore you are constantly watching the clock. I am guilty of this myself, and have countered it by starting the Stirling run early on purpose, to get the most from the castle when I get there.

Just approaching Stirling Castle's front door, where the top of the Great Hall can be seen (it's the white-walled building). Time to stop and admire the views and get a well earned breather for a wee ten minutes, and the ice cream van parked outside the castle is a permanent feature and a godsend on a really warm, sunny summer's day.

The Wallace Monument – looking from Stirling Castle – which was built to commemorate William Wallace, of course. A man whom I regard as the real true Scottish patriot; unlike Bruce, he was not acting out of self-interest.

I can honestly say it was worth all the effort, for it is a truly magnificent structure and place to visit. The views alone are something else, and Historic Scotland has people dressed up in period costume, telling stories and informing you about the place as you go round. The show-stealer is probably the great hall, built by James IV, who was probably the best of the Stuart monarchs. The tapestry ceiling on his bedroom is absolutely stunning. Also worth a look is the old military museum to the Argyll and Sutherland Highlanders. Reading accounts from the young troops about fighting the French is very harrowing. One young trooper wrote how the French fought well, being on home soil, and how we had no right to be there. He went on to say a great many men fell on both sides during one battle. It seems to me that Britain has not changed its outlook to the rest of the world since.

So, after a great tour of the buildings and battlements, it's back out the door and onto the old steed. Now, it's time to bear in mind what I told you earlier and get onto the pavement on the way down. It's a steep,

Another view looking northwest from within the castle, with distant Stuc a' Chroin and Ben Vorlich sitting right in the centre, on the horizon. It is a great place to visit, and I overheard a couple of Aussie tourists talking the last time I was there. One said to the other, "We don't have anything like this at home!" I think that says it all.

STIRLING CASTLE RUN

Going through just one of the many tight passageways within the castle, which is full of great wee nooks and crannies.

This is the stunningly ornate ceiling of the king's bedroom, I think, and what a work of art it is. It will keep you looking up at it for quite a while. Also within the castle, there are people dressed up in period costume, telling stories and describing how life used to be. So, all in all, it is a most enjoyable wee tour round the place. Thoroughly recommended.

teeth-chattering descent if you don't, and it's not easy to appreciate the old gold round about you on the way down if you stick to the road and the cobbles.

The next 10 miles on the way back I always find the hardest part of the whole run, till I reach the top of the Tak Ma Doon Road. This won't include the start, of course, for it is a very steep plummet down through the old town of Stirling, and is as picturesque and pretty as it is on the way up. Yes, it's a very dramatic swoop to start you off down the narrow cobbled road, and if anything it is even more charming than the ascent. It is just one lovely old place after another, and they guide you back down into the town centre.

RETURN HOME VIA KILSYTH

Follow the road back out onto Albert Place, and turn left to begin the journey home. This runs you onto Dumbarton Road which swings right onto Port Street. You'll find yourself cutting through some fine old tenements and buildings here – most are grey stone, but some are made from red or near pink brick, to make for quite a colourful spectacle. There is a good wee baker's on the left here, just before you get to the lights, and when you do get to the lights, it's best to carry straight on (signed local B-8051). This will lead through a fine-looking old part of town to the big St. Ninian's roundabout.

From the roundabout, make tracks for the Bannockburn Heritage Centre by taking the A-872 for Denny, by turning right. The plan here is to find the small back road that leads off the A-872 and takes us back over to Carron Bridge. Now, this is a lot easier to find than would be first imagined, for two reasons. The first is that it is well signposted, and the second and more significant, is that it comes right after the Bannockburn Heritage Centre itself. The new centre has only recently opened, and I have been informed that it is a fantastic, virtual reality experience, and one to enjoy. 2014 is, of course, the 700th anniversary of the battle. The entrance fee is £11 per adult and £8 per young 'un.

As for the actual battle itself, it was – as I stated earlier – absolutely crucial to keeping Scotland independent,

The 10 miles from Stirling Castle to the top of the Tak Ma Doon Road is the toughest section of the run, I always feel, though it isn't without its charms. Here, we are on a delightful stretch heading towards Carron Bridge.

castle to Edward Bruce if no relief came for him by the midsummer. So, a gentlemen's agreement was reached between the two. This gave the English king, Edward II, ample time to raise an army and head north to relieve the castle.

The gentlemen's agreement was not to Robert Bruce's satisfaction and he was angry at his brother for agreeing to it. However, it had been done, and the English had to reach and relieve Stirling by the 24th of June to prevent the castle falling into Scottish hands. Despite a lot of infighting in the English hierarchy, it was a very impressive army that did march north, and among their knights was Sir John Coymn of Badenoch, who was the only son of the Red Comyn – the very man Robert Bruce killed in Greyfriars Kirk, Dumfries, in 1306. Sir John was out for revenge. The English arrived on time, having made Falkirk by June 22nd. Accurate figures are difficult to get, with some historians putting the English Army at 2 to 2½ times that of the Scots.

as was the Battle of Stirling Bridge by Wallace 17 years earlier. Bruce had one big advantage that Wallace did not have, and that was that he was not facing the Hammer of the Scots himself, Edward I, but his son, Edward II. He was nowhere near the warrior that his father was. The action came about because Edward Bruce, Robert's brother, had laid siege to Stirling Castle around lent time in 1314. The English commander, Sir Phillip Mowbray, actually agreed a deal that he would hand over the

The battle was fought over two days, with the most famous incident occurring just before the main action started on the first day. The nephew of the Earl of Hereford, Henry de Bohun, who was riding ahead of his companions, spied The Bruce, who was also alone and out in front of his men. He decided to seize his chance for glory and charged with his lance. The Bruce, armed with only an axe and on a smaller horse, stood his ground and wheeled away only at the last moment, before standing on his stirrups and then slicing de Bohun's helmet and head in two with one blow. Thereafter, despite being heavily outnumbered, it was good tactics by The Bruce that won the battle, forcing the English – especially their cavalry – into a bend in the Bannockburn and allowing them no room to escape or manoeuvre.

It was a very bloody affair, with as many as 10 to 11,000 English infantry being slain, along with 700 cavalry. Scots casualties are put at between 400 to 4,000. Edward II made good his escape to Dunbar Castle, but most of his army were routed and they also lost a good many men on the retreat south. Much to Edward II's chagrin, Sir Philip Mowbray kept his word and handed over the keys to the castle. And so with that, ended the Battle of Bannockburn and a two-day encounter that sealed Scottish independence till that "Parcel of rogues in a nation" sold us out in 1707. I look forward to my first visit to the new heritage centre.

Just passing Loch Coulter Reservoir on the road to Carron Bridge. It has taken a fair wee bit of climbing to reach here, but the next stretch of road taking us right to the Carron Hotel will mostly be in our favour. It is a most enjoyable ride to there, and as a lot of it is downhill, it allows a fair bit of recovery before the climb up the Tak Ma Doon begins.

In the meantime, it's back to the job in hand of getting home, and it begins with turning right then left at the centre and joining the New Line Road, where the sign says 6 miles to Carron Bridge.

So, we're back out in the fields again and making our way straight as a die at first, back over the M-9, and then climbing gently into the hinterland. It gets very nice again, too, for a while, as we hit the softness of the farms and fields, and the road snakes slightly upwards and away. All's well and good as we enjoy the level road sandwiched between the Fiveyates Wood and the large Caulbarns Farm and its fields. The road has been nice and easy-going, but just watch out for a wicked wee double bend coming up about now. The dip that goes along with it will sure test your bike-handling skills, take it from me. Now up ahead on the hillside, you may start to notice sloping woodland, and it is towards that we are heading, with more pleasant rolling through the dairy fields.

Just about to ford the ford on the Tak Ma Doon Road, before the hard climbing begins in earnest. The ford itself always looks a bit tricky and awkward, but I've never had any bother all the times I've been through it. On this occasion, we're doing it in very wet, damp conditions.

A prominent and signposted big right swing in the road is followed by a little lift, which is a bit of a warm-up for the main climb to come; that starts when we eventually reach the first trees belonging to Canglour Wood. Nothing too fierce, I might add, just a long, straight rise in among the trees that continues for quite a while, till a sort of Y-junction comes upon you. Odd, too, in the fact that there are two direction signs here both pointing to Carron Bridge, with slightly different distances on them[1]. We keep left and pass up through what was the remainder of the wood; cutting has left it looking like it's just gone 10 rounds with Ricky Burns.

We finally turn left at the top of the trees, and we're back out onto the open heath.

This road must be popular with the local riders, because I meet a lot of them coming the other way whenever I'm on it. The road itself continues bolt straight out onto the moor now, and following on it you can see

---

1 - One says 4 miles to Carron Bridge, and the other says 3½. I make it 3 exactly.

how it will rise again in the distance as it draws level with Loch Coulter Reservoir, sitting down on the left. Once more it's rough and ready sheep fields for company, and away to the right the modern day scourge of the high ground, wind turbines, wave a stiff arm at you and say "How are ya?" Much huff and puff now, to get yourself up and over the last wee rise for a while, and enjoy not only the view of Loch Coulter but also the road ahead.

A fair wee bit of fun can be had up high now, as the gradient is to your advantage. And you find yourself firing fast down past Easter Buckieburn Farm, on a tight and twisting, narrow toboggan run, which will require a bit more oomph from you to pull up and out of the dip that takes you over the Buckie Burn itself. After a little more twisting and turning, you'll require even more oomph to get you up the tough wee rise that takes you then past Shielwalls Farm. That done, then the fun can begin again, because you can once more fly, with gay abandon, down beside dry stane dykes of quality, on good tar, and enjoy the road taking you finally down to Carron Bridge.

Across the shallow valley ahead can be seen the start of the Tak Ma Doon Road, rising up and over the ridge in the distance. At the same time, the wonderful B-818 can be seen running left, falling away east, to take you to Denny. The road will steepen on the final approach to the Carron Bridge Hotel[2], forcing you to hit the brakes hard to come to a safe stop at the crossroads. This signals the end of a very enjoyable flying finish to this section of high moor road, though we're not by any means on the low ground yet. To get there, we must first climb up to the top of the Tak Ma Doon, and this will prove a tough wee climb, especially this late in the day.

Right at the crossroads is the white, solid Carron Bridge Hotel itself, which was a former stopping-off point for the old cattle drovers of yesteryear, some of whom had come from as far as the Inner and Outer Hebrides. Here, they would rest up and graze their beasts, to allow them to put on a few pounds before taking them to market in Falkirk or Glasgow. As you ride between the hotel and the bridge itself, you will notice a small smattering of huts just like the ones at Carbeth. I dare say these are retreats for the bodies from Kilsyth, or maybe even Denny. It's a lovely old bridge, the Carron, and over it you go as the river murmurs under your wheels. It's dig-in time for the last time today, for the old Tak girl is always a toughie.

Now, coming this way is nowhere near as long, as sustained, or as steep as it is coming up from Kilsyth, but still it's no picnic either. It tends to rise in stages, with each one kind of feeling a little longer and harder than the last. The first of these sees you entering North Lanarkshire, as you think, "Christ, here we go again" and you get the old legs going one more time. But once over the first rise, it's recovery time, with a gentle downhill and calm ride passed the Faughlin Reservoir. This small dam nestles quietly up here in the Denny Muir among the rough, high meadows and the big conifer plantation that you are just about to ride through.

You pass among its young firs as you take on the second rise, which again is followed by a gentle descent, this one having at its bottom a rarity nowadays, which comes in the shape of a ford. You are advised to slow down as you reach it, but it's usually no problem to ride through the small burn. After this, another rise, going up through very high pink lupin-like flowers which grow wildly by the roadside. You'll find it's really nothing more than a thin slither of tar the old Tak road, which is hardly surprising as it started out as an old drovers' road way back in the first place.

We're getting near the top, but are not quite there yet, and there is still a bit of a meandering climb in front of us. It wouldn't feel so bad if we hadn't so many miles in the old legs, but soon a sign is spied for the viewpoint car park and we're…Up. Nice one! Nice one indeed, as the sweeping view, from the refinery fires of Grangemouth to the soft fields all along the Kelvin Valley running to the west, will reinforce. The height you've gained, however, is just about to get cashed in pronto, and the other side of the Tak Ma Doon will prove to be a similar animal to the one we've just come up. By that I mean it will drop then level, drop then level repeatedly. But on the Kilsyth side it will do so much more profoundly and for a whole lot longer.

The action starts right away with a speedy wee drop and bend before it straightens and levels, then the road banks hard left and falls quaintly and gently over a stone bridge, crossing another burn. Ahead, the black and white arrows warn of tight bends, but they don't tell you how steep they are, and you scream down them towards and past Berryhill Farm. As always, the road is at its

---

2 - The hotel has a sign on the door saying we don't fill water bottles and the toilet is for hotel patrons only. Expect no succour.

STIRLING CASTLE RUN

The main A road that carries us back to Glasgow from Kilsyth is the A-803, and although it can be fast and busy with traffic a lot of the time, especially once we reach Kirkintilloch, it can be wooded and pleasant to ride in its early stages around Queenzieburn.

crappiest just when it's at its steepest. So, show a bit of caution here, and also at the next steep drop that occurs just as the golf course comes into view. Hang on for dear life, as again the road surface is at its poorest right here. However, just when you could do with a breather, you get one, and the road levels out and straightens for quite a bit, alongside the course.

That is most of the steep ramps negotiated safely, and you can now take your hands off the brake levers and give the old wrists a rest, for a minute or two at least. When you enter the trees ahead, the road will bend right and then start to descend again, though not at any alarming rate. It will fall fast, yes, but at a controllable rate for some distance through the woods. You know you are coming near the finish when the houses are reached, including a great, old-style, black and white painted house sitting on the right. As you pass it, the final steep, curving, ramp-like section of the Tak Ma Doon does exactly as it says on the tin, and plonk! It drops you right into Kilsyth. Onto the A-803 to be exact, and that is a rather convenient road to be dropped onto, for me at least.

It means that I can actually stay on the same road without turning left or right till I am over the Clyde by the Albert Bridge. Straightforward and simple. Another nice one! So, right wheel it is and away we go. Now, there has been a settlement here at Kilsyth for a lot of centuries, but that isn't noticeable right away. No, it's some 70s concrete houses that greet you, begads (well mostly), but only at the start. As you head down to the big roundabout at the bottom of the Airdrie Road, a quick glance left – as that's all you'll have time for – allows a fleeting glimpse of the old town centre, and not any old town at that. For this is reputedly the birthplace of that most Scottish of pastimes, curling. Bet you didn't know that, and even if you didn't, what the hell.

After the roundabout, a little bit of a pull-up begins as you head up and out of the western end of the town. If you have been returning into a south or south westerly wind, you will already be feeling the benefit of dropping all that height.

Very often in the Scottish mountains, a drop of only 200 feet can really make a difference when you are being buffeted by a strong wind. Well, it's the same even at road level, and I'm always glad to drop down into Kilsyth if I'm into a headwind. So, you take your leave of Kilsyth and head out into the fields, but not for long, as you soon reach the small village of Queenzieburn. It mostly comprises buildings that predominantly line the right side of the road, and its main claim to fame is that it is the birthplace of one Janette Tough – better known to all as wee Jimmy Krankie. And no, I'm not going to say "Fan-dabi-dozi". Oh Christ, I've just gone and done it.

So, a curve and a fly takes you quickly through the place, which you leave after passing an old farmstead. You then find yourself back out in the fields of the Kelvin Valley. Surprisingly, a lot of it is very rough indeed, fit for nought by the looks of things, these are the pastures that lie to the left on the very floor of the valley. The fields on the right that begin as the ground slopes upwards are more like you would expect, and used for dairy and the like. Being on the valley floor, the road only rises slightly when it does, but curves enough to keep it interesting; the old A-803 is no bolt-straight baby, I assure you. On one such rise ahead, you enter both the unnoticeable Auchinreoch and East Dunbartonshire, all at once.

On the other side of the rise, there is a bit of a straight, mind you, and a very undulating one at that. Off to the right is the side road for Milton of Campsie. Just beyond this, and just before you enter Kirkintilloch, you pass a monument known as the Martyr's Stone. This solid, big tablet commemorates the death of two Covenanters in 1683, who I think are actually buried (coffinless) in the field behind. This would be in keeping with the time, as anyone convicted and executed for covenanting crimes was treated like a common criminal. The incident came about when a group of soldiers, who were escorting a prisoner to Edinburgh (Alexander Smith), were set upon by a group of local men near Inchbelly Bridge.

The attackers were successful in freeing and then escaping with the prisoner. The soldiers, now very angry, rallied themselves and decided to pursue the attackers who had headed off in the direction of Auchinreoch. On searching the area, they discovered John Wharry and James Smith sitting in a wood. They were taken prisoner and then transported to Glasgow. Both men were unarmed when found, and the only evidence against them was that they were in the general area at the time. Unfortunately, this was enough for a conviction, and both received a very brutal sentence.

This included having their right hands cut off first, before being hanged. Though, like William Wallace, they may have been cut down before death, so as to prolong their agony. Some locals had made coffins for the men to be buried properly in, but the commanding officer, a Major Balfour, broke the coffins in pieces. He was the very man who had cut off their hands. Both were then taken back to the scene of the crime, to be hung in chains. I assume that Alexander Smith was a captured Covenanter, and it's no surprise he was rescued about here, as Kilsyth was known to be a stronghold for extreme presbyterianism.

You will shortly cross Inchbelly Bridge itself, just before you arrive in Kirkintilloch. Now, we don't actually see much of Kirkie itself, as we only really skirt the edge of the town if we stay on the A-803. This is a bit of a pity because it can be quite picturesque in the centre, particularly around the canal. I doubt that was always the case, because with the coming of the canal and then the railway, Kirkie became a real leading light of the industrial revolution. This initially was weaving, but then the real heavy stuff got started, with not only iron and nickel, but coal mining taking place in the surrounding fields. Its main claim to manufacturing fame most likely is that it used to make the famous red post and telephone boxes, no less, with production only stopping in 1984.

Previous to that, Kirkie right from the word go seemed to be of strategic military importance. Certainly, the old Romans realised this and they had a fort here, all part of the Antonine Wall's defences, of course. The Clan Cummings built a motte and bailey castle here in the 12th century and the English used it for a garrison in later years. It was actually commanded by Sir Philip de Mowbray at one time, the very man who was in charge of Stirling Castle during the Battle of Bannockburn.

And on a most disappointing note, we will finish this history lesson, because it was from this castle that

STIRLING CASTLE RUN

soldiers were dispersed to capture William Wallace at nearby Robroyston in 1305. Unfortunately, they were successful. The castle was destroyed on Bruce's orders during the Wars of Independence and the land hereabouts given to the Sheriff of Dumbarton, Sir Malcolm Fleming, a Bruce supporter. Hence the reason that this land is still to this day in the realm of Dunbartonshire, whereas previously it belonged to Stirlingshire

For us, we run past the modern-style houses on the way in, which leads us to the Eastside roundabout. Go straight through (second exit) and run up to the lights that lead you onto the Glasgow Road, going through a small industrial area to get there. This comes complete with the modern car dealership, flags fluttering for effect.

Go straight through the lights and run along a fairly modern stretch of carriageway. The road starts to get a bit busy from now on, but there's still plenty of room at the moment, so no real problem. There are modern types of industrial buildings on the right, with trees obscuring the town on the left. When we get through the next roundabout, it means we are on our way out.

The run out follows the pattern of so many other towns nowadays, beginning with the older, traditional stone houses before passing the very modern estates the closer you get to the town boundary. And so it is with Kirkie, before the fields meet you again. You've now, just for the record, left the home town of Moira Anderson and where former champion boxer Jim Watt lives.

There now begins a long and gradual, open, draw up through the fields towards Bishopbriggs. Long, meandering, and slow climbing straights now follow, only broken when the road swerves lazily as it crosses the Forth and Clyde Canal just at the Stables pub. To the right, always acting as a distant guide, are the Campsie Fells, showing a steep and solid flank.

This would be the same steep and solid flank witnessed by centurions and troops of the mighty Roman Army as they manned the Antonine Wall, whose course we have been following ever since we arrived in the Kelvin Valley. The open, fieldy climbing stops when we reach the Torrance roundabout, because the road then follows, bolt straight, the high stone wall of the Cadder Cemetery for as far as the eye can see. We are a lot more enclosed now, but not claustrophobic by any means. We go straight through, heading for Glasgow of course, but should you suddenly become overwhelmed with a burning desire to visit any friends or relatives who are currently incarcerated in Low Moss nick, then turn left at the Torrance roundabout to do so.

The rest of us can carry straight on to the next roundabout, the Cadder itself, and by doing so enter the suburbs of Bishopbriggs. The A-803 continues flat and straight through the bungalows and semis that are home to the good people of this rather large town. A town that got its name when the land was granted to Bishop Jocelin in 1180, by King William the Lion. Surprisingly, it struggled to grow for a long time, the Briggs – as it is often known – and was in danger also for a long time of being swallowed up by Glasgow and becoming merely a suburb. However, eventually it got going and retained its independence. Nowadays, it has commuter town written all over it, but in the past it had mining and quarrying to support its own community. The 1920s saw the mines systematically close, and it was the big expansion programs of the 50s and 60s that saw the town's population balloon.

The long, flat straight only ceases when the road starts to drop down through big old houses into the town centre, or Bishopbriggs Cross as it is known. It's a real hustle and bustle place, so keep your wits about you now, as cars are coming at you all ways. Or so it seems, because there are so many side roads feeding in from all directions here. Even when you get clear of the busy wee shopping precinct, it's very advisable to continue to look sharp, because the busy road down into the north end of the Toon – as Glasgow is known – now begins. It's still single carriageway up until and just after the Colston Road junction, but then the dual stuff starts, as downhill you gather momentum through Springburn. It's probably best to gather as much momentum when going through Springburn as you can muster (only kidding!).

Now, the next mile or so, from here to the top end of Glasgow's High Street, will be ridden on a very busy dual carriageway, nothing too pretty, especially as you run down past the high flats of Sighthill. The one saving grace will be the St. Rollox railway building on the left, which is a lovely old Victorian job and was the place where a lot of the grand old steam engines were built. Between it and another three yards in this area, they enjoyed an incredible 25% of the world's steam train production. They were real Clyde-built. During the war, they produced – among other things – the gliders for the D-Day assault here.

There now follows a hairy wee manoeuvre, when you have to go from the inside to the outside lane, to avoid running onto the motorway. You are flying down at this point, and having to look over your shoulder at speed is never the easiest thing in the world to do. Especially as mucho motors will all be heading in the same direction, on the same road, at the same time. However, you must get over, and where there's a will, as they say.

As we come out the other side of the motorway's flyover, at the top of the High Street at the Royal Infirmary (on the A-8 Castle Street, to be pedantic). This immediately catapults us from the new urban hard edge to the oldest part of the city no less. Even parts seemingly attached to the modern, square-built Royal are grandiose and ancient. A lot, if not all of these parts, have recently been restored, and the place is looking all the better for it.

It's a real busy junction and stretch of road that you find yourself in amongst now, with all the traffic coming off the M-8. So again, stay on the ball and use the eyes you have in the back of your head to keep safe. Things get a bit quieter after you pass the Cathedral and the oldest house in Glasgow. The Cathedral, looking dark and magnificent on the left, and the Provand's Lordship House dating from 1471, directly across the road from it on the right. Great also is the old blue police box (a real Doctor Who

It's all one road, no turning left or right, all the way from Kilsyth till you cross the Clyde on the Albert Bridge. Here we are on the High Street in Glasgow, just approaching the Tolbooth steeple. A fine sight she makes, as we enter the oldest part of the city.

job) that sits on the junction with John Knox Street (never heard of him). There now comes a beautiful fall down the High Street, that follows the curves of the grand, red sandstone tenements that take you down to the corner of Duke Street.

It really is a wonderful whoosh down, and I actually much prefer to come up this section than go down it, just to get a bit more time in amongst the old. In complete contrast, the left side beyond this is now full of high rise, ultra-modern blocks, built by Strathclyde University, to house their students (mostly Chinese, as far as I can tell). This makes a good contrast with other stuff around, because this is you heading into the Merchant City, which is another part of Glasgow's oldest district. They've made a good job of restoring the Merchant City, most of which you won't see from the High Street, but that doesn't matter. Ahead, stealing the show and rightly so, will be the Tolbooth steeple.

You will go right below this old medieval needle as you run up to Glasgow Cross. It is a beautiful, striking, stone structure, complete with blue, square clockface and weathercock. It was here that the public hangings occurred in the old days, and this is you now in the traditional centre of the city. The city centre itself started to move further west with the coming of the industrial revolution. Before that, the road running off to your right, the Trongate, was a main centre for commerce. It was here that everything coming into Glasgow via the Clyde was weighed and taxed. Tron is an old Scots word meaning weigh scales, after the weighbeam used for the job.

Ahead of us now is more of ye olde, in the shape of the Saltmarket. It has a right old, dark, and dank look to its beginning, what with the old tenements and the dark exterior of the Tollbooth Bar, which sits below the old rail bridge that once carried the trains from St. Enoch's. Under it you go to carry you down towards the Albert Bridge. The Saltmarket was known for its wool

And finally it is the Glasgow Road that welcomes me back into the old home town. Sometimes, though not always, you can be really glad to get back home from a long run, depending on how you feel. But regardless of how much you have suffered on any run, within half an hour of getting home you will be buzzing again. Guaranteed.

production at one time and not, as its name suggests, anything to do with the white stuff. It also had a very bad reputation for slums and its associated ills at one time, too.

What I can tell you is that nowadays it sure has character. And I can also tell you it runs you conveniently onto the Albert Bridge, which will carry you across to the south side, just as it has done for many before you in its 140-year history. It still looks in good nick, but recently they announced a £2 million upgrade to restore it to its former glory. Fine by me.

Once across, I make a right turn and start to head for Paisley. This starts off on Ballater Street, before running onto Norfolk Street, but the majority of the return is done on Paisley Road West. Now, from the Albert Bridge to Paisley Road Toll, you tend to ride past a bit of the city that has either a tough or tired look to it, and I suspect that a lot of this area will come in for a good bit of regeneration, once we finally get clear of the so-called credit crunch.

After joining Paisley Road West proper, we skirt along flat and at a fair old skelp, towards and through the tenements and fruit shops that abound around Ibrox. I always seem to go really well at this point, due to the feeling of being in such a tight corridor, perhaps. This stops for a bit as you cross over the M-8 and run beside Bellahouston Park, but resumes once again when you get back in among the tenements at Craigton. A slight rise brings you up to the junction with Mosspark Boulevard, and then you gently roll down to the junction with the Berryknowes Road.

Mind how you go from here till you're past the equally mega-busy crossroads at Crookston Road, for this mile-plus stretch of road is never quiet. There are cars flying in from all directions and angles, from side streets to filling stations, and also many motorists involved in the risky manoeuvre of pulling in and out from the shops. I've always managed to get through here unscathed, but it's a bit of a mystery how.

When you get past Crookston, you're as good as back in Paisley and things definitely ease off a bit. You go through another long corridor, but this time it's the bungalows of Ralston and not the tenements of Ibrox that fire you along. All is still flat and fast, and that's just fine, because the old legs aren't looking for any sort of challenge this late in the day. But then a sneaky one soon presents itself.

It comes in the shape of the long and deceptively tough draw-up past Barshaw Park, and phew! This wee bugger certainly lets you know how many miles you've done. There is an equally long descent down the other side to give you time to recover, however, which is pleasantly done between the park and the very beautiful villas that line the road here. A final flat straight runs you into Paisley centre, and for this tired rider there is one final sting in the tail, with the tough, steep climb up the Munt waiting for me at the top of Causeyside Street and Calside. It makes a big difference to know that this is the last hard haul of the day as you start your run up to it, as does the new tarmac that helps you force your way up as you turn the cranks on it.

With the last curving twists of the Munt behind me and my heartbeat starting to decrease, then it's finally cool-down time, with just a couple or three easy rises between me and home. And with the approach to the old front door, a great 70 to 80 mile run into our distant past comes to an end. Hope you enjoyed it, and could I just say that if doing this run in future, try and pop into the Bannockburn Heritage Centre when passing. Who knows? It might just get you fired up enough to go out and vote for independence the next time. Remember the men of 1314.

Liam Boy

CARRON VALLEY RUN

VIA KILLEARN
66.9 MILES
4.25 HOURS
ASCENT 2960 FEET
2938 CALORIES BURNED

VIA CAMPSIE GLEN
65.1 MILES
4.25 HOURS
ASCENT 3340 FEET
2915 CALORIES BURNED

OS LANDRANGER MAPS 64, 57..

ROUTE SUMMARY

ROUTE START

Paisley Rd West
George V Bridge
Saltmarket
High St
Springburn Rd
Bishopbriggs
Kirkintilloch

Kilsyth
Tak Ma Doon Rd
Carron Bridge
Gonachan

Fintry
Killearn

Strathblane
A-81 Or Mugdock
Milngavie
Clyde Tunnel Or Renfrew Ferry
Paisley

ALTERNATIVE START 1

Clyde Tunnel
Dumbarton Rd
Byres Rd
Bilsland Dr
Springburn Rd
Auchinstarry

ALTERNATIVE ROUTE

Crow Rd B-822
Lennoxtown

ALTERNATIVE START 2

Paisley Rd West
Ballater St
Cumbernauld
Stepps
Twechar

Kilsyth

THE CARRON VALLEY RUN

TO THE EDGE OF THE HIGHLANDS

I am about to describe a run here that is almost totally contained within other runs, mostly the Stirling run, but have decided to accord it separate status. That run is the Carron Valley run, and the reason being is its popularity and importance. Especially for, though not exclusively to, riders who live north of the Clyde. For the boys and girls who stay on the north side of Glasgow, the Carron Valley can provide very quick access to some great scenery and climbing in no time at all. So much so that when doing it, especially at the weekend, it is very rare not to meet other riders, unless the day happens to be an absolute howler.

For me, this is a run that comes in about the 60 miles mark and I will offer a couple of alternative routes, to provide some variety, should you be in the mood for some serious climbing or not. This will all be done in very beautiful and rugged country, right on dear old Mother Glasgow's doorstep, and will bring home to any former city slicker just how truly beautiful is the country they live in, though perhaps they weren't aware of it until they started cycling.

Most people from this neck of the woods, and there are plenty of us here, will have only seen the uniform southern face of the Campsie Fells from a distance, with no idea just what lies beyond. Well, let me assure you, when you do find out, you are in for a very pleasant surprise.

The overall plan is to head out to Kilsyth and then go up and over the Tak Ma Doon Road. This is followed by returning through either Killearn or Lennoxtown, and then using either the Clyde Tunnel or Renfrew ferry to make it back to Paisley. As we are not going all the way to Stirling this time, the overall distance will be about 20 miles less, and that is enough to make this a run that can be done on even the shortest days of the year. I particularly like taking it on when there is an easterly wind blowing, and this airflow is most predominant during the colder months. This means I have a tail wind on the home run, so I have often found myself up in the Carron Valley during winter time.

But don't get me wrong here, it is a great run all year round and is an absolute pleasure to do on a glorious summer's day, when you are in short sleeves and taking on the gradients of the Tak Ma Doon and Crow Roads. These two big climbs should be enough to give any rider a great day out and work out, and have been used by many when they are preparing for big trips to the Alps and such like.

Now, for me the easiest and most straightforward way to get to Kilsyth will simply be to retrace my tyre tracks on the route that I used to return home on the Stirling run, all the way to the Carron Bridge Hotel. This is the way we will take on this occasion, as it will be the first time we have ridden this route in this direction. But I will offer a couple of alternative suggestions as well.

The two other approaches that I will mention will be done for two reasons. First, to avoid the busy section between the Saltmarket in Glasgow and up to where the A-803 Springburn Road meets Colston Road. Second, as not everyone is starting off from Paisley, the other approaches could be more suited to their needs.

So, we better get cracking, and after my usual high carbohydrate breakfast before a long run and my ritual of morning stretches, I'm saddled up and out the door. Let me just say that I only have a breakfast of pasta or beans on toast if it is a big cycle day. Ordinarily, I would not take in so much high energy food if I was not going to burn it off on the day.

Remember that carbohydrate is full of energy. If you're not going to burn it off right away, you will store it in the body as fat. So if you're not training or riding that day, you don't need to take in a lot of energy. It is better to take more protein instead, or less carbo if you are taking some, just to keep the old weight in check. Nutrition is a very difficult thing to get right, and precise advice is not an easy thing to come by as you will find out for yourself, should you ever go looking for it. I'm no nutritional guru by any stretch of the imagination, and I usually avoid carbohydrates on my sedentary days, and only stock up on them when exercise is imminent. During riding it's also fine and recommended to consume carbs, and remember, any carbs taken within 20 minutes of ending your run won't go on as fat, but will be stored in the liver as glycogen.

And the stretching? I stretch every day and recommend you give it a try as well, as you will feel much better for it and notice right away a loosening up of the old joints and muscles. Further to that, the benefits to a cyclist are worth the effort, for it will mean that you have more flexible hamstring muscles, and this helps produce a better, more powerful, and efficient pedal stroke. On top of that, if you don't stretch, then bear in mind that your hamstrings will tighten and start to give back problems. As they are now getting larger and more powerful, they are able to pull your lower back out of position. For these reasons, I cannot recommend enough the benefits of at least stretching your legs, but it will be for your own benefit if you do an all-over stretching routine at the same time.

As I was saying, we're out the door and away. It's magic to get on the old machine and get going again, no doubt about it. And today I want to make my way out the Glasgow Road and head for dear old Glesca Toon.

Now, I can dive into Paisley centre and go through the cross, or even take the more direct route of Mill Street. But I don't particularly like Mill Street, because it is part of the Paisley ring road system and therefore always mega bloody busy. I do use it, of course, from time to time, especially when returning along Glasgow Road, but am always glad to get through it. A favourite alternative to the centre that I use when Glasgow-bound is to wind my way through the schemes on the south side and access Glasgow Road by Hawkhead. This involves following three fairly long east/west running roads that serve me well here.

The first is Glenburn's Donaldswood Road, which I'm on within a minute after leaving the old homestead, and it leads down and onto Falside Road. This at one time housed the old Brown and Polson's factory, which went the same way as the rest of them. Falside leads to the Neilson Road, on which a quick left/right shimmy runs me onto the wonderful-to-ride Lochfield Road. God knows what loch they are talking about, for it must have been filled in when they built the houses. After a slope up, the grand old Lochfield scheme is ridden through and then it's a flat fly round the bends as you pass the playing fields (which may formerly have been the loch). You then pass between the houses of Hunterhill and Dykebar.

The traffic lights mean you have reached the Barrhead Road, and by turning right onto it and then left at the roundabout ahead, you gain Hawkhead Road. It's a good old flying start right down this rather interesting road, I do declare; a road that contains a lot of this, that, and the other. A jumble of assorted industries and land

CARRON VALLEY RUN

Looking across the wheat fields of Arkleston Farm from Arkleston Road towards the high flats of Knightswood, behind which sits the Campsie Fells. The noticeable dip in the Campsies behind the flats is the very route taken by the B-822, the Crow Road, which I often use when returning from the Carron Valley run and is one of two main options. Kilsyth is the target town on the outward journey, of course, containing the Tak Ma Doon Road, and if going via Arkleston it means I'm using the Clyde Tunnel then Bilsland Drive, Ruchill, to gain access to the A-803 at Springburn, before heading up through Bishopbriggs.

uses as diversified as one could possibly imagine. It includes, amongst others, a former hospital, a very large cemetery, an equally large chemical works (soon to close), headstone engraver, filling station, fuel dump, and a great hump bridge to take you over the railway and into the lower residential part of the road. Take any of the next three roads on the right to run you, over uncountable numbers of bloody speed bumps, onto the Glasgow Road just after Barshaw Park.

For some reason or other, the residents in these three streets of Ralston have had the misfortune to have been plagued by those ridiculous bumps, which seem to be overdone to say the least. Why Renfrewshire Council put in so many of these things in the places that they did, completely defies logic. After all the years of waiting for tarmacadam and other road surface materials to arrive to make our journeys smoother, no sooner have we got them than some loon ball council officials decide to put in man-made lumps that would put any cobbled road surface to shame. Why? You would have thought that the potholes were enough to slow down all but the most determined of boy racers. Even on a bike, the speed bumps are a bloody pain in the arse.

Still, once on the Glasgow Road, we are on our way uninterrupted and heading out of town. This will happen before you realise it, because most people assume that the boundary between Paisley and Glasgow is at the bottom of the Crookston Road. Not so; it is a little bit earlier than that, at the bottom of Kelhead Avenue. Now, if you are a bike rider like me who doesn't do red lights, then just be a bit extra careful at this junction as it is always so busy. Again, I know that all the road safety campaign brigade will be tut-tutting and wagging a finger at my irresponsibility with not stopping at red, but I'm not bothering my arse what they think. I can judge when it's safe to go, and don't need a nanny state telling me what's good for me. We have too much of that bollocks going on nowadays.

One of the main drawbacks when heading through the city on a cold winter's day is trying to stay warm because of all the stop/starting at lights. You don't get this problem when heading through less built-up areas, as you can for the most part keep moving and keep up a good core body temperature. This is another reason I do my best to keep moving, regardless of the traffic light's colour. Some car drivers take offence when they see a bike rider cruise through red, but they can sit in their warm, dry vehicle unaffected by the conditions, they are not exposed to the elements like us poor souls. So, undeterred, I'm through the busy Crookston Road crossroads and heading along Paisley Road West (PRW) now.

Coming up shortly will be the first section of shops, just after the next junction with Hillington Road South, and it's here you really must keep watch and be very wary of all around you. The amount of activity makes it an absolute must to be on your guard, especially for drivers pulling out from the shops or the filling stations across the road. After only a short respite of residential, you will hit the next really busy stretch round about the shops at the bottom of Berryknowes Road, and again look sharp for hazards. Once through this, though, things do get quieter as you glide over the rise ahead that will provide a springboard to fire you down through the tenements at Craigton.

However, the big roundabout attached to Helen Street sees the need for caution and vigilance once more, but the open dual carriageway following it is breathe easy time again. Now, when you roll up to the lights at the end of Bellahouston Park, on the left will come into view the main stand of Ibrox Park. The old Teddy Bears have not had their troubles to seek of late, and despite all the infighting and financial woes the club has gone through, the old stadium building maintains a dignified front. Some people might find that statement odd coming from

The Clyde Tunnel is only one option when making for Kilsyth, and for years my preferred choice was to take Paisley Road West and then head up the High Street for Bishopbriggs, or go via the Cumbernauld Road to Stepps. This is PRW at Ibrox with its good-looking red sandstone tenements lining the way.

someone like me, who has an Irish Catholic background, bearing in mind Rangers' biased past. But at least that is now a policy no longer operated by the club, with regard to the playing staff at least, courtesy of Graham Souness. I personally have no time for that crap. It's time to leave all that sectarianism in the 17th century where it belongs and move forward, though that's easier said than done for some.

I love the fine old tenements that follow on Paisley Road now, and they lead into the tight corridor of the ones at Cessnock, which is a place where I always seem to go so well. Just before you reach them, Edmiston Drive will come in and join you over your left shoulder and you flip onto the A-8 from the A-761. Not that you notice, right enough. So, tally-ho it is, all the way along till you are almost guaranteed to get stopped by the traffic queuing at Paisley Road Toll. You know when you are nearing this important big Y-junction, because you will spot the magnificent golden angel statue on top of the La Fiorentina building from quite a distance away. Despite its prominence and beauty, there is surprisingly a bit of dubiety as to the creator.

The next section of road goes under the high Kingston Bridge and round onto the waterfront. Not the prettiest part of town, but I suspect redevelopment is not too far in the future for a lot of this place. It leads us to the George V Bridge, which is a lovely and easy way to cross the Clyde on its low spanning arches. It provides great views downstream to its younger, less attractive neighbour, but may not be as old or as different to the Kingston as you may think. It was finished and opened in 1928, which was much later than planned; the original year to start building was 1914, but the First World War held up the show. And despite its stone appearance, it is actually made of concrete with a granite façade as a finish. It does the job of getting us across most splendidly, where we turn right and head on under the Central and along Clyde Street.

This leads onto the Bridgegate (pronounced Briggit) and into the oldest part of the city. First, we start off on the Saltmarket, whose tenements and demeanour just ooze old, which is fine of course, but not so the traffic. It will be real hustle, bustle, and stop/start the minute you meet the Salty, and this is the only drawback with coming this way. The surroundings are most splendid, however, with of course that striking sentinel of yesteryear, the Tolbooth steeple, again stealing the show. It will immediately grab your attention over the old, now defunct, rail bridge that crosses the road and was once part of the St. Enoch station system. I absolutely love this area, especially the bit round Parnie Street that curves so exquisitely round on the left-hand side.

It contains my favourite camera shop and things like a model shop (though I don't build models). The premises on the Salt itself also carry character, like the pawn shop, the Tolbooth bar, with Billy Bilsland – one of our most famous bike men – having his store further down nearer the Albert Bridge. It isn't only the Tolbooth steeple that represents old Glasgow here, for just to the right is the Mercat Cross. This structure is not only for show, but is one of about 620 in the country that was granted to a town by a bishop, a baron, or even the king himself, and signified that a certain place was legally entitled to hold a market (mercat comes from the Scots pronunciation of market) or regular fair.

This cross is actually a replica of the original which was removed in 1659, and the one you see there today

CARRON VALLEY RUN

Just approaching and about to cross the Clyde on the George V Bridge, and a fine looking fellow he is. Once over, I never go straight up onto Hope Street as there are simply too many buses on that route, but will instead turn right along the Clydeside and make for the Saltmarket.

didn't actually get built till 1930, though the steeple is the real McCoy, being built in 1626. It was the place they carried out the hangings in the old days, you will be warmed to hear. The rest of the Tolbooth building was demolished in 1812 but the steeple survived. Just for the record, the condemned man was taken out of a small window and onto the scaffolding that would be on the Trongate side of the steeple, I think. Here would be where he took his last breath.

In fact, Glasgow cross is not only a former meeting place for traders, but is also one where beautiful old structures and buildings meet, too. The Mercat building, which stands behind its namesake cross on the right, and the grey Royal Bank building directly across the road from you at this point, which curves elegantly behind the Tolbooth steeple, are two buildings that would really stand out in their own right in any other situation.

So, in the midst of all this grand history, we sail over the cross and start to make our way up the High Street. A short section of very modern student accommodation is passed on the right, some of which is very stylish, before we re-enter the old again. When coming down the High Street on the way back from Stirling, I mentioned

Just approaching the Tolbooth steeple on a very busy Saltmarket, as it always is, and the traffic from here right up to Bishopbriggs is the only drawback with coming this way. It's one of the reasons I started to look for alternative routes to get me to Kilsyth.

how I love to climb up the top half of this street, and that is true. I always enjoy its rising curve between such beautiful, old, red sandstone tenements.

Adding to the character of the setting here are the small shops and services that occupy the bottom tier of the buildings. On the right-hand side, this seems to be predominantly faith healers and fortune tellers, and I strongly advise you to avoid the latter. I'm about to make my own psychic prediction here and say, "All that will happen will be you will come out a few pounds lighter and be none the wiser." So there you go, that's your reading from me.

Just sit down and purr your way up this pleasant path, because it will all come to a bit of an abrupt halt when you round the corner and come to a stop at the Cathedral lights. You're guaranteed to run into some serious amount of traffic here, that's for sure. The enforced stop, however, does allow you time to take in the surroundings.

Not any old surroundings at that, I might add pronto, because once again we find ourselves sandwiched between the two oldest buildings in the whole of Glasgow. On our left, almost close enough to touch, will be the Lord Provand's House (1471) and across the road will be the Cathedral. Now, a lot of the old stuff including the Lord Provand's place has had a bit of a facelift in recent times and therefore doesn't look its age, but not so the great Cathedral itself. It still possesses a lot of its black, sooty old walls that contrast stunningly with its bright green modern roof panels. It dates from the late 12th century, well before the Reformation, and I'm not able to do its history justice here. I can say that I do admire its age and grandeur every time I ride by.

THE SPRINGBURN ROUTE

Now, the reason that there is so much traffic in this vicinity, will be because we are so close to the M-8 and therefore most of the cars will be coming from or going to that thick blue line. We now touch Castle Street and have to do a left/right turn to take us onto the A-803 (Springburn Road). This manoeuvre is executed once we draw level with the Royal Infirmary, which is itself a very grand and impressive building. This part of the hospital was built in 1914 and replaced the original from 1794, though of course there were major additions to the place in the 1970s. The hospital's most famous son was a surgeon called Joe Lister, who noticed how many of his patients died from infection rather than their injuries, and he introduced cleaning with carbolic acid for surgeons' hands and instruments.

Today he is regarded as the father of antisepsis, though he is only one of a handful of men from this very hospital to contribute greatly to modern day medical practices. On a broader front, this is only one field where we old Scots have contributed to greatly improve the world. There will be more of that later, but in the meantime let's get up the Springburn and on with the show.

So, after going left then right at the Castle Street lights, you head under the motorway by a surprisingly attractive underpass. You will be beneath a gantry saying A-803 Port Dundas-Springburn, and the brown walled tunnel that takes you under couldn't be more pleasant. We are still in busyville at the moment, and will continue to be so till we reach the junction with Colston Road.

In the intro I mentioned just how heavy with traffic this place can get, which is what you will find on the dual carriageway that rises up past the Sighthill high flats. Across the road sits the grand old St. Rollox building, and I can only imagine what its Victorian architect would make of the modern tower blocks which blight the landscape only a stone's throw away today. Much tut-tutting, I suspect. When you clear the rise ahead, you not only get a bit of respite on the way down, but also get your first view of the Campsies. A pleasing site they make, too, and after passing through the junction and rising once more, still on dual carriageway, you pass under Hawthorn Street, being carried on the bridge above.

THE WEST END ROUTE

The reason that I mention Hawthorn Street is because this can be a very good way to gain the A-803 and Kilsyth from the west end of Glasgow. This artery can also be used by someone from my neck of the woods who has negotiated the Clyde by either the Renfrew ferry or Clyde Tunnel. Hawthorn Street is merely a continuation of Bilsland Drive that starts at the top of Queen Margaret Drive and then runs through Ruchill. Queen Margaret, in turn, is a continuation of the Byres Road, all part of the B-808. It has to be said that this area, what with the Dumbarton and Great Western Roads, is also one busy baby and you will find yourself manoeuvring through heavy traffic at some point or another. However, once you get onto Queen Margaret, there is a cycle lane and things start to ease off a fair bit.

I like to approach on this route from time to time, as it makes for a nice change of scenery, and also I absolutely love the start to Bilsland Drive the way it begins under the rail bridge with a rising swish between two dark and curving high walls. Once on Bilsland, continue to make your way east along a street that does somewhat have a look and feel of old Glasgow about it, and this is despite the fact that a lot of regeneration, some very noticeable, has taken place here. The high flats of Springburn and beyond will act as beacons to guide you towards your target as you near the junction with Balmore Road. Once across, you're onto Hawthorn Street itself and into palatial Possilpark. Rise gently up between the new, and not so new, houses and buildings, till you arrive at the slip road that will glide you down onto the Springburn Road itself.

Here we meet up with the route coming up from the High Street, and now that we are all back together again, we can make our way up towards the Briggs. It's all still broad and open at this point, as the old Springburn girl is still dual carriageway, and there isn't too much in the way of commerce or accommodation hemming us in on either side. Things do start to narrow as we approach the crossroads at Colston, and once over that we've just crossed from Glasgow District into East Dunbartonshire. That is the busy section more or less behind us and, apart from one time when some stupid – would you believe female – driver[1] cut the nose of me whilst hurrying to turn left, I've never had any bother on it. It isn't a long section into the bargain, so is over fairly quickly.

THE STEPPS ROUTE

You may want to avoid coming this way altogether, and might find the west end isn't your best end and doesn't suit you either. If that's the case, then you may want to approach Kilsyth by the area that lies just to the northeast of Robroyston. I usually access this by heading for Stepps on the old Cumbernauld Road, and then taking the Lenzie Road, which is well signposted, about halfway through the town. I have used this way more than any other, just for the record. Having said that, I

---

1 - Only kidding, I tend to find women drivers more patient, generally speaking. She incidentally was turning into Everard Drive. "Oh, shut that door!" If you're too young to remember Larry Grayson on the *Generation Game*, you won't get that gag.

CARRON VALLEY RUN

The third and final approach route that I use to reach Kilsyth is via Stepps and the back roads beyond Muirhead and Chryston. This entails coming across to the edge of Glasgow's east end and heading up the old Cumbernauld Road, the A-80. The above photo shows the Jury's Inn Hotel on Jamaica Street, seen from the south end of the Glasgow Bridge, which means we didn't cross on the George V Bridge but carried straight on heading for Bridgeton.

must be honest and say I don't know the area particularly well, and usually I just head in the general direction of Kilsyth and use the Campsies as a guide rail. In other words, I didn't know how I was going to get there; I only knew I was going to get there.

This strategy, if you could call it a strategy, more often than not resulted in some great, country, back road riding, and on one occasion I even ended up going under the Forth and Clyde Canal by a most exquisite narrow tunnel. You have the option of either checking a map before you attempt to come this way and therefore plan a route, or simply follow your nose and the Campsies and leave it to chance. Either way, you'll get there and enjoy it enroute.

So first we must get onto the old A-80 Cumbernauld Road, and you could use Alexandra Parade and turn left at the end of the parade to do that. This, however, would mean you would still need to ride up the High Street, and that's fine if you so wish. The parade itself becomes a beautiful red avenue of sandstone, once you've had your brush with the Royal Infirmary and the old Wills cigarette factory.

But on the other hand, should you want to completely avoid the High Street altogether, then don't cross the George V Bridge when you arrive on the Clydeside from the southwest. Instead, stay on the southside and continue onto Ballater Street (A-74), which will run you past the Gorbals. When you arrive at the junction on the edge of Glasgow Green, don't go straight ahead and through that bastion of loyalism, Bridgeton. No, turn right and head into the new stuff. Now even I don't recognise this part of the town any more, and can actually struggle when taking a hire through here, even to Celtic Park. All this redevelopment has been done in preparation for the Commonwealth Games (God help us!) and fortunately we barely touch the new roads, which are barren and soulless.

They do have some natty wee cycle lanes attached to them, if I'm being honest, but still we get out of there fast by taking one of the first lefts and turning onto Dunn Street (the B-763), which is signposted for Dennistoun. The B-763 is to all intents and purposes the Cumbernauld Road, despite its several guises and name changes on the way up. It more or less runs us directly to where we want to go in a general northerly direction, with Celtic Park quickly coming into view. I have to say that although I want independence, I don't agree with the SNP's ban on political banners at sporting events, and I admire those who defy such censorship. So, it's hats off to the Green Brigade. Long may those leprechauns' lums reek. I'm not taking sides in a blue/green, them and us scenario, no. I'm talking about free speech and expression here.

This is more of this political correctness gone mad here. The men in charge, certainly at Celtic, want all the history to be forgotten about in the name of political correctness and profit. Everything that has gone before is not to be mentioned and is to be swept under the carpet if it doesn't suit their modern corporate image. I know I said earlier that it's time to look forward and leave the sectarianism in the past, and that is true. However, for some football fans, their club is the emblem and channel of all they are, and it's through that that they express themselves. For many, especially Celtic and Rangers fans, it's one of the most important things in their lives. How else can they make a political point? Talk to their local MP? Who the hell wants to talk to their local MP? For that reason and that reason alone, once again I say, "Up the Green Brigade."[2]

Despite so much major regeneration being done all around here, there is still enough of the old stuff about to remind me of late seventies Glasgow. As you trundle northwards, it may strike you that the east end is a real hotchpotch of everything, with apparently no overall long-term plan for the place having ever been devised.

---

2 - I know that it is UEFA & not the Government who fine the club for flying political banners, and can understand the football clubs' problem with that alone.

At the start of the Cumbernauld Road (the A-80) at Riddrie, you do come very close to Barlinnie Prison, which sits on your right-hand side just before you cross the motorway. Every time I ride past it I do feel a sadness that life has come to this for so many people. On one occasion, as the photo shows, I went much closer than usual and discovered that below every white barred window is the cell number painted on the outside of the building. This must be for identification purposes, I assume.

Things just seem to be built here, there, and everywhere, whenever or wherever they were required. I certainly get that impression as I move from Fielden onto Millerston Street. But as Duke Street is approached, normal service is resumed, and you meet up with the well planned-out, old tenements of Dennistoun and Haghill.

Although this might be the most suitable way to approach Kilsyth for some riders, others may just be looking for a quieter alternative to the Springburn route. This was initially why I would prefer to take the Stepps and Robroyston way. However, even coming by the B-763, you will find that round about Duke Street things do start to get busy, because of traffic coming and going from the M-8. In this case, it will be from Junction 14 Blochairn/Carntyne. It's fair to say that if you must make your way across the city, like I do, then there is a good chance that at some point you will hit a busy section. This is until you manage to suss out some quieter way, with a bit of planning, and or trial and error perhaps.

We don't have to suffer the heavy stuff for too long, though, because we've now joined the Cumbernauld Road in name as well as in body, and to stay on it we must get into the right-hand lane up ahead and break right at the lights. This takes you slap-bang into Haghill and another set of lights, and another right turn keeps the Cumbernauld lad under your wheels, only now this is officially the A-8. You've also just met up with the Alexandra Parade option, for your information.

Now we are required to turn left up ahead, and for me this is the start of the Cumbernauld Road proper. At one time this was a mega busy route, before the Stepps bypass was built, and though I did ride it back then, boy, was it a nerve-jangler.

The thing that marks the Cumbernauld chappy (now the A-80) out from now on will be its long, long straights, and from the word go you are onto one. Away ahead, you see him rise gently as he takes you up through the scheme of Riddrie, whose most famous landmark is the Bar-L. You don't see the prison early on, as you make your way through another one of Glasgow's 1930s housing schemes. Yes, Riddrie is very Mosspark/ Knightswood to begin with, and that's fine of course, but then the road once more must rise to enable it to clear the motorway. At this point, a look to the right will reveal the walls and chimneys of our best-known nick. I find that looking at any building to do with the penal system is a bit upsetting, to say the least. Especially when all the connotations and ingredients about the why's and where's are taken into consideration.

There are the inmates who have had their freedom, and in some cases, lives taken from them, a lot of it to do with circumstance. Let's not forget the victims of their crimes, of course, who can often be forgotten, especially by the judicial system. Being such a lover of the outdoors myself, and even at this age in life still being able to do what I want when I want to a great extent, I find the thought of long term incarceration absolutely abhorrent. Even just the look of the place is enough to leaden my thoughts. It's very disappointing to think that life has come to this for so many people, and it gives you food for thought as you cross the M-8 and level out near Hogganfield Loch. Before you reach it, you pass the Provanmill Road on the left, containing Big Art's Ponderosa[3]. I'll be surprised if Historic Scotland hasn't bought it by now.

It's a fair size, the old Hogganfield Loch, and it pleases as the road bends round it on its way into Stepps, which lies in North Lanarkshire. The long, thin line of the road continues, now nowhere near the busy beast it once was, and just to totally put you at your ease, a cycle lane is marked out on the road, would you believe? The bungalows cheer you along, as the A-80 draws you into the older village centre, and there seems an eerie quietness about the place, as though something is missing – even though the bypass has been in place for years now. The turn-off point is nearing when you see the old footbridge ahead which spans the road, though now its services

---

3 - Gangland figure Arthur Thompson's place of residence.

aren't needed nearly as much, and you take a left at the lights onto the well-signed Lenzie Rd (the B-757).

It's a right old leafy lane, the Lenzie lady, that's for sure. Big, old houses, with big, old trees, in big, old gardens, that's what you'll find down this road, and oh so nice it is. The road's style adds to the pleasure with its curves here; the first one, right, has a rusty old pole on which the attached sign says Lenzie 3. The second curve, left, drops you delightfully down and out of Stepps, into the fields and under the M-80 bypass. The long descent to the roundabout will open up a wide and wonderful view of the Kelvin Valley. This is the first time that I will be enjoying the greenery if I come this way, and after all that traffic and urban block, the airiness and the tranquillity are such a joy.

The run down through the fields on this road does make all the effort worthwhile and the Lenzie Road is one of the highlights when coming this way. No effort required, as we're on the descent, of course, and already you can spot the Campsies losing height and falling away as they become the Kilsyth Hills in the distance. So, if you just intend to wind your way to the bottom of the Tak Ma Doon, now is a good time to keep your eye on the fells, as you can use them, just a bit, to help guide you.

Down into the quilted patchwork of fields you go, and the real follow your nose fun starts the other side of the roundabout. The new Lenzie bypass will take off away north, but we want northeast and so head off in that direction, which is straight ahead.

You are sure to enjoy what is to come, and the way is obvious at first as you only have one option to take. It will lead you wonderfully winding round old battered-looking farms, climbing as it goes, which will give you a great view over the new road and way beyond. You'll find yourself heading east along high, bleak roads, lined with a few wind-battered trees, which will lead to a crossroads at the Lindsaybeg Road. Go straight across, which is signposted for Stoneyetts, and this leads into very similar and equally enjoyable terrain. The back roads again climb up, only this time they take you beside the new M-80 and, much to my surprise, to an isolated row of houses called Viewfield Cottages. These, I was informed by a resident, were initially built to house staff for the former Stoneyetts (mental) Hospital that was close by, and which closed in 1992.

Viewfield Cottages are well named, as they do afford great views due to their height, and the road now takes a severe swerve left, which is because the road straight

Following your nose through the country lanes between Muirhead and Kirkintilloch can provide a lot of pleasure and enjoyment, and some old Scottish industrial history to boot. Here we are close to the old Stoneyetts Hospital, approaching the distinctive lump of the former Wester Gartshore pit bing

ahead is blocked. At one time it led to the hospital itself, which had opened in 1913. As you fly down from the height, in the near foreground will be the unmistakable shape of the pyramid-like Wester Gartshore pit bing. It is an enormous heap, and for a great part is covered in sizeable trees, some of which must have started growing in 1950 when the pit closed. It had opened in 1872 and had two shafts, both going down to a scary 274 metres. The mine was the scene of a dreadful explosion in July 1923, when eight men lost their lives. With its size, shape, and trees covering it, the bing actually resembles the natural feature of Dumgoyach Hill near Strathblane (we pass it later).

The Wester Gartshore pit bing from close up, and for a pit slag heap I must say it is a very striking landmark and rather a handsome-looking fellow. In fact, it's been there for so long now that it is almost entirely covered over by trees, which gives it a very natural appearance.

Now, the general rule at this stage is that whenever you are presented with a choice of routes, turn right. This will include the T-junction you arrive at just after crossing the Luggie Water by a delightful wee stone bridge. At the end of this road, you emerge from the hinterland onto Mollins Road that runs alongside a lot of big factories, and this is the end of the real backwater riding, unfortunately. I always really enjoy that stretch, and have taken the odd left turn when riding through it in the past, which will simply take you back into Kirky.

Now that we have emerged from stage one, to continue on our way it's probably best to head for Twechar. This is done by turning north (left) on Mollins Road which will lead to the Drumgrew roundabout.

This is the first of two roundabouts sitting thereabouts, and it's no bother to pick up the Twechar road, as it's very well signed. There now follows a great, leafy, fieldy sweep round and into this lovely wee place which is entered after a slight rise and dip. Bear right when you do enter, and go past a fair bit of history in this old mining village. It was the men from Twechar who manned the aforementioned Wester Gartshore mine.

There is its lovely old village church on the left, and also signposts for the Antonine Wall and its Barrhill Fort ahead on the right. The jewel in the crown is the bridge up ahead that crosses the Forth and Clyde Canal. As it is equipped with flashing lights and barriers, it's safe to assume that it swings in some way to allow canal traffic through. One thing's for sure, it makes for a very colourful and picturesque exit.

Turn right on the B-8023, which goes delightfully along beside the canal all the way till you reach Auchinstarry. The old quarry here is a firm favourite of the rock climbers and is very scenic itself, then another picturesque short climb takes you into nearby Kilsyth and the start of the Tak Ma Doon Road.

That is probably about the most straightforward way to access Kilsyth from Stepps, but it is only one windy way amongst a few windy options, and I have had a lot of fun and pleasure finding my way around there every time. You may want to go exploring yourself and try something a bit different. Don't let me stop you. In the meantime, I am going to return back up onto the Springburn Road and continue to carry on describing the most direct route. I'll see you back in Kilsyth soon, at the bottom of the Tak Ma Doon.

SPRINGBURN ROUTE (CONT.)

So, after the Colston junction, the Springburn Road then becomes the Kirkintilloch Road and it drops us down quite nicely into Bishopbriggs Cross. Be prepared for more hustle and bustle in and around this small shopping centre, for there is always plenty going on. There are also some wonderful old Victorian buildings in the vicinity – the first one being the police station, which you pass just before reaching the cross, and the tenements of the cross itself also date from that period. But it will be the library and its wonderful square clock tower that will steal the show. I'm glad to say that it survived the war, but only just. Around midnight on the 7th of April, 1941, those carnaptious combatants in the Luftwaffe paid us a visit, and almost scored a direct hit.

The library at that time was the school building, and one of its annexes was being used as an air raid shelter-cum-first aid post. Five people were killed and more injured when a bomb hit it, narrowly just missing the main building itself. This was around the time of the Clydebank Blitz and the like, and the Jerries were hammering us big time. No-one is quite sure why Jerry targeted the place, as we weren't on talking terms with Big Hermann Goering at the time, but it may have been because what is now Low Moss Prison was at the time RAF Bishopbriggs.

We leave the centre by a pull-up, still in the realms of the old Briggs, and that means we have big villas with big hedges to ride through until we are on the level.

The road now straightens way out in front of us, in a long line of street lamps that run bolt straight towards the Campsies through the newer part of town. These are the big 50s and 60s developments that saw Bishopbriggs blossom, and it is an undeviating gentle slope down, of about a mile in length, that finds us at the Cadder roundabout and on our way out of town. Now it's the turn of the Cadder Cemetery wall to guide us bolt straight towards the Torrance roundabout half a mile away, and with that we're out into the fields. Quite a scene awaits us here, for we are clear of all obstacles blocking our view, and it allows the width of the Kelvin Valley to be appreciated.

The broad valley floor stretches out before us, one in which the flatness of the fields are only broken by two separate tree lines, which follow and therefore give away the position of the canal and river. Beyond them, the

CARRON VALLEY RUN

Things open up and traffic eases off once you get through Bishopbriggs Cross and start to make tracks for the now-in-view Kilsyth Hills. The A-803 carries us all the way to the bottom of the Tak Ma Doon, and does so with next to no climbing into the bargain.

floor curves up to become the Campsies, which I must say impress in a very uplifting way. Even Kilsyth will be visible from here, its houses seemingly nestling on the hillside far away in the distance. You can also make out the approximate position of the Tak Ma Doon Road, just from the lie of the Kilsyth Hills.

There now follows a great bit of road riding for us on the 803, as it goes long and down towards Kirkintilloch, still in a very open and airy situation. With such a gentle, lengthy glide in front of us, it's time to sit up on the bars and enjoy the payback for the climbing done on the way up and through the Briggs.

The long straights on the road are only interrupted about halfway down, when you bend big over the Forth and Clyde Canal and pass the Stables Inn positioned right on the canal towpath. This splendid old place of succour at one time did exactly as it said on the tin and provided not only rest and refreshment to the boatmen, but also to their magnificent big Clydesdales as well. It is a most impressive, solid, big building, whose quaint old pub sign tells most pleasingly and accurately of its past.

As you proceed down through the fields towards Kirkintilloch, you will of course be unaware that you crossed the line of the old Antonine Wall, just before you crossed the canal. You are actually now running parallel with it, as it formerly ran through the field on your right-hand side.

You will from time to time pass signs pointing to it, or old forts belonging to it, as you make your way through the Kelvin Valley, because it came this way, going for

Between Bishopbriggs and Kirkintilloch, we pass over the picturesque Forth and Clyde Canal. Don't forget that the towpath on the left can be used to reach here, and even as far as Kilsyth itself, from near the Renfrew ferry if you want to avoid the traffic altogether. Just remember that it isn't tarmacked the whole way, though.

39 miles (approximately)[4] from Bowling in the west to Falkirk in the east. The wall was the brainchild of the then Roman Emperor Antoninus Pius, who ordered its construction in 142 AD. The plan was to push north from Hadrian's Wall and adopt the same tactic of placing a barrier the breadth of the country, thus extending the Roman Empire even further. There is very little left of the Antonine, as it was only held for about 20 years – unlike Hadrian's, which was the Romans' frontier for about 300. This is the reason that there is still so much of Hadrian's left, as it was held for so much longer and was a much more formidable structure.

That's not to say that the Antonine was in any way not up to the job, because it took about twelve years to build, with the 2nd, 6th, and 20th Legions doing all the building. It was a stone construction with turf on top, and had a defensive ditch out in front, some of which can still be found today. But not in this particular stretch as it happens, so *tempus fugit*[5], we must make haste to the town of Kirkintilloch itself.

This is done on the last of the slope, taking us onto the level when we enter the houses, and all's looking well-to-

---

4- The distance given for the Antonine Wall is usually recorded between 37 to 39 miles long.

5 - It's Latin for time flies.

CARRON VALLEY RUN

The Martyr's Stone tells of more grisly Scottish Covenanting history, and you pass it on the A-803 shortly after leaving Kirkintilloch. The sentence meted out to the two men named on the stone was barbaric, and I for one doubt that they were actually guilty in the first place.

This delightful old mile post outside Lochwood Cottage at Auchinreoch on the A-803 lets you know how far you've come, and how far to go. Not long now till Kilsyth, just another couple of miles.

do as we head bolt straight for the Peel Park roundabout that guards the west end of town. Once again, just like we did when returning from Stirling, we only skirt the edge of Kirky, keeping on the A-803.

This runs us past the commercial edge of the town – a really colourful affair, what with the yellow and red of the National Tyres place sitting right beside the blue iron sheds with bright orange doors of the builder's merchants; quite a display, I think you'll find. The show-stealer in amongst that lot will be a rather space age-looking, silver metallic building, with a round part of its side seemingly cut out for some reason. The company goes by the strange name of Guala Closures, and I was so intrigued as to what they did, I had to make an effort to find out.[6]

Now that we are older and wiser, we run up to the lights at the bottom of Milton Road. We carry straight on, now on the Kilsyth Road, and pass the start of the Strathkelvin cycle track just before the funeral directors'.

The track runs all the way to Strathblane, covering just over 8 miles, and is a possible approach route from that neck of the deck. For the most part, it is fit for purpose, being tarmacked and smooth into the bargain at that, but one short section is a little bit muddy. For that reason, it would be advisable only to ride it on a machine with mudguards, and be prepared to give it a wash after the run. Another word of caution when using this track is that in my experience it is heavily used by dog walkers,

---

6 - They are in the aluminium business. and are of Italian origin

so you may find yourself constantly having to slow down for them as it's a narrow path, though it does have some nice touches from yesteryear. The show-stealer is Milton of Campsie station; last used by the public in 1951, would you believe?

Now it's back to the road. When we pass the cycle track entrance, we soon reach the Eastside roundabout and head out of town, with the well-to-doness of Kirky showing no signs of abating.

Just after we leave, and even before we get to the Inchbelly Bridge, we have the option of taking the more scenic, though slightly longer, B-8023, which will get us to Kilsyth via Auchinstarry. This will, of course, link us up with the Stepps route and also take us past the exquisite narrow tunnel under the canal that I mentioned earlier (it's signposted Tintock).

This B-road has the major plus of running right alongside the canal for a few miles, and simply can't be beaten for charm. I recommend it and use it more than the direct A-road. Up ahead, though, when staying on the main A-803, is another useful approach route I will mention just before we reach it, and that is the A-891 Antermony Road, coming in from the left through Milton of Campsie. This gives access from as far away as Bearsden and Milngavie, and is a very scenic way to approach Kilsyth from that neck of the woods.

Here we now bend about the early rough fields in the Kelvin Valley as we make tracks towards Auchinreoch. We pass the old Martyr's Stone as the road straightens

The A-803 isn't the only way to get to Kilsyth after you pass through Kirkintilloch, incidentally. Just after you leave Kirkintilloch, you can also use the B-8023 that will take you past Twechar, and run you picturesquely alongside the canal at times as well. It is a quieter option and a much more interesting road to boot, and it provides good views of the houses of Kilsyth as you make your way along, before it brings you out at Auchinstarry quarry.

out and undulates past the side road from Milton. This is us once again going through the sparsely-spread Auchinreoch, and I always enjoy the rising bends ahead that give a bit of elevation to better appreciate the surrounds. The fields on the left that are the early foothills of the Campsies look lush and cultivated, whereas the ones on the valley floor, which I suspect are part of the Kelvins floodplain, are rough and reed-filled. The bends lead us up past Lochwood Cottage, outside which you will find a delightful old, white mile post, with black painted hands pointing in both directions. From here the shallowness of the Kelvin Valley is very apparent.

We drop down and carry on through a similar landscape, till the rise up into Queenzieburn begins. And this time I will definitely not mention Fan-dabi-dozi or even wee Jimmy.[7] The red roof tiles on some of the houses make the Queenzie girl a colourful fly past, as it only takes a bend to pass through it. The place always looks slightly bigger when going this way, and you can also see how the trees on the hillside behind encroach right into the houses. This, coupled with the low-lying cottages out in front in places, does make for a bit of a picture postcard look. We leave this one-sided village behind, and find we are only a field's length away from Kilsyth now. We enter that quickly, of course, and when we do, we find that the road sits high early on and allows us a good view over the rooftops of the town centre.

There is a great, square church tower with a blue clock face, rather like the one in Old Kilpatrick, that will rise above all else here. The road drops down to a main roundabout now, and if you had taken the Stepps route, you have a high chance of approaching along the road from the right. Not far now to the start of the Tak Ma Doon; it's just up ahead and straight through the roundabout. It will only take a minute or two to reach the start of it, so steel yourself well for the toughest climb of the day. It is well signposted, so there is no chance of missing this old drovers' route, and as you make the turn left, remember, low gear now! Dig, dig, dig in early, for the first ramp is upon you right away. It's maybe a good idea to get of out the saddle for this one, or not if that's not your style.

Now the bad news is that the Tak Ma Doon climbs for nearly 2½ miles, and within that it contains about four

---

7 - In case you haven't read the Stirling run, Queenzieburn is the birthplace of Janette Tough (wee Jimmy Krankie).

Arriving in Kilsyth from the direction of Auchinstarry, and behind the houses sits the Kilsyth Hills containing the tough Tak Ma Doon Road climb. Get ready for it, for its four ramp-like sections will test you to the full unless you are in really good nick.

really steep sections. However, the good news is that they are all short ramps, and that they are all followed by either flat or much easier, longer sections. This, thank God, gives you plenty of recovery time and that's just as well, for chances are you'll need it.

As I said, you are already on the first one, though it isn't the worst you'll find, as you curve up past a great looking old black and white house (I've actually seen the guy out painting it). He is a cricket-loving Nottinghamshire lad, who on one occasion was good enough to fill my water bottles. Howzat!!!

The initial, right swerving ramp soon lies back and leads onto a long, gentle rise through the trees. This goes on for quite a considerable distance, and at one point the trees give way to hedges and sheep fields, allowing good views across the valley of the Kelvin to the right. Finally, after more continuous slight rising, the road leaves the trees once it turns left, and heads north, flat and bolt straight, beside the Kilsyth Lennox Golf Club. The bunker to the side of the 7th green looks an absolute demon, by the way. Ahead, the sparseness of the hillside is obvious, but so too is the big, ugly quarry on the right-hand side, whose presence is quite imposing.

Despite this, you barely notice the damn thing when you are descending the road, even though you aren't on a steep section at this point and have time to look around. The quarry itself runs the length of the golf course, right to the end of the flat stretch that you're on. Now you're into serious roughsville, for some of these fields don't look fit enough to even hold sheep. Most are and do, but no time for sightseeing now as a second and tougher ramp has to be tackled, and the road surface doesn't help the

Steep climbing on the Tak Ma Doon, but thankfully every steep section is followed by a more forgiving gradient of road, allowing a fair wee bit of recovery to take place. However, still expect your heart rate to almost reach its maximum, especially on the bends just after Berryhill Farm.

Now, just round the corner you will see the road rise through a series of S bends, but what you won't realise at first is just how steep is the bugger to come. This is the crux of the whole climb now, so get ready to really force your way up it and to continue to do so once you round the corner. Your heart rate monitor will be showing well into the 190s on this one, which means I'm into zone 5 on my computer.

The road now goes flat level (*Merci*!) as you feel the effort hit you full on, just as you clear the last. Harsh is the going and harsh is the landscape, with stumpy, wee trees, rickety, old fences, and rusty, old iron gates for company. Admittedly, they do have charm, as does the wee stone bridge that takes you over the burn ahead and brings you onto another climb – much easier than the last two, you'll be glad to hear. The road turns to the right and travels along a flat section as you contour the hillside. Ahead, the fires of Grangemouth and the River Forth are seen, so you know the top is near, and it only takes another three undulating rises to get you up there. These aren't too painful, but having said that, I'm always glad when they're over. When you pass the viewpoint car park, you're up.

cause. Force your way up this one and then settle in for the curving, easy meander of a climb up to Berryhill Farm.

It's all nicey-nicey as you swerve between the stone walls, guiding you up ever higher; well, it is once the old breath's back. And who said this climbing lark isn't fun? Not me. I'm in my element here. When you get past this high, isolated, fantastic old farmstead, take a look to the right, and on a clear day you should glimpse Tinto Hill.

Hello, Denny Muir! Or something like that. Bleak maybe, but a welcome sight nonetheless, and what did you expect 322 metres above sea level? Fields of

CARRON VALLEY RUN

On the descent down to Carron Bridge on the Tak Ma Doon, and a great wee dip doon it is too, with a real old blast from the past in the shape of a ford to get through as well. It is with a lot of pleasure and much relief that this stretch of road is usually ridden. The Ochils are the hills in the distance.

The Carron Bridge Hotel junction will be the main turning point and change of direction on this run. So, if you have been battling against a strong north easterly wind, then now it's behind you and you're flying down the B-818. This picture is taken from the Stirling side, so the Tak Ma Doon is actually the road to the right of the hotel. Beside it, you can just about see the great old, rusty iron signpost that sits there. Remember, the hotel will not let you fill water bottles or use their toilet. Welcome to Scotland!!!

strawberries? If you did, you're in for a shock, because it's a drab, uniform brown carpet of long grasses and mucho green conifers belonging to the Carron Valley Forest that will greet you. To the right, they rise away towards Darrach Hill, which you see as you take your way round what little plateau road there is, before the descending starts. It's a rip-roarer when it does get going, and all done on that same slim slither of tarmac that brought you up. I often wonder at this point just how the old drovers managed to control their cattle on the descents of the Tak Ma Doon. It must have been mayhem at times, especially as the old Highlanders didn't have a lasso to their name.

As you hare down on what, for the most part, is pretty smooth tar, the white of the Carron Bridge Hotel can be seen, as well as the Ochils in the far distance. So, too, when the light is right, the Wallace Monument. Haring down indeed and hanging on for the thrill, that's what's happening at this point; never a dull moment on the old Tak boy. This includes the ford ahead, though it is advisable to hit the anchors before entering the burn. The ford always looks real dodgy, but I've never had any bother crossing it in the past.

Another slight rise, then its back on with the fast show, as down past the Faughlin Reservoir we plummet. This natty wee dam, nestling up here, is somewhat spoiled by a big, ugly, iron railing supposedly protecting it. The broken old walls that follow restore some charm, however.

Only another twist or two takes us into Stirling District and to the Carron Bridge itself. It's a beautiful old structure, made up of two lovely arches, and built way back in 1695 to replace the former ford that was here. Nowadays, the Carron murmurs quietly below, and that is due to it being somewhat subdued ever since the dam was built about a mile upstream. Like all old bridges, it's pleasing to the eye and pleasing to ride over, as it propels you down amongst all the wooden huts that line the riverbank here. They guide you up to the hotel and the quaint old crossroads that brings you to a halt. It is a most fitting, lopsided affair – the crossroads that is, not the hotel. The hotel[8] of course was a stopover for those old cattle herders, who must have been glad to see the place – even more than me.

The long, hard road down from the Highlands must have taken its toll on them as well as the cattle, and of course they used the stopover here to allow some grazing and fattening of the beasts before heading for market. The modern road signs, give direction and distance to Stirling, Denny, and Fintry, but they're all no match for the old iron signpost, which is still standing and just about readable. We want to go left for Fintry and that puts us on the B-818. 8 miles the sign tells us, and what an 8 miles it is; one that will simply fly by and will seem the shortest 8 miles you've ever ridden. So, off we go then down the telegraph road, or rather up the telegraph road,

---

8 - As mentioned in the Stirling run, the hotel has a sign on the door saying they don't fill water bottles and their cludgie is out of bounds. You have been warned.

I should have said, for there is a pull-up, though not a steep one to begin with.

This leads us past what few low-lying fields there are here, and alongside the Carron towards Carron Valley Hamlet. I assume these were the very pastures that the old drovers themselves used for their cattle. Once past the name sign, you will initially only meet a house or three on the way to the reservoir itself, which is reached by a ride through some real rough ground. This is filled with conifers, reed-filled fields, some so overgrown that you can't actually see the ground. So, if you like your scenery a little on the wild side, then you've come to the right place.

The dam wall will appear right on cue on your left, and just to give it a bit more impact, the dome of Meikle Bin will be sitting right behind it. The dam is a classic design, built in 1939, and is at its best after a very high rainfall, when water cascades spectacularly over the top and down its smooth, grey face.

Now, for me this run really begins when I turn left at the Carron Bridge Hotel, and it gets better by the mile.

Fly fishers can often be seen bobbing about on the water on the Carron Reservoir as you fly past on the great B-818, and as you are up fairly high at this point and perhaps wind-assisted and pumped up to hell with the ascent of the Tak Ma Doon Road, then I do mean you will be flying – both mentally and physically.

This is especially so when I draw level with the start of the reservoir, and a flat, broad blast of blue hits you full in the face. The contrasting green from the carpet of conifers, belonging to that all hillside-encompassing Carron Valley Forest, gives the water's blue even more

Carron Valley Reservoir with the pointed Meikle Bin behind, and what a lovely picturesque spot it is. I absolutely love the place and always look forward to getting here when doing this run. No wonder it's so popular with bike riders, and the highlight of the run I always feel.

of a sparkle. To the right sits a row of solid, white houses that have the 1930s stamped all over them. They look like they were plucked from Knightswood and planted here, for the purpose of the water workers, I assume. The last one in this row is occupied by the Carron Trout Fishery, and their rowing boats can often be seen bobbing about in the water as the fly fishers pit their wits against the brownies and rainbows down in the depths.

My, my, what a scene of gentle, lapping calmness exists here, all isolated from much of the modern-day vices, save for motor cars and satellite dishes. No shops or amenities are to be found within this hamlet, and I wonder just how different it actually is from 1939. It will take the next 3 miles of riding to clear this lovely,

Contouring round the Carron Reservoir at its west end, and just about to swerve round the waterside bends ahead. This is easy riding and high pleasure time into the bargain, and a very well-earned reward for all the effort to get here.

scenic high dam, and it starts off with another slight rise, which is just fine as it gives some elevation to appreciate the surroundings even more. The fields on the right run up onto Craigannet Hill, and are very bare, windswept affairs. They do have character within them, comprising stone walls, crags, and thinly-spaced, windblown trees. Very *Wuthering Heights*, I must say, so keep your eye open for Heathcliff.

Most of the fields contain sheep, but not all. Some do still hold beef cattle and I'm glad to see that old tradition of grazing your cattle is still alive and well here. The road drops back down to the water side after its early lift, and the narrow corridor of trees that exist between the road and the reservoir always allows glimpses of glinting chinks to get through. As for the dam itself, it follows a dog-leg course, bending round to the right, where a lot of the forestry this side has now been chopped and leaves the usual scarred landscape. In contrast, on the far bank the evergreens are all standing to a tree, through which you must trek if you want to climb Meikle Bin. The view of the reservoir is an excellent one from its trig point and I thoroughly recommend it. It does stand rather grandly on the far side as it towers above all around it.

You access the Meikle from the dam's western end, which will come into view shortly after you pass through the bends at this stage and then run onto the road's straighter sections which follow. The bends are taken right at the water's edge and are pure magic, as is this whole stretch, up high away from everyday cares and worries. Go internal for a moment and let the feel-good factor kick in big time, which is payback for all your effort and expense laid out so far. In the distance, the Fintry Hills start to make their presence known, and will do so even more the closer you get to them. Just as you clear the dam wall, you also pass that wee back road heading off to Stirling that takes off at an acute angle over your right shoulder.

On the dip down in front of you will be the fields of Todholes Farm on the right, and they look so well cultivated that I think whoever had the job of knocking them into shape really had their work cut out. The infant Endrick Water runs through them right in front of you at this point. You've not quite escaped the conifers of the Carron Forest entirely yet, for there is still one more small batch of them to go, which contains some sort of fenced-off waterworks yard. However, the great wee stone bridge over the Endrick ahead does take you out and up into open fields and into an entirely different landscape altogether. When we clear the rise we're on, it's fresh and airy all around, as we find ourselves out frolicking with the Fintries.

The scene you are about to enter seems more like Cumbria. In front of you will be fields and dales, filled with white woollies and stone walls running off away into high pastures and the likes. It is a glorious pastoral show, let me assure you, soft and wild all at the one time. Most noticeable will be Double Craigs crag, so razor gilt-edged dead ahead, but the Campsies across the valley also play their part in adding grandeur to the scene. In the middle of it all, cutting through the blanket of easy green, will be our tarry guide, the B-818. And as it drops down swiftly here, it will become very apparent as to why I called it the telegraph road earlier. Our constant companions have been the uncountable poles carrying the telephone wire the whole length of the road from the hotel, apart from the stretch by the dam where no bugger lives.

The high wire acts like a lofty guide rail, as we begin the plummet down from our current height. And a warning has to be issued here, because the road surface is in such a state that it is very advisable to exercise a fair bit of restraint. So bumpy is the going that on one occasion my pump fell out the frame on the way down, but that is the only thing to mar this dazzling descent. Stone walls line either side as the road falls through the fields, long and luscious, only levelling temporarily when it reaches Spittalhill Farm. This is a real bonus, for it is such a stunning setting, just the way that the white farmhouse sits in front of the majestic stone pillars of Double Craigs crag. I always slow down to admire it and catch my breath, but only momentarily, because the road will start to descend once more, this time all the way to the valley floor.

It soon crashes through a wonderful woodland stretch before emerging out into the fields again, and a stone dyke says 'follow me'. This you do, most enjoyably, with a sway down into the small cluster of houses leading to a very tight left-hand bend. This is followed by the bridge that re-crosses the Endrick, which is another fine old stone specimen, and with a lovely leafy roll-up to the junction ahead, you arrive at the Crow Road (B-822) at Gonachan Cottage. Now it's make your mind up time, because we have two choices on how to get to Strathblane from here. The left takes us over to Lennoxtown and the sign says that's 7 miles away. The right takes us through Killearn and that's 7½ miles away. Distance-wise there is very little in it, only about a mile, but as for feet of ascent, that's a different matter.

KILLEARN ROUTE

If we decide to go via Killearn, then we turn right and batter along the flat, straight Crow Road, which quickly passes the Fintry village sign. Of the two options, this is most certainly the more low-level, though even on the valley floor it is a grand situation. You can't help but feel dwarfed by the scale of the Campsies and Fintries either side, both seemingly just a field's width away. The village sign proves to be a bit of a false start, because once you pass only a handful of buildings, you suddenly find you're back out in the fields again. It takes a bit more rising on

Having cleared the Carron Reservoir, there shortly begins the great, long, thrilling descent down to the valley floor towards Fintry. The scene resembles something more akin to the Yorkshire Dales than it does to the Scottish hills, with stones walls running up the hillside marking the boundaries of the sheep fields, and all in all it is very pastoral and pretty. Just watch out for the road surface in places here as it is very poor at times, and don't forget you will be hitting high speeds on the descent.

bloody awful tarmac to enter the village proper. On the way there, the mighty Ben Lomond puts in a welcome appearance.

As for Fintry village, well, it's no eyesore that's for sure. A Main Street of pretty white cottages, with lots of quaint old village touches exists here. Like the must-have red phone box, well-worn garage, and a lantern-filled traffic island, which takes some beating. Look out for the half bike that is bolted onto the wall of and advertising the Fintry Inn. It looks like an old Raleigh racer. They must get a lot of passing trade from us bike riders, I imagine.

Not much more than a saunter down the Main Street will be required before we exit out the other side, and even then it won't be the last blast from an ensemble of pretty farms and crags. That's because just to the right as you leave, you will see Kilunan Steadings, looking every inch the des-res farmhouse. Behind this sits high Stronend, the pointed rocky nose which acts as the Fintry Hills' vanguard. And with that sight now passed, it's westward, me boys.

It's approximately 6 miles from Fintry to Killearn, though it always seems a lot longer. But it's not a problem. It's not hard going, as it's delightful country road riding all the way, with only a dodgy road surface from time to time making our life just a little bit difficult. The Endrick Valley starts to open up quite markedly from now on, as the steep Fintries are left behind, and it's now a gentle rolling rising hillside that disappears up

CARRON VALLEY RUN

One of the highlights on the descent of the B-818 down to Gonachan will be the sight of the striking Double Craigs crag, which sits most picturesquely behind Spittalhill Farm. The white farmhouse definitely adds to the scene, and the crag looks absolutely stunning when it gets caught in low evening light, as in the picture above.

onto Ballindalloch Muir. That's not the case on the left, however, as the Campsies stay with us for a long time yet, but never too close. An early section of wooded curves leads out onto open farmland, which is full of stony wall-lined wanders.

The Campsies play one of their ace cards when they show off the Corrie of Balglass, which is a wonderful, big, natural scoop, and can't fail to impress. Some much more substantial stone walls lining the road are picked up now, and that signifies that we are approaching the grounds of Ballikinrain Estate – one time the home to Sir Archibald Orr Ewing, former Conservative MP for Dunbartonshire. This was a post he held for 24 years, starting in 1868.

Now, I went into a fair bit of detail about Sir Archie in the Stirling run, so won't do so again, but suffice to say we are talking stiff upper lip here, big time. The old estate's touches are still very evident, like the rather grand gatehouse, the estate workers' houses, and also some great deciduous trees that you ride along through. Some of them must date back to the time of Sir Archie himself.

The road between Ballikinrain and Killearn is also wooded in many places and offers great views across

The lower bends on the Crow Road are visible from the still high B-818 just before it drops steeply down and over the Endrick Water and then rolls up to the T-junction with the B-822 at Gonachan. Turn left for the Crow or right for Fintry.

Turning right at the Gonachan T-junction is the easier option to get to Strathblane, because there is a lot less climbing than going over the Crow Road, though the distances are almost identical. Shortly you have the pleasure of riding through pretty Fintry with its white walled cottages and gardens, before the slightly longer stretch of road to Killearn begins.

you when you do run in, and all's pretty now. We are going right through and returning home via Strathblane this time, but if you wish to use the Stockiemuir Road and Erskine Bridge, then it's best to turn right at the big white church and descend the B-834.

Staying on the Balfron Road will take you past Killearn Kirk and up to the big swing left that will run you down Main Street. Just before you take the turn, you will become aware of the very noticeable tall grey monument to the village's best known former resident, George Buchanan. Again, I mentioned him in

this soft, shallow valley, with Balfron's houses clearly visible as they sit undisturbed on the slope opposite. The B-818 finally comes to an end at a rather exquisite wee junction as it abuts with the A-875, where the road runs off at an angle in several directions, including one going to Balfron Station. We turn left here, and curve and climb up before riding the last field-filled mile into Killearn village itself. It's cottages and kirks that greet

the Stirling run and won't go into detail this time either, nor do I want to, given his part in our pretty young queen's downfall[9]. The fall down Main Street doesn't lack drama, as it's tight, speedy, and has a Campsie canvas as a backdrop. After dropping down through the lovely homes on the brae, don't forget to grub up if you need to, as there is a Spar and Co-op hereabouts.

A rise and leafy lane takes you pleasantly out of Killearn and onto a fantastic long, angled descent that seems neverending. Dumgoyne looks its best as you fly past turreted Westerton Farm on the way down to meeting the mighty A-81 coming in over your right shoulder. No need for caution here, as the angle is just perfect and the road straight and true, allowing you to get down on the bars and enjoy some safe high speed. This continues for quite some time till you reach Dumgoyne junction and run onto the 81 just before Glengoyne Distillery. What a scene the road is here, as it double bends by the whisky's white walls, with the impressive dome of Dumgoyach Hill dead ahead. It all makes for a most splendid sight.

Just after leaving Fintry, a great scene presents itself on the right with the rocky nose of Skiddaw crag, and above, the rockier tip of Stronend, both appearing simultaneously above Kilunan Steadings. It makes for a very impressive sight to send you on your way down through the fields to come.

---

9 - He gave evidence against Mary Stuart at her trial in England.

CARRON VALLEY RUN

It's broad, open, bonnie riding for a lot of the way between Fintry and Killearn, with a fair wee bit of swerving and just a little upping and downing on a road that seems to go on a lot longer than expected. That's not a problem, however, for it is a lot of fun on this none-too-hard stretch, with only a few bad bits of road surface to go over.

The Campsie Fells make a very scenic backdrop as you drop down Main Street, Killearn, and another major change of direction in the run is made at this point. So, if you've had a tail wind from Carron Bridge, then you will be heading back into it all the way to Strathblane at least. You won't notice this at first, however, for you are quite sheltered in the village, but once back on the A-81 then, boy, you will be fighting hard again.

Now you know me well enough by now to realise that the A-81 is a road I hold in the highest esteem, due not only to its profile but also to where it leads. But even I have to admit that the next few miles on it are rather tough going. It starts off well enough, what with the distillery and all, followed by some curves as it enters the woods, but then the going gets tough, very tough.

Well, it does if you have a lot of miles in your legs and you just happen to have turned into an east wind again. The road surface is a bit on the poor side here as well. A fairly long pull-up begins in the woods, which isn't hard or sustained, but it's a continuous rise that will carry on

Just the slightest glimpse of Loch Lomond can be had when you come in on the Balfron Road on entering Killearn. You are back in Prettyville when you enter this well-to-do village, which has stores and mores for refuelling should you need it.

After the superb effortless glide out of Killearn, with its fantastic scenery of both Dumgoyne on one side and the Highlands on the other, behold Dumgoyne junction. Now it's back onto the A-81 and it's a tough stretch of road to Strathblane and beyond. Get ready to dig in hard.

SPEED!

even once you have entered Blanefield village. It is pretty all the same, what with the trees on the right and the fields running onto the steep Campsies on the left side.

You will also notice the traffic having increased as well, even before you dig in for the climb that must be taken when you meet up with first houses in the village. It's nice when you do level out once more and find the time to admire the place and get your breath back. Now you seamlessly roll into Strathblane village and come to the mini roundabout outside the Kirkhouse Inn. If you had decided to take the Campsie Glen option and return via Lennoxtown, then the road on the left is the road you would arrive by, which is the A-891. It is an absolutely fantastic climb and descent coming that way, and to take it makes for a great day's climbing if combined with the Tak Ma Doon. To start it, we need to return to where the B-818 meets the B-822 at Gonachan.

Once the climb up through both Blanefield and Strathblane has been taken, then the mini roundabout that also greets the arrival of the A-891 coming in from the east is met. The 891 can also be used to get to this point, of course, which would entail turning left at the Gonachan T-junction and climbing the Crow Road over to Lennoxtown

CAMPSIE GLEN ROUTE

Now, get your climbing legs on here and get ready to be seriously entertained by the climb over to Lennoxtown on the Crow. If it's a warm summer's day, the short sleeves are on, and you've just battered the Tak Ma doon, then think Beltran. I repeat, think Beltran[10]. That great wee Spanish climber would be in his element here and you will be, too, as you get yourself onto some early, tight, steep bends and begin this one in Pyrenean style. Close to the road on the right sits the steep sided Gonachan Glen, above which sits the high dome of Dungoil and both of these add a feeling of real ruggedness to the setting. The road straightens out as the angle eases a bit, but not by much, as the upper and rougher sheep fields keep us company. And it's still tough going as we pass the entrance to Townhead Farm further up again.

About halfway up the Crow Road, the B-822, after turning left at Gonachan instead of right for Fintry and Killearn. Expect a lot more climbing on this route, but what a climb it is. Done by many and loved by all, it's a classic day out going over the Tak Ma Doon and Crow on the same day.

The steepish gradient continues, about 7 or 8%, till you work your way through the next set of higher bends, which are beautifully wall-lined. Meikle Bin now puts in another appearance and he is such a striking fellow, what with his double-topped dome above his coat of conifers green. The gradient finally eases down to about 4% when you cross the Clachie Burn Bridge, with its colourful red and white warning-lined sides. Get into a faster rhythm now, to eat up what's left of the extra 800 feet of ascent that going this way adds to the overall tally. No real

---

10 - Manuel Beltran, he of Banesto, Mapaei, & lastly US Postal fame.

CARRON VALLEY RUN

If you manage a look back over your right shoulder once you gain a bit of height on the Crow Road, then you will be rewarded by the excellent views of the distant Highland mountains. They make an awesome sight.

The enticing slender rising bends ahead keep so much out of sight and make you want to follow, just to find out what's hidden from view. The road keeps disappearing round slanting ridges that cut in from both sides now, as ever higher we follow up into a wild-looking wasteland of blanket brownness that grows and spreads ever more as you contour over the Campsie Muir. When you swing alongside the conifer-clad side of Lecket Hill, you run beside the source of the River Carron and it gets just a little ravine-like, what with the crash barrier beside the road and all. You know you're near the top when you pass a small wooden house called The Neuk that looks like a bothy, but isn't. The road makes one final smooth rise up, and if you thought up till now was bleak, you ain't seen nothin' yet.

The district boundaries are either side of the summit and you cross back into East Dunbartonshire again, where there now begins a mirror image of what you've just done, only downhill this time. It's those same disappearing meanders, just sloping gently at first, that you follow with the same anticipation until you pick up the Kirk Burn on the left, and then things start to get serious. You round a bend and then bang, it's crash

problem with that, of course, as we are well up for it as always. Long and easy at this stage goes the old Crow Boy, and an apt name for this road is Crow, as it just speaks high and harsh. But it now runs angled smoothly for us, as all the hard work's done and we can turn a fast cadence through brown grass and past conifer.

It's chocks away as the drop down off the top of the Crow Road is about to begin. The early stages are a bit hairy, to be honest, but once the big left-hander at Jamie Wright's Well has been negotiated, it's plain sailing all the way down into Lennoxtown.

On the plummet down the early high dips of the Crow Road, and remember to get ready for the big sweeping left-hand bend that approaches real fast. This stretch should get the old butterflies going a bit, just so you know.

barriers ahead, and in the distance way below, the valley floor just and only just comes into view. This gives you some idea of the drop ahead. It was approximately 3½ miles to the top and it will be the same to the bottom. Then the road straightens as it starts its drop and it's Geronimo! (Or use your own war cry!), because 45 mph won't take long to reach here.

As the fall starts fully, the Kirk Burn becomes a ravine on the right and the battered old warning triangle (barely readable) warns it's a 1:8 descent. Fortunately, the road isn't in any way technical at this point, just a few slight undulations, but as you pass the viewpoint carpark, get ready for a massive big swinging left-hand bend. Get the anchors on for this one, unless your nerves are of the steel-made variety, and once you come out of that bend, what a descent you've got in front of you. An unbelievable length of a slanting drop is about to take you right down the side of the Campsies, at a rate and angle that even the most timid of descenders can relax and enjoy. No need for nerves here, just get low on the bars and enjoy following the swaying crash barrier all the way down this sensational hillside, till the lower, tighter bends are reached just before Lennoxtown..

As good as the Crow Road is to ride when coming from Lennoxtown, in my opinion it is by far and away much more superior to come this way. You can, of course, make your own mind up on that yourself, but whichever is your preference, you're sure to enjoy the steep crags above and the patchwork of fields below as you come down effortlessly on the old Crow at this point. If this is a winter's day, then expect to be bloody cold by the bottom. Other than that, only the bottom bends will require a bit of care, as you drop down into the houses of the village. You can continue on the B-822 till it meets the main A-891 at the Black Swan Inn, but for me it's better to take a right down Lennox Road and cut out the dog leg. This takes you through older houses that may have been purpose-built for a workforce at one time, or more likely replaced housing purpose-built for a workforce.

The reason I say this is because Lennoxtown was at one time, and for a long time, the site of much industry. It was, in fact, a purpose-built settlement to accommodate workers for its big cotton print factory. This sort of replaced the earlier corn mill. After the cotton print factory, came a chemical plant, one of whose founding members was Charles Macintosh (he of the rainwear fame). Quite an inventor was our Charlie (he came from

Once safely down from the Crow Road, the A-891 Strathblane Rd then carries you rather more gently west to join up with the Killearn route once you enter Strathblane. This might not plummet you down like a banshee, but it is a most pleasant road to ride all the same. Ahead can be seen the striking lump of Dunglass, which we are just about to ride past.

Glasgow), because he also had a hand in the development of tarmacadam. It was the ability to build roads fast that

CARRON VALLEY RUN

helped make the spread of the mighty British Empire a whole lot easier. After the chemicals came the nail-making factory, which I think was the last big employer here. You wouldn't know about any of that now, of course, as it looks such a quiet residential place.

We will turn right and enjoy the scenes and the curves of the 891 for the next 4 miles to Strathblane, though there is an alternative route in the shape of the cycle lane that follows the line of the old Strathkelvin railway, should you wish to use it[11]. This will run you all the way to the old manse in Strathblane itself, which sits right across from the kirk, which is where you will find the start if you wish to use it when coming the other way. Either way, it will be a delight to make your way there, and it begins with a very scenic slight rise on the Glen Road, going up past a lovely row of arched doorway-fronted, red-roofed bungalows. Behind these slopes is the striking steel line of the crash barrier protecting the Crow Road, and quite a sight it makes as it cuts right across the whole front of the Campsies, glinting in the evening sun, if it's that time of day.

Right from the word go, and all the way along, the Campsies provide a most beautiful soft backdrop to the white farmsteads and fields that separate the road from them. The road itself rarely rises the entire length, but simply curves and turns continuously along the narrow valley floor. After leaving Lennoxtown, you quickly enter tiny Haughhead, after you cross the Finglen Burn, and pass a sign beside a big old driveway, saying Schoenstatt[12]. I often wondered what this was, so I took the time to look it up. You're soon be back out in the open and tootling along, and it is a tootle at that. Just purr beside the hedgerows and stonewalls, and as you do, keep your eye open for a great old rail bridge on the left, under which runs the aforementioned cycle track.

You'll find this just before the road curves and takes you up past Blairtummock, which was a former farm, I think. And now dead ahead, sitting in the middle of the upper Blane Valley, is another striking-looking, former volcanic plug, I assume – Dunglass. As you roll towards it, it gets better looking by the minute and is as dramatic and stunning as its better known neighbour, Dumgoyne. It's what you call a lump of rock. The road starts to become less curvy as Strathblane village approaches, though it's just as pretty and pleasant, and the finale comes in the shape of a perfect glide down past the church which stops at the mini roundabout. You've just rejoined the Killearn route now, and with that it's time to head for home. No sooner have you negotiated the roundabout than you are faced with another choice as to the best way to Milngavie. You can either stay on the A-81 by going straight ahead, or go via Mugdock by turning first right. As always, you won't know what suits you best till you try both.

MUGDOCK

The advantage of Mugdock is that it is the quieter option and the more scenic overall. Is it easier? Eh, no. As I said, turn first right onto Dumbrock Road and then first left onto the well-named Old Mugdock Road. Start to climb, climb, climb, and bloody steeply at that, up the brae lined with houses, old council-looking types, and then disappear round a couple of steep bends and out onto a level, thank God, country lane. The cars on the A-81 can be seen across the meadow on the left, as you now pass small lakes (one known as the Mill Dam) and grand gardens belonging to homes of substance. There are no

Once Strathblane is reached, there are two possibilities to get us back to Glasgow. One is the main A-81 Milngavie Road, which is nice enough in itself, especially the way it falls long and leafy down past the reservoirs, but it has a tough start out of Strathblane. The second is the Old Mugdock Road, which climbs steeply up to Mugdock Village and is a quieter, more scenic, but harder route. Dumgoyne shows well from high up on the Old Mugdock Road in the photo.

---

11 - Turn left at the first roundabout, then right before the bridge to access it.

12 - It is a Catholic movement, founded in 1914 in Germany by Father Joseph Kentenich. Schoenstatt means beautiful place.

Once Mugdock Village is passed through; then a spectacular view down onto Mugdock Reservoir appears. Quite a sight it makes before the plunge down starts; and it's pretty all the way.

miners' rows in Mugdock, that's for sure, though we're not actually quite there yet. There is a bit more heathland to ride through and another wee short steep ramp that must be taken, before we finally rise up to the junction.

Single lane, high heathland riding can only be good for the soul, so just relax now and enjoy your edgy skirt with this lofty village. You know that the next stretch will all be in your favour, not only in gradient but in beauty as well. The gardens here, well some of them, actually contain that grandest of tree, the pinus sylvestris (the Scots pine). Also, don't be too surprised if a gardener or two tugs his forelocks as you ride past, such is the way of the wealthy.

Now, when you come out the other side, you will almost immediately get a sensational view down to Mugdock Reservoir below, nestling among its firs. And then hold onto your hat here, for you will be down at it before you have a chance to shout Geronimo this time.

Just in front of you is a wicked left turn that is unbelievably tight, and once round it, it's whoosh!!! You're flying down passed the dam wall, all hairy and airy. Just as well the road's as straight as a die here, for there is speed aplenty about us now and then some, me boys, let me tell 'ee. You now batter and clatter down the Mugdock Road, into the room and kitchen residences of Milngavie, and come out at the lights on the Main Street (the B-8030) at Marks and Sparks. If you feel the need for a bit of calm after that, don't worry you're just about to get it. Turn right and roll down the road to the Burnbrae roundabout. This also has the A-81 coming into it on the left side, and it's just as easy, if not easier, to reach here by staying on the main A-road from Strathblane.

CARRON VALLEY RUN

A-81

Now it is also a bit of a tough pull up even when sticking to the main drag coming out of Strathblane, and if you came via Killearn and have been climbing into an east wind ever since Glengoyne Distillery, then you will be glad to get to the top of this one. It starts off with some good-looking, wooded, but steep double bends that get you up onto the higher muir, but the road isn't finished climbing yet, not by a long chalk. It continues to rise and rise, and feels a bit of a neverending job, with always one more bend to follow up, till at last you draw level with Ardinning Nature Reserve and the road tilts in our favour. It is very rough-looking over the high marsh of the reserve, but becomes leafy and pretty when you flip out of Stirling District and enter East Dunbartonshire again.

Just like the Mugdock option, there comes a watershed and it's payback time for all the hard ascending. Here, the fun starts down some great tree-lined double bends, made all the more dramatic with double white lines in the centre. It's a swoop-and-bank job as you take the curves that will open up a great view of Glasgow halfway down, and then you swoop and curve some more, till the long straight run down beside the reservoir begins. On this side, the wall belongs to the Craigmaddie Dam, and it's hard not to be in awe and enjoy the run down under this long, leafy canopy. Yes, a very long and welcome slope that holds only one bend in its possession, and brings you most speedily into the residences of upper class Glasgow as it takes you towards the crossroads.

Coming down the Mugdock Road and entering Milngavie that way. The solid, moss-covered stone walls that line the road give this avenue a real air of old quality, and it is a delight to pass between them.

This time it's the Renfrew ferry that will be used to get us across the Clyde, and I always enjoy using it. In its heyday it was a vehicle-carrying ferry that must have also carried thousands of people across each week. Despite the fact it is now a shadow of its former self, I'm just glad it's still running.

Go straight through and follow the road, always slightly downhill, through the bungalows and under the rail bridge to meet up with the Mugdock route at the Burnbrae roundabout.

Now we start to head south, as things noticeably busy up, and I am glad that the red-coated cycle lane is here for a while at least. It disappears all too quickly as we get in about Asda, and then we're on our own from hereon in to the Clyde Tunnel. It isn't too bad at first, as we are on fairly wide roads as we roll through the lights at Kessington, but then we're onto the Switchback and, boy, is it heavy. After the initial wee pecker of a climb to get you up from Canniesburn Toll, it's along the long, undulating, gentle rollercoaster carriageway of this main artery, and you won't be in any doubt as to its importance. You, your bike, along with Tom, Dick, Harry, and Harriet, will all be travelling along the old Switchback in a more than merry flow towards the gaping mouth of the tunnel.

Looking upstream from the Renfrew ferry when it's in midstream. Yarrows is only one of three shipyards left on the Clyde now, and you can see a frigate in for some repair work, which is hardly surprising as they mostly do defence work nowadays. It is hard to believe that the Clyde was once the shipbuilding heartland of the world, and I believe it turned out an incredible 30% of the entire world's shipping at one time.

CARRON VALLEY RUN

Just approaching the Renfrew slip, and it means we have been carried safely over the Clyde by the Renfrew ferry, just as it has done for countless people for hundreds of years. Long may it continue.

follows in the shape of the long, angled pull-up to the Govan side. It can be a bit of a drag, but only if you're well dehydrated by this point, which I usually am.

Despite that, we're soon breathing God's fresh air again and glad to be back on the flat, even if it means riding by the Govan sewage works (I was using the term 'fresh air' loosely). For me, the industrial home straight begins with going past the Sou Gen and all the old heavy industry-type places along the Govan and Renfrew Roads. This includes the King George V Docks, then we make our way long and straight past Bells Whisky plant towards the big busy roundabouts of Braehead.

Quite often, when coming back, I will avoid Renfrew altogether by returning through Hillington Industrial Estate and using the Arkleston back road to return into Paisley. The advantage of this is that Arky Road runs quite high through the fields and affords great views back across the city and to the hills we climbed over an hour or so ago.

The initial disadvantage of going via Arky Road is getting through the very busy section from the A-8's Braehead roundabout to the sanctuary of the industrial estate's quiet roads. It's not a long stretch, thankfully, and begins with taking the A-736 under the motorway and onto Hillington Road. Stay alert here till the first roundabout is reached, and turn right behind the Shell filling station. Again, turn right at the wee mini roundabout that follows, and you're feeling safe on Kelvin Drive. Relative quietness can even make the surrounding factories seem appealing as I fly along and through another roundabout taking me onto Mosslands Road. A big left swinger introduces the top end of Penilee Road and also the fields on the right that represent the green belt between Glasgow and Paisley.

When you take the first turn on the right, just before the traffic lights on the rail bridge, you are on Arkleston

That won't come, of course, till after you've had the tumble down to big, bad Anniesland Cross, from where it will be the Crow Road that will take you on in from there. Anniesland Cross is what you call a bloody junction, no two ways about it. Even I don't fancy running red at this one, but the thought has crossed my mind.

Anyway, once safely across by the green light, keep well tucked in on the left – just to be on the safe side – as you run between Jordanhill and Broomhill, and get close to the river. To access the tunnel from the main A-739 is very straightforward. Once you've gotten through the lights at Victoria Park, head straight for the tunnel mouth, where you will see a cycle path – although signed – slip off discreetly to the left onto Balshagray Drive.

Turn right and run down to the bottom, which leads via the pavement, to a cute wee underpass that takes you out onto Dumbarton Road at Fountainwell Square. This is all rideable, so no need to dismount. When you do emerge out the other side, the beginning of the tunnel's cycle lane is just round Fountainwell to your right. Curve round, press the buzzer, and await that Open Sesame moment when the iron bar doors swing open. Into the white underworld below the Clyde we begin to descend. Down and down we plummet, starting off to the side of the road tunnel, before ending up right beneath the cars. Always keep everything under control during the descent, as it's a tight lane we're in and we know what

105

Road. It's one that I find most scenic and pleasing. The fields either side of the road are long and fertile, often they are ploughed or holding crops all erect in a swaying, fair blanket. There is a long straight rise up to and past Arkleston Farm, where the view across red Clydeside is a stunning one of hills, high flats, and smoothed urbanisation. A wicked left-hand bend brings you to the top of Gallowhill Road, always heavy and dramatic-looking with the big railway line running its length. A mini roundabout holds court at the top of the road right in front of us, and I always turn left and meander through the old Whitehaugh area of the town.

This is Paisley's sort of Knightswood, and by a twist and turn or three through birches and bushes, the Glasgow Road is encountered again near the Grammar School. Now there is only the challenge of Calside and the Munt between me and home, and I try and pick the easiest way through the town centre, which will vary with the time and the day of the week.

On returning home, you will learn to have a recovery strategy in place. This might take the shape of an actual, usually expensive, cycling-specific recovery drink or a homemade equivalent. Me personally, I can't wait to get my teeth into a tin miner's or Cornish pasty. Hope you enjoyed the run this time and we'll be back out again soon. Till then, take care.

KILLEARN-CAMPSIE LOOP

57.1 MILES
3.54 HOURS
2920 FEET/ASCENT
2442 CALORIES /BURNED

Now, a great way to do the Campsies without going all the way to Kilsyth is to do the loop from Strathblane via Killearn to Lennoxtown, or vice versa. It will, of course, include the long climb over on the Crow Road. It is a very popular run, as far as I can gather, probably more popular than the Tak Ma Doon Road. Whichever way you tackle it, it's a good workout, and you can throw in an approach or return via Mugdock to add even more variety. You're sure to meet many other riders on your travels, especially if it's a weekend ride.

Give it a go. *Liam Boy.*

FALKIRK & SLAMMANAN

VIA LONGRIGGEND	VIA DENNY & GLENMAVIS DIRECT
72.3 MILES	72.6 MILES
5.38 HOURS	5.33 HOURS
ASCENT 2100 FEET	2900 FT/ASC
3317 CALORIES BURNED	3583 CALORIES BURNED
	OS LANDRANGER MAPS 64, 65
	OS LANDRANGER MAPS 64, 57, 65

ROUTE SUMMARY

ALTERNATIVE ROUTE	MAIN ROUTE	ALTERNATIVE ROUTE
	Clyde Tunnel	
	Dumbarton Rd (East)	
	Byres Rd	
	Queen Margaret Dr	
	Bilsland Dr	
	Springburn Rd	
	Kirkintilloch	
Tak Ma Doon Rd	Kilsyth	
Denny	Bonnybridge	High Bonnybridge
	Camelon	Falkirk
	Falkirk	High Falkirk
	High Falkirk	
Limerigg	Slamannan	Limerigg
Longriggend	Upperton	Caldercruix
	Greengairs	Plains
	Glenmavis	Airdrie
	Coatbridge	
	Bargeddie	
	Shettleston Rd (A-89)	
	Saltmarket	
	Albert Bridge	
	Paisley Rd West	
	Paisley	

FALKIRK & SLAMMANAN RUN

CANAL COUNTRY

This is a run that is in many ways completely different from anything we have done already. It largely involves making for Falkirk via Kilsyth – though there is a great variation to that – and then heading up onto the old mining moors around Slamannan and Limerigg, before falling back down to Airdrie and Coatbridge. Thereafter, it is the long-running arteries of Glasgow's east end that return us busily but safely back to Paisley. Just over 70 miles of riding out east makes for more than just a nice change of scenery, as I do most of my riding in the west. It also takes us on a wonderful historical trip. This, too, has variation, as it isn't only our old industrial past we ride through, but also a famous battle of the '45 rebellion no less.

I first got the idea for doing this one due to several factors. One, believe it or not, was sheer curiosity. I simply wanted to find out what the road was like if you turned right at the Carron Bridge Hotel and headed for Denny, instead of the usual turn left. And I was not disappointed with what I found. This is not the main approach route, some may be glad to hear, as it involves a major deviation and a lot more climbing, but it's one helluva way to get to Falkirk. Also, looking at an O'S map and wondering just what it was like up and around Slamannan, got my curiosity going, as well as wanting to take a personal trip down memory lane, by paying a visit to Longriggend remand centre.

I never had the misfortune to spend three weeks in the place – one of Her Majesty's boarding houses – but some of the guys I grew up with did. So, on occasion, I made the long trip up into the bleakness to pay them a visit. However, by the time I made my first run up there on the bike, I was surprised to find that the place had already closed. I'm sure it will be missed by no-one.

So, there is a lot to ride past and see on this 70-plus miler. It comes in roughly four stages, and we won't get any of it covered by sitting on our arse, so it's stretch, grub up, inflate tyres (every run, don't forget), then out the door we go. Now, I will have an additive in the water bottles, in the shape of a zero tab[1], if it's a summer run, but will often just run on fresh water in winter time. This is due to the winter run – which, of course, is no less arduous; in fact, it's often harder – being done at a lower tempo.

I will also change my on-the-road grub, depending on the temperature and season. This consists of just Mars Bars and Topics in the winter, but as these would melt summertime, I will switch to cycling-specific energy bars and Torq gels for the long hot runs. I have mentioned this strategy before, but intentionally do so again just to get the message across. I personally have a real sweet tooth and enjoy a Mars and a Topic when I'm on the move. In fact, I often wonder if I do these long runs in colder weather just to enjoy the sweet treats, which I don't ordinarily allow myself.

The first stage of this one, for me, will be to take the exact same route to Kilsyth that I used in the Carron Valley run, all the way to the bottom of the Tak Ma Doon Road.

So, the usual drill will now be applied where I don't describe the route fully, because I did that in only the last run, but will merely include a brief description for those who haven't read Carron Valley and want to do this run first instead. The general bones of that is fairly straightforward, involving only one dog leg, crossing over the Clyde on the George V Bridge, after running along Paisley Road West when we leave Paisley on the Glasgow Road. This is you on the great old A-8 till you cross the river, then after heading for the Saltmarket, you make your way up the High Street, before picking up the A-803 Springburn Road and you're on your way to Bishopbriggs. Don't forget that this point can also be reached by using either the Renfrew ferry or Clyde Tunnel and then making Bilsland Drive, Ruchill, your approach artery.

One of the reasons I like to come that way is because of the views I get when heading for the tunnel by riding along high Arkleston Road. This makes a nice, scenic, quiet change from the busier Glasgow Road, and I usually gain the Arkleston by heading straight across at the Barshaw lights once I've ridden down Hawkhead Road. This in turn is gained by using the south Paisley roads of Donaldswood, Falside, and Lochfield, which allows me to

The new massive Queen Elizabeth University Hospital is unmissable across the wheat fields of Arkleston Farm, as Arkleston Road is ridden, heading towards the Clyde Tunnel. It means that Glasgow's west end will first be the approach route used to get us onto the A-803 Springburn Road, before heading out into Bishopbriggs, then Kilsyth and ultimately Falkirk.

completely avoid the town centre's mayhem. Once onto the Arky, the field-filled views of the city and even the Kilsyth Hills way in the distance, get you in the mood for what is to come. It's quite a start, I must say.

Arkleston Farm, which is ridden by on the right and which sits on the road's highest part, is a place that reminds me of a Van Gogh painting, especially when seen from the M-8 motorway as you're driving along. The surrounding wheat fields, whether in full crop or stumped, are long and eye-losing, always drawing your gaze deeply into them. Admittedly, the Hillington Industrial Estate that follows isn't nearly as pretty, though it is fairly safe and quiet. The same can't be said for the mega-busy stretch of road that must be ridden to take

Looking back across the wheat fields to South Arkleston Farm and the Gallowhill high flats from the Penilee Road, and we're just about to enter the relatively quiet roads of the Hillington industrial estate. I say relatively because soon we have to negotiate the mega-busy roundabouts that service the Braehead shopping centre, and the difference in traffic volume will be very noticeable. You're quickly through, however, and then it's a quick batter along the Shieldhall Road to the tunnel.

---

1 - I find 1½ tabs per bottle about right.

us past Braehead shopping centre and also along the Shieldhall Road to the tunnel.

Once we emerge from the tunnel on the other side at Whiteinch, it's also a fairly straightforward dog leg manoeuvre to get us onto Bilsland Drive. Turn right and continue along the impressive, though always traffic-heavy, Dumbarton Road, till you can turn left onto the Byres Road (B-808), and this you follow all the way to Springburn.

Again, I urge caution, and ask you to keep your wits about you until you get onto Queen Margaret Drive and the safety of its sort-of cycle lane and noticeably less traffic. The university area of Glasgow, like the university areas of all big cities, has a vibrancy all of its own, and with it, it carries the danger from motorised transport. When crossing the Maryhill Road, however,

Going under the rail bridge on Hawthorn Street, gives a real feeling of old tough Glasgow. We're just about to join up with the Springburn route

that magnificent old arched rail bridge and its curving wall that follows, welcomes you into the north of the city, and the great ease that carries you from Ruchill into Possilpark via Hawthorn Street.

This rather forgotten corner of Glasgow does make for an interesting approach, and I prefer it to the all-out mayhem of the High Street any day. The new houses on Bilsland Drive have rather skilfully been built in the same style as the older ones round about, and this adds to the continuity and feel of old as you purr passed Ruchill Park. As always, the distant high flats of Springburn act as your marker to keep you moving in the right direction, as Balmore Road is approached and crossed. After that, the toughness of the north end of

FALKIRK & SLAMMANAN RUN

town is seen and felt. However, there is a great rail bridge to ride under before the bright red sandstone buildings bring some quality into the frame, as you near the modern slip road for the A-803.

When you meet up with the Springburn Road, all the navigation is over for the time being, because it is a straight run from the moment you pick up the 803 right to Kilsyth, and beyond for that matter. This carries you not only through the Briggs, but also Kirkintilloch and Queenzieburn enroute. In the last run, on the way to Kilsyth, I mentioned a picturesque-looking row of low cottages in Queenzieburn, which sit right on the main road, but what I didn't notice at the time was the stone-carved date of their construction, which sits above one of them. 1891 can clearly be seen, and I was informed by a

Looking across the meadows to the Kilsyth Hills from the A-803, just after the Torrance roundabout and before the long drop down to Kirkintilloch begins. This is one of the last kind of pretty pastoral scenes you will witness on this run, as it is more about former gritty industrial landscapes and high barren moors than picture postcard places.

local man that they were a miners' row.

The men of this row would have worked in the nearby Twechar mines, or further afield perhaps. I mention this because, for the majority of this run, we will be riding through what was a major coal mining area. The roughness of the terrain gives the game away in a lot of places. Across the valley at this point can be seen the houses of Twechar, and above them Barr Hill. This was a major Roman fort sitting just behind the Antonine Wall, and will be one of two (of the best) that we ride close to today. It is a great view from the top of the Barr, and you can see why the Romans chose to make a fort there. It's a quarter of a mile walk up a track to get there, so it's not

A view of the former mining village of Twechar from the old Roman fort of Barr Hill. Running alongside the canal is the B-8023 which is a good alternative to the A-803 to get to Kilsyth, and one I use often. We've now entered the Kelvin Valley, a former heavy industry stronghold, and the canal – along with the railway – would have been used to ferry the coal away to the foundries of Glasgow and Coatbridge. The rest of the run over to Falkirk and then back via Slamannan, Monklands, and Glasgow's east end, runs through a similar old industrial landscape.

for road bikers, but it is worth a walk up sometime, if you like your history.

Now, about 23 miles will see me arrive in Kilsyth, and with that the start of the Tak Ma Doon Road. When you reach here, an option is open to you should you wish to use it. By that I mean it is possible to access Falkirk via Denny, and this entails climbing over the Kilsyth Hills to Carron Bridge and then heading east on the B-818. In fact, you could, if it suits, come over the Crow Road from Lennoxtown, or even make the big loop round by Killearn, to get to Denny that way. Either of these two ways certainly makes for a great day out on the quiet roads. For me, the Tak Ma Doon is the most practical option if I decide to enjoy going via the other side of the hills. However, to stay on the A-803, is the faster, easier, though no less entertaining option, and I recommend using both. I guarantee you won't be disappointed with either.

So, that is stage one of the run over when we reach the Tak Ma Doon. Now, it's time for stage two.

DENNY ROUTE

If you do fancy going via Denny, then turn left and start to make your way up the four ramp-like sections and 2½ miles of the Tak Ma Doon Road. It's one you know well enough by now, as we've climbed and descended it already. Without coming this way, the amount of climbing is just over 2000 feet, so it won't be beyond a reasonable climber to handle this pull-up as well. Once over the top, really enjoy the swerve and slip of the tar down to the Carron Bridge Hotel, with the views of the Ochils ahead. And when the crossroads at the hotel squints sideways at you close up, turn right. The sign says 4 miles to Denny, and what a four miles it is. It is this stretch in particular that makes it worthwhile to come this way.

Now, four miles, even if it's top-notch riding, isn't a lot of payback for a hefty pull-up on something like the Tak Ma Doon. So many guys and girls won't feel it worth the effort to come this way. That is fair comment. The stretch from Denny to the

Leaving behind the Carron Bridge Hotel after re-crossing the River Carron on the B-818, and we're heading for Denny. After just a little bit of climbing, done on wonderfully gentle rising bends, the great fall down through Fankerton and Stoneywood follows, and it is a great – albeit too short – stretch of road to ride. This makes the climb up on the Tak Ma Doon worth it, I feel, though some may not, but it is a great variation on the more direct A-803 to get to Falkirk.

FALKIRK & SLAMMANAN RUN

Three Bridges roundabout, where we rejoin the A-803 route just before Camelon, doesn't exactly set the heather on fire. So again, some will understandably feel that it is only worth their while to come this way if they decide to make a real day of it by coming through Killearn or over the Crow Road from Lennoxtown. And again, fair comment. I only decided to include this way because it was one of the reasons I got interested in the route in the first place, and also because I know how good the drop down to Denny on the B-818 is. So, in my humble opinion, it is worth a mention.

Right from the word go, when you leave the Carron Inn, you know you're in for a belter, just the way that road re-crosses the river on another beautiful old stone bridge and leads you up the hillside again. It is a magnificent big swerving start over this single-arched spanner, where a look to the left as you cross will show the low Carron quietly running away through the bleak. A climb-up now begins; one which is a gentle affair, and which rather dramatically has black and white painted crash barriers guiding you round several sensational bends. These are there to keep you from plunging down into the River Carron, which starts to take off down a wooded glade. Unfortunately, it finishes all too soon when you crest out at a handful of houses which are known as The Topps.

A large stud farm sits nearby, and there are horses everywhere as you begin a rather surprisingly tentative descent. Even this soon levels out into a long flat straight, which only finishes when you reach pretty Northshields Farm. It's a really green, pleasant, and again surprisingly open countryside you ride through, and after Northshields the descending begins in earnest. It's all been worth the wait as you helter-skelter round tight bends and over bridges, rounding fast hedgerows and the likes, firing fearlessly down into the waiting Fankerton. Already the Grangemouth fires have told you you're in the Forth Valley, and the blue back of the Fankerton name signs lets you know you've also dropped into Falkirk District.

Now, if you expected roughsville, you're in for a pleasant surprise, because Fankerton is a rather well-to-do looking wee place. Wee indeed, for no sooner have you arrived than you're out again, and with a dip and a dive, you're battering down to Stoneywood. This at first seems a little bigger than Fankerton, though it's hard to tell as you are moving so fast; it does seem to be of similar ilk. The last time I passed through, it looked like a building site, with new houses going up left, right, and centre. There is also a new big roundabout to go through, and even that wasn't finished. On leaving Stoneywood, you pass under the square box bridge carrying the M-80 above and you level out in Denny.

On entering, you will abut the A-872 at a T-junction. Turn left, following the Stirling sign onto Nethermains Road, and run through the houses to a roundabout. Forget the left for Stirling this time; instead, go straight through for Denny town centre (A-833). Be ready for just a little hustle and bustle up to the traffic lights, where we want to turn left to take us to Camelon. It is a tired-looking centre which the town has, no doubt about it. Rather unsurprising, as this was a former heavy industry stronghold of iron foundries, brickworks, and coal mines, of course.

When you arrive in Denny from Carron Bridge, you're back into the towns of the industrial revolution. This one certainly falls into that category, as it was also a former heavy industry stronghold. Nowadays, it also unfortunately has a look of decay about it; well, the centre does, with the big block of flats in the photo looking like they belong in Communist Russia. When the old industries went, they were never replaced, and so it's taken many places a long time to recover. We are about to turn left onto the A-883, which will take us flatly all the way to the Three Bridges roundabout at Camelon, where we rejoin the other route.

The town centre's row of shops look like they belong in a housing scheme, as opposed to their actual position, and the flats on the right that sit above them wouldn't look out of place in Leningrad. At the lights, though, the fine old Denny kirk saves the day, as we turn left and head out of town, once more on a down slope. When you get through the unusually-named Herbertshire roundabout, you are more or less onto the flat plain and fields of the Forth Valley. Now it's a totally different landscape that hems in the road on both sides, with broad, rich, gentle green fields providing the blanket to ride through.

It is also a little bit busier than we were used to up beside the infant Carron, and it's not particularly pretty or pleasant. You roll under the M-876, on its way to the Kincardine Bridge and the likes, and the ever-increasing flatness will become markedly more noticeable once you pass through the big Checkbar roundabout. The great-looking Larbert Bridge sits just to the left of the roundabout, magnificently spanning the Carron. Here the road also becomes longer and faster into the bargain. Electricity pylons appear in numbers, as they carry their flow from the Forth-based power stations, and it is this more plain-like, power-packed setting that brings you

When riding through Kelvinhead on the A-803 just before crossing into Falkirk District, the valley looks hard and gritty, with the remains of old slag heaps from yesteryear still visible on the slopes across the canal. It was the arrival of the canal, and later the railways, that allowed these areas to open up to industry in the way they did.

finally to the Three Bridges roundabout.

On the way, there is a disused railway line running along beside you on the right, which is fairly interesting. It tree-clad embankments and impressive old bridge stanchions break the monopoly of the flatness, for sure. It leads towards our meeting with the A-803, which is the more direct route from Kilsyth to here, and one that avoids going over the Campsie Fells or Kilsyth Hills. It is a route that has its own charm and interest, however, especially the way it continues through numerous small settlements enroute to the Three Bridges. I guarantee that you will get as much pleasure from this way as you would the Denny route.

FALKIRK DIRECT (A-803)

Now, if you don't fancy going via Denny, then carry straight on when you pass the Tak Ma Doon Road and stay on the A-803. An entertaining wee few miles is about to come your way, which won't be that obvious at first, as you run fairly flat and straight out the far side of Kilsyth. This, like a lot of the places round about, was a mining town in the past, and I've already mentioned in previous runs about its links with extreme Protestantism.

The road here runs in similar straight vein to the way it did in the early part of the Kelvin plain, but then it starts to entertain a bit more, with some curving and dancing dips, just as it approaches the tiny hamlet of Kelvinhead. There are signs of old slag heaps and the likes sitting across the valley at this point, and their blackness can be seen even to this day, despite Mother Nature's green attempt to cover man's handiwork.

Kelvinhead seems to consist mostly of a row of white semi-detached houses sitting on the right, behind which sits the valley floor containing the canal, which is in view. I asked one resident why the houses were built here in such an isolated spot, but she was unable to provide an answer. This was despite the fact that she had in the past made an effort to find out herself. So, being none the wiser, we carry on, straight and undulating into Falkirk District. Ahead, the rooftops of Banknock's houses have already been spied, and we shortly enter the village. So far so good, as we're purring along nicely at this point, no problem. Now, the way that the road sits just off the valley floor, on a bit of a slope, tends to lend it a bit of interest, what with is twists and rolls. And as it isn't too taxing at any point, it is a most enjoyable jaunt at this stage.

The good news is that there is more of the same to come; especially as you swerve and rise past the beautiful old farmhouse at Auchencloch. Then quite a good view of the valley can also be had as you enter Banknock. It is solid-looking old council houses, typical of hereabouts, which greets your arrival. The show-stopper, however, is the white, turreted Glenskirlie House Hotel that was once the residence of the Dobson family, who owned a nearby foundry. The Cannerton was the local coal pit providing work for the miners, and both the canal and railway provided the transport system for coal removal at one time.

I don't know if it's my imagination, but the houses in not only Banknock, but also the other small towns we are

FALKIRK & SLAMMANAN RUN

about to ride through, still seem to possess that uniform line and look that you associate with the miners' row. So, more old industrial history is met enroute just before we slip seamlessly into Haggs, where the name sign is needed to inform you of this, as there is no space between it and the former village. A rather spectacular crossing over of the M-80 comes next, and it isn't often that a motorway looks good enough to stop and admire, but this one does, with its old railway bridge spanning the road to the south.

The way that you instantly enter one small town after another is what gives this route so much interest and character. It is rare that this sort of thing happens in our sparsely-populated rural areas. Haggs, I assume, was also a mining town, and again I say that because of the way the housing lends itself to the row mentality. This is especially true of a distinctive row of houses that lie off the main road to the left at an acute angle; they are of a distinctive light brown colour, as are a lot of the other houses in the area. The fine-looking Longcroft Inn was up for grabs as I passed (if anyone fancies becoming "mein host"), then you continue on the long fire-through completely unhindered.

The straight you are on has taken you past a lot of modern houses on the right-hand side, but again the left has very distinctive miners'-looking low cottages all along its length. They bring you towards Dennyloanhead (DLH as its known), which is entered on a soft dip that allows us a glimpse across the now gentle valley floor to our right. The low harshness of the early Kelvin Valley is now long gone, as a richer, greener landscape of fertile fields and big farms has replaced the sheep and reed-filled flood plain that we rode through only a few miles back. It will eventually dawn on you that you have slipped unknown from the Clyde into the Forth Valley without any real climb of consequence. This is another real bonus of coming this way.

Now, there is nothing old about the houses that greet you on your arrival in DLH, as is often the way nowadays, with modern developments skirting many town edges. But with a rise and a curve later, we find more traditional attire. Then an interesting wee fork in the road is soon met, which is managed by a mini roundabout, right beside ye olde Crown Hotel. We take the right fork for Bonnybridge and Falkirk, as always keeping us on the A-803. Along the road at the point where the older houses stop and another new grand white development begins, means you've left Dennyloanhead and entered Bonnybridge. Again, the new houses soon give way to the older, and you get to enjoy a pleasant skirt round and through the suburbs on the Bonnyfield Road.

This takes you onto the High Street, which leads you down quite a dramatic wee slope into the town centre. At the start of the slope, we pass a couple of old inns, the Cornhill and Royal Hotel, before we cross the Bonny Water Bridge, which I assume is where the town name came from. It's a real happening place, the town centre; surprising for such a small settlement. What is important to us, apart from the normal services of grub and juice, is the roundabout, smack dead centre in the middle of it all. This is because it actually offers us two ways to get to Falkirk: either left to stay on the main A-803 and head for Camelon direct; or turn right for High Bonnybridge and go in on the B-816.

If you go left, it's hard to imagine just how much of an industrial town Bonnybridge once was, as all you see going this way are a few houses. The town, incidentally, had numerous iron foundries and other interests as well, including chemicals, paper, wood, and the ubiquitous brickworks. The pride of place, however, was the Smith and Wellstood Foundry, which brought the American hot metal stove to Europe. It was that fine old stalwart the Forth and Clyde Canal that transported the goods to Glasgow. The whole area, because of its position and transport links, became a main hub in the industrial revolution, and Bonnybridge was certainly part of that hub. Now, if you're happy to stay on the main road, turn left.

A-803 FALKIRK CONT.

The run out of town on the Main Road sees normal service resumed, with a great straight flow past old council houses and an old red phone box thrown in for the usual good measure. Next though, we find ourselves back out in the fields for the first time in a while, and as we speed through them on the mile or so to Camelon, we spy that magnificent structure of the Falkirk Wheel. Its great, grey, steel circles steal your focus away from the road ahead, and why not? It's as impressive a piece of engineering as you are likely to see the world over. It has a practical purpose, as well as just looking good, in as much as it transfers boats from the Forth and Clyde to the Union Canal.

Meeting some modern transport now when we cross over the M-80 at Haggs. In the distance, however, can be seen the impressive bridge that carries today's railway, while the Forth and Clyde canal passes under the motorway in the mid-distance. The motorcar, along with all its highways, has totally superseded everything that has gone before, including the bicycle of course. But I'm happy to say the bike is making a strong comeback.

The wheel opened in 2002 and replaced a flight of canal locks that had done the same job for many years. At the same time, we pass the nearly as impressive but equally strong-looking farmstead of Wester Carmuirs, with its solid stone wall in front and big trees filling its garden, just before we drop down to the Three Bridges Roundabout. This joins us up with the route from Denny. From the Three Bridges, we dip under the two colourful rail bridges ahead (I assume the other bridge belonged to the now defunct rail line) and enter the busy-busy of Camelon. It is tenements and houses (brown coloured) all along the right-hand side, and more industry and commerce than you can shake a stick at on the left.

Yes, it's a seemingly endless procession of car dealerships, bus garages, Tesco's, Aldi's, and anything else you care to mention, holding the left flank. All serviced by the now chock-a-block A-803, and you wonder just how in the hell it got so busy all of a sudden. Things ease off a fair bit when you get through the Camelon roundabout, passing the fine Falkirk Court building on the way, then you pick up a red-painted cycle lane. Keep your eye open for the Roman Bar, another indication of the Antonine's presence as you go along here. It was hereabouts that a large find of Roman coins was discovered, and I believe this was due to the fact that the Romans had additional camps in the area, as well as the Antonine Wall.

The red cycle lane blossoms into a full-blown red bus lane once you pass through the Rosebank roundabout up ahead, and it means you have entered Falkirk. This is done once you have crossed the canal for the last time, right beside the old Camelon distillery. The canal itself ends disappointingly not far from here, when it rolls into the Carron rather unscenically just before the motorway, if my memory serves me right.[2]

It does not do justice to this rather wonderful man-made waterway, which did so much in the past for the areas it passed through, particularly as it is so serene and scenic in many other places along its way. For the record, it finally opened in 1790 after several halts in its construction, and it meant that many towns along its 35 miles length now had an avenue to the outside world. This was duly exploited by numerous industries, which still continued to use the canal even after the arrival of railway, though perhaps to a lesser extent.

In the past, I have ridden to Falkirk and back in a day, when using the canal towpath, and it's a great way to get from west to east, traffic-free and with pleasant scenery into the bargain. I can pick it up once I cross into Knightswood and Yoker on the Renfrew ferry. I normally use my mountain bike for this particular jaunt, as a lot of it isn't strictly on tarmac and can get a bit muddy in places. That is the reason I haven't included the canal as an option in any of the runs. However, it is rideable on a road bike, and therefore can be used as an easy and safe escape route back home to the west, should you require it. I personally have used it when I am out on my training bike and have left it late and have no lights, or when the wind has become really strong.

It is also a great escape route if you are just totally canned and need an easy artery to get back without any climbing. A lot of the towpath is tarmacked and therefore makes for clean, fast riding; some of it isn't, though, so I wouldn't take my best machine along it at any time. But I'd have no hesitation with using the mudguard-sporting training bike. A lot of the canal and its path have been greatly restored with National Lottery money in recent years, after it had fallen into gentle decay ruin following its official closure in 1963. Long may its lum reek, for I cannot think of a more pleasant saunter than going along the towpath on a mountie on a warm summer's day.

Talking of lums, we pass right under the high chimney of the Camelon distillery right after we have crossed the canal, and it is a reminder that it just wasn't heavy

---

2 - I haven't ridden it end-to-end for a few years now.

industry manufactured here. Whisky distilling was also big in Falkirk, and Bonnybridge, too. The old mill-like distillery building has kept an air of enchantment about it, despite its derelict state, and I hope someone buys it and does it up soon; it would be a shame to let it go to rack and ruin.

Just approaching the roundabout in the centre of Bonnybridge, and this is an important point in the run. Here you have a couple of choices on which way to continue to Falkirk. Turn left to go in direct on the A-803 via Camelon, or turn right to go via High Bonnybridge and then in on the Tamfourhill Road.

Now, I read somewhere that Falkirk, or "Fawkirk" as it's pronounced locally, was voted the country's most beautiful town by television viewers, and on the strength of the road that we now cycle down I can believe that.

It is a great downhill flyer in the safety of the red silent bus lane that brings us through manicured gardens of pines, and lawns with des-res dwellings of age and show on either side. Very nice, I must say. Big stone walls and rhododendrons complete the scene that finds us falling into the equally quaint town centre's edge. Unfortunately, we don't get to see the very centre itself, which is reputedly just as pretty, but just skirt round the modern ring road, which isn't inspiring, to say the least. Before we get onto that, though, there is a chance we will get stopped at some lights and this gives us time to admire some of the cobbled lanes and arched passageways hereabouts. They are most splendid and pretty, all set among the light sandstone buildings to your right.

Now, we are going to go from Falkirk centre right up onto the high muir above and head for Slamannan on the B-803. Simple as that. We are swapping the A-803 for the B-803. This won't be a problem even if you haven't done your homework or studied a map. The way to Slamannan is very well signposted and will be obvious to you the moment you approach the centre. On the drop-down, get over to the right-hand lane and tuck in safe as you roll up to the lights. You are about to go round a bit of a helter-skelter piece of road that will take you past a modern, hideous (though necessary) big car park and Debenhams. This will require you to flip from the right-hand lane to the next one left, which can be done with ease.

Now, Slamannan, Shieldhill, and the B-803, are all still well signposted, so keeping on the right track won't be difficult. Just one final left turn where the big Erskine Parish Church sits, will take you up to the end of the more tranquil Cochrane Avenue, where the signs for the High station are met. Now shortly, when we start to head for Slamannan, I will go on at some length about the battle that took place in Falkirk during the 1745 rebellion. This, as any historian worth his salt will know, was not the only battle to have taken place in this town.

Old meets the new here when you see the Falkirk Wheel as you speed from Bonnybridge to Camelon on the A-803 after taking the left fork at the Bonnybridge roundabout. This most impressive piece of modern engineering links two canals – the Forth and Clyde and the Union – and replaces the many locks that did the same job in the past. The wheel itself is a wonderful sight, I must say, even from quite a distance away.

Just about to enter the town of Camelon by passing under its bright blue bridge, and then Falkirk is only a short hop away. If coming by the A-803, there hasn't been a lot of climbing so far, and a fairly speedy journey can be had once you get beyond all the traffic lights of Glasgow and Bishopbriggs. However, the 803 isn't the only route you can take to reach Camelon. If you want to mix the rural with the urban, you can take the Tak Ma Doon Road when you reach Kilsyth, or even come via Killearn, or the Crow Road from Lennoxtown, and make it a really varied run.

In the July of 1298, an English army, under the Hammer of the Scots Edward I, defeated the Scottish army under William Wallace.

The Scots were again greatly outnumbered, as they were the year before at Stirling Bridge, and Wallace – without the support of his main tactician, Andrew Murray[3] – was forced to flee with many of his men to the safety of the nearby Tor Wood, whereafter he made good his escape. A lack of support, and also treachery by other Scottish Nobles, undermined the great man on this occasion. And with that sad thought in mind, the second stage of this run ends, just as we begin to make our way up onto Falkirk and then Slamannan Muir. Initially following the sign for Falkirk High station, this will take us in the general direction we want to go.

This also means turning right out of Cochrane Avenue, which keeps us on the B-803, and once we round the first bend at the primary school, the climbing has already started. Beginning the third stage will involve a short steep climb as you snake round the early bends, ignoring the sign for the train station now, and keeping to the left as you hit the ramp-like section on the early part of Glen Brae. The sign says straight ahead for Shieldhill, but we get in the right-hand lane for Slamannan.

---

3 - He had died of injuries he received during the battle of Stirling Bridge, unfortunately.

The good news is that when you do turn the corner, the gradient relaxes considerably on Slamannan Road itself. Just as the old lungs start to calm down after the turn, you go over the railway bridge almost immediately.

The station lies just to the right. However, to the left is a rail tunnel. When this tunnel was being excavated for the line in 1839, the workmen came across a large burial chamber. This was one of two main burial pits that were dug after the battle here in January 1746; the 17th, to be exact. This was the lower of the two pits and you will shortly ride by the upper one, which is contained in Dumyat Drive, just up ahead on the right. For it was on Falkirk Muir on that day that the Jacobite Army of Charles Edward Stuart (Bonnie Prince Charlie), under the leadership – for the most part – of his second-in-command Lord George Murray, defeated a Government force (Redcoats) under the leadership of the irascible Lieutenant General Henry (Hangman) Hawley.

Hawley and the majority of Government troops had been based in Edinburgh. The Jacobites were based in Stirling, besieging the castle. Now, the Redcoats had decided to base a food and fodder store in Linlithgow, which was roughly halfway between the two camps. This was perilously close to a sizeable Jacobite covering force under Lord George's command. The prize was so tempting that the rebels captured the town on the 13th and began loading their booty onto carts. As luck would have it, the Redcoats had decided to make the opening move of their military campaign for that year on the

This is the Forth and Clyde canal as it runs through Camelon looking in the direction of Falkirk; as always, it makes a very pretty sight, but especially on this stretch. It takes a slight diversion off the A-803 to see it at this point, but it's worth it all the same. You can just about make out the chimney of the now disused Camelon distillery, which we will ride by shortly as we enter Falkirk town.

exact same day. A sizeable force, Hawley's 1st division, was heading west under the command of Major General John (Daddy) Huske.

News reached Huske that a Jacobite force was in Linlithgow and he set off in hot pursuit, splitting his force in an attempt to try and trap the rebels. This was all in vain, however, because word reached Lord George of what was afoot, and he withdrew his forces in time, escaping across the River Avon by its only bridge. The fact that the rebels slipped away, rather than staying to stand and fight, gave Hawley and the Redcoats' high command the impression that the Prince and Lord George would not give them battle. This was exactly what Hawley's predecessor, General John (Johnny) Cope, had thought the previous year before his defeat at Prestonpans. Hawley was about to make the exact same mistake.

In fact, when he (Hawley) moved himself and the rest of his men towards Falkirk in the next couple of days, his main concern was that the rebels would try and slip away before he could get to grips with them. It never crossed his mind that he would come under attack. Just to be on the safe side, he stationed a large number of dragoons at Larbert Bridge, which would have been the rebels only way to cross the River Carron. In the meantime, he was made most welcome in nearby Callendar House – the home of John Boyd, the 4th Earl of Kilmarnock. This was despite the fact that Lord Kilmarnock was actually out with the rebels at the time.

Lord Kilmarnock, incidentally, was no dyed-in-the-wool Jacobite, far from it. He only joined the rebels out of expediency, as he was heavily in debt to many local tradesmen and the only way he saw out of his predicament was a victory for Prince Charles, so threw his lot in with the Jacobites[4]. It was a make-or-break move that ultimately cost him his life after Culloden. His wife Anne, Lady Kilmarnock, had strong Whiggish sympathies, however, so the warm welcome that Hawley and his men received there was most likely genuine.

On the morning of the 17th, when the rebels were seen on the move, Hawley had left Callendar House at 5am in plenty of time to rally his troops, despite tall tales of his being caught on the hop and galloping to the battlefield without his hat or wig, or some nonsense like that. This again had a similarity to Cope's conduct at Prestonpans. when stories told of how the early Jacobite action had caught "Johnny" Cope sleeping. Not so. Despite an early morning sweeping action by the rebels, Cope was wise to it and had already turned his troops to face the threat.

And so it was with only thoughts of cutting off the rebels' escape that General "Hangman" Hawley sent his troops up onto Falkirk Muir to intercept them on their way to England, or so he thought. The advantage of using high Falkirk Muir to attack the Redcoats was the idea of Lord George Murray. This natural vantage point was also recognised by the Romans, and that is why they built the Antonine Wall along its lower slopes.

Lord George had brought his infantry and cavalry down from Plean Muir in the north, and swung them round to face Falkirk. This also gave them the advantage of having the wind and rain at their back, for the day that had started off so brightly was now a foul one. This meant that the Redcoats were not only coming uphill to face the fearsome Highlanders' frontline, but that they also had the wind and rain in their faces.

Ironically, it was the very poor conditions and fading light that ultimately saved the Government forces from total annihilation. The Highland charge worked its magic yet again and saw many, though not all, Redcoat units turn and flee for their lives. It was said that the Royal Scots (Redcoats) were in such disarray that they ran round units who were behind them, to escape the battlefield. So bad was the weather that Jacobite commanders were unaware of just how well they had done and how much damage they had caused to the enemy, that they never pressed home their advantage. So, a great chance for all-out victory in the '45 was missed.

In the aftermath, when Hawley learned how many senior officers were killed, he realised what had occurred. Several junior officers paid for the defeat with their lives, and true to form, Hawley sent his hangmen in amongst the rank and file to teach them a lesson. He, unlike Cope, never faced a court martial for his incompetence, but without doubt it was he and his vicious nature that contributed greatly to the Hanoverian defeat. It was said of him afterwards that "General Hawley had neither knowledge nor conduct to command in general battle; nor had he room in the affections of officers and men that could make him hope for success".

As for Prince Charles, he admittedly became a drunken woman-beater in later life. However, in his defence, I would say that had he retaken the British Crown he would have been a totally different man. It was Lord George Murray's idea to turn back at Derby that cost the Prince his victory. The Prince was for going on and

---

4 - Prince Charlie's men were called Jacobites because they had initially been followers of his father, James. Jacobus is the Latin for James.

As we approach Falkirk centre on the Camelon Road, we want to get ourselves over to the right-hand lane, where we will ultimately swap the A-803 for the B-803 as we head for Slamannan. It's as simple as that; we keep the same road number, only the letter changes. We are about to hit a short stretch of ring road, but it's just a case of follow the signs for Slamannan and the B road. This makes route-finding easy, very easy, even if you have never been here before. The long climb up onto Slamannan Muir is about to begin as we leave the low ground behind for a while.

taking London. He (the Prince) narrowly lost the decision by only one vote. There are many schools of thought as to whether he would have been successful had he continued south. I, for one, firmly believe he would have been, and can only wonder what might have been had the vote gone the other way.

As you continue to ride up the Slamannan Road, ever gently rising in a south west direction, you are actually cutting right through the battlefield itself. The aforementioned Dumyat Drive and upper burial pit can be accessed by turning right at the roundabout ahead and then right again into Dumyat. There isn't much to see, as the pit itself is unmarked and is merely a patch of grass surrounded by a ring of trees. This same roundabout, the Lochgreen, can also be reached by an alternative route from Bonnybridge which avoids all the hustle and bustle of Camelon and Falkirk town centre. It includes a couple of great character-filled climbs, and I thoroughly recommend giving it your attention.

Falkirk centre isn't the only way to access the road to Slamannan; when you reach Bonnybridge, you can take the right fork at its roundabout and head up into High Bonnybridge. This is you on the B-816, and what a journey back in time this is. You immediately go over the canal and under not one but two rail bridges, which gives some idea of the transport system that was here to service all the old industries. This is further reinforced when you pass the large pit bing belonging to the now-closed Rough Castle open mine. We're talking seriously gritty here.

FALKIRK & SLAMMANAN RUN

HIGH BONNYBRIDGE ROUTE B-816

From the small roundabout in the centre of Bonnybridge, right in amongst the triangle of stores, turn right onto the B-816 instead of left for the A-803, and begin a great wee climb up through this small town's industrial past. Incidentally, it is very easy to link up the Denny approach with this way, by merely turning right when you meet the A-872 in Denny and entering first Head of Muir and then Dennyloanhead from that direction. After which, the turning for Bonnybridge is very well signposted. By taking the High Bonnybridge route, it will be much more obvious that here was a place which was as well served for heavy industry as it was possible to be.

The evidence isn't slow in coming and neither is the quality of the climb, because just after the first wee chinking pull-up round the corner, it's over the Forth and Clyde Canal you go. What a site this waterway is, no matter where you meet it. Its long, slender aqua line just charms time and time again, and here is no exception.

It's not only the history attached to the industrial revolution that you will find in High Bonnybridge, as these great old direction signs show, but also the mighty Roman Empire's furthest frontier as well – the Antonine Wall. The Rough Castle fort requires a diversion onto a fairly good track, but it's worth it.

The red and white barriers with warning lights add some extra drama to this swing bridge crossing. Further up, once we pass the Antonine Primary School, it's through the works and houses before we pass St Joseph's RC Primary School. It warms the cockles of my heart to see we are still segregating our children on religious grounds in the 21st century[5].

Next comes a great wee rail bridge – an iron, square job, not lacking character – and this is passed under with glee. The fun's not over yet by a long chalk, because there is a long, straight rise through the upper houses that ends in a gentle climb-up on Church Street. Here's where another twist and turn by the road starts, just as you reach a magnificent-looking, high-sited, old place of worship. The bends take you under a second rail bridge – an arched one this time, and all the more exciting for

Going under the first of the two rail bridges that you encounter on the road up through High Bonnybridge, and it is a most enjoyable rise, in my opinion. I really like the old feel that this place retains, and it is a very entertaining easy climb up.

5 - In all honesty, though, I believe it is Celtic and Rangers and not school segregation that keeps sectarian tension high in West Central Scotland.

The ditch that was attached to the Antonine Wall at Watling Lodge requires no diversion to see, however, as it runs right beside the Tamfourhill Road (the B-816) which carries us into Falkirk. It is a fantastic sight, sitting in its wooded glade, and to think that the legions actually patrolled this very spot so long ago is amazing.

its yellow and black warning band round the curve of the arch, and almost single-lane size. Motorists toot their horn as they approach, to warn drivers coming the other way, so be on your guard going under it[6].

Once under, another rise and twist sees you come up to some more of those great antiquated Antonine Wall direction signs that inform you that by turning first left, you will come to the Watling Lodge in 2 miles. Incidentally, by turning left you will stay on the B-816 as you run along the Bonnyfield Road. No sooner have you made the turn than you pass a big, ugly work of some sort. This is put in its place with regard to being an eyesore by its next-door neighbours, which are the slag heaps from the nearby Rough Castle open cast mine. Rough Castle is also the name for the Roman fort attached to the Antonine, which sits nearby and below. We passed the direction sign for it on the way up, just after we crossed the canal.

Now at this point, with so much heavy industry right beside you, it is understandable if you thought that whoever named this road Bonnyfield had his tongue firmly stuck in his cheek. Not so. In fact, Bonnymuir is the name of the muir you are now running through, and hence the road name. To prove my point, there is a plaque accompanied by a low-flying saltire, just a short distance away, that not only informs you of this, but also of a skirmish that took place on the muir in 1820. This was between some radical workers and British Army cavalry. Two of the militants later paid for their lives in Stirling, for their part in the small-scale uprising. They were John Baird from Condorrat, and Andrew Hardie, a Glasgow man. The skirmish became known as the Battle of Bonnymuir.

Now the scenery does improve with regards to the surrounds, however, when you shortly enter the Rough Castle Community Woodland. This contains an assortment of wonderful birch trees – some aged, twisted, and contorted into fabulous shapes. Not so good are the distant views, though, and this was a bit of a disappointment for me when I first rode this way. I imagined that there would be great views across the Forth and all, when I first looked at the map for this one. And as I made the first climb up from Bonnybridge, I thought and expected the same. Not so, I'm afraid. The quietness is nice. The woodland is nice. And even the way the road curves is nice. Fair enough, but the views don't come.

Never mind, because there is some seriously great history coming your way very, very shortly. You may have already sampled some if you paid a visit to the Roman fort[7] on the way up at Rough Castle. I say that because it is actually possible to bear left after the canal and visit the site, though admittedly you must do so on more of a track than a tarmacked road. There's no need to double back, as you can actually carry on, along this track, and run under the railway, then up through Rough Castle wood, and join the Bonnyfield Road that way. Now, you may be saying to yourself, "Hold on Liam Boy, I thought you didn't do off-road routes" and you would be right. I don't.

However, in this case, I include the possibility of visiting Rough Castle as an exception, because it is such an ancient and wonderful sight. The track itself is blocked

---

6 - No need for caution now, as a set of traffic lights have been added.

7 - You can see the ditch from the track, but you would have to get off the bike and walk to see where the fort was positioned.

FALKIRK & SLAMMANAN RUN

off to cars halfway along, and it is more than rideable on a road bike – especially your training machine, of course. So, whether you come by the Rough Castle track or up and along the B-816, you're sure to be entertained and enjoy the bends through the woodland here. If you don't visit Rough Castle, you still get to see a bit of the Antonine Wall, or rather its defensive ditch, a stretch of which you encounter on the way down the long slant of the Tamfourhill Road. This starts just after you cross over the railway this time, on a modern, hideous, concrete slab-sided, traffic light-controlled, somebody-should-have-been-shot-for-it bridge.

Once over (try not to look)[8], a great long freewheel into Falkirk begins. On the way down, you have predominantly woodland to your left and the upper housing schemes of Falkirk on the right. Already though, behind the houses, you would have seen some of Falkirk Muir. One wooded section does exist on the right, however, and within this leafy glade sits the aforementioned ditch belonging to Rome's first line of defence. Wow! Just think that the legions actually walked this very way, in the place you are at now. I find it a real mind-blowing experience to visit these places. This was the site of the Watling Lodge West. I am truly glad for what there is of the Antonine left, but I just wish there was more of it.

We continue on our fly-down into Falkirk, still on the Tamfourhill, which is mostly a wooded glide on its lower half, and come out at the bottom of the road in front of a couple of big high flats. Do your best to ignore them and turn right onto Greenbank Road, and get ready for a great climb of superb character. As you follow the Greenbank Road up, you will immediately spy the magnificent big red-bricked rail bridge that the road takes you under, the very line that runs to Falkirk High station. Once under, it's a curve, a climb, and under the canal behind you go. Then the road rears up stallion-like for a short stretch, towards a picture postcard, perfectly positioned, wee green (leaf-covered) cottage.

The road will then slip and swerve between the row of houses that follow, before lying back as it runs up between the hedgerows to the Lochgreen Road. It's getting high now, and a left turn on the Lochgreen will not only take you into the houses again, but also to its namesake roundabout on the Slamannan Road. On

Once clear of Falkirk, you're on up onto the high ground by way of a long meandering pull-up, but not before you pass through another area of important Scottish history – the site of the Battle of Falkirk during the '45 rebellion. This starts as you near Falkirk High station and finishes approximately when you pass Seafield Farm. The higher you go on the B-803 means the views get better, as can be seen here with a look back to the two Southern Highland Munros of Stuc a' Chroin and Ben Vorlich.

the way there, you pass a memorial to the battle of the '45, which is a rather uninspiring sandstone needle that wouldn't do justice to a custard pie fight, never mind a major event in Scottish history.

Coming to the roundabout, of course, means we've met up with the other lower route and we now begin our journey up onto the muir proper. As the muir itself is neared, all the lovely long row of houses get left behind. It has been no great hardship to ride the Slamannan Road thus far, despite it being a very long climb, and when the muir is reached, it levels out in your support. Here you're into the rough, no doubt about it.

---

8 - At the bridge, that is.

Away to the left from the ever-rising B-803 Slamannan Road can be seen the River Forth and Longannet power station. They make an uplifting combination as the road gradient eases and you can settle in and enjoy the ride again. All the climbing for Slamannan has been done, and if you are making direct for Coatbridge by staying on the B-803, the hard climbing's over for the day. If you want to return via Limerigg, however, there's a tough wee climb still to come to reach that village.

The bleakness will be apparent from just about the word go, and at the end of the fairly straight section the road will take a dramatic swing left and plummet down and over the Glen Burn. However, just as the road starts to make its big swing, you will notice a track running dead ahead, which leads to Seafield Farm. This farmhouse was actually in existence during the '45, and one of the Prince's cavalry units, Elcho's horse, would be coming right towards you at this point on the day. The Prince himself made his standpoint only a few hundred metres up from the farmhouse; the very spot would be just up on the high ground to your diagonal right.

It's a screamer of a dive down towards the burn, and two steel television masts stand slim and tall on the hillside

Approaching Slamannan on the B-803 and it's done on long easy bends, making it a most relaxing approach at that. It will be a fairly fast hurl round to the town, and if the weather's good even these old mining muirs can seem very pleasant.

above. It's up on these moors that all our TV transmitters live. At the bottom, another swerve is required, this time to the right, and then a long draw up through the trees soon follows. From the point that you leave Falkirk till you reach Slamannan will be about 4 miles long. This always seems longer, probably because you are climbing for a fair bit of the time. However, at no point on the way up is it steep or sustained. So, through the lower woodland section we climb quite easily and emerge out onto sheep fields that are greatly enhanced by the trees, old and steadfast, that line the edges of many of them.

The road continues to head south, undulating and even dipping as it does, before it rears up rampishly and then makes a big swing west. This section runs straight and flat, and ironically the heather-clad muir to the right reminds me very much of Culloden. Great flat swathes of brown heather appear on that side, before another twist and rise south carries you past an old, high, abandoned works. Its red-bricked, square chimney looks very much like it belongs in another era, and I'm not sure what the place did but I suspect it was possibly a brickworks or fertiliser manufacturer. Just at that, the white flank of the Slamannan houses appear across the broad fields on the right, and the road makes some great sweeping curves towards them.

This is followed by a dip and a rise to enter this high, old mining town, which although it has a bleak approach, is brilliant, too. Behind the town sits still higher ground, and also sports pencil-thin, high TV masts. An old graveyard with a manse-like house greets your arrival, but the old soon gives way to hard-looking urban block. This is especially so when you come to a halt ahead in the centre of the town at a T-junction. This point tends to give the impression, more than any other, that Slamannan – or Saint Lawrence as it was once known – has seen better days; and these were a long time ago, too. The rest of the place, other than the centre, doesn't look too bad, in my opinion.

Unlike a lot of the settlements hereabouts, Slamannan started off more as an agricultural place, though a loose one at that. But the coming of the steam train in 1840 opened up all the coalfields round about for exploitation. Then it was a boom town.

At the junction where you now find yourself, sit two former hotels – the Royal, which is now derelict; and the Saint Lawrence, which is now a pub. Both of these were built to accommodate the numerous visitors to the town back in the mid-1800s. Pits and miners' rows sprang up everywhere, as miners flocked to the area for work. Nowadays, the shops and flats across the road look like they belong in a Paisley housing scheme as opposed to a village centre.

From this junction, the plan is to head back west to Coatbridge and return home from there. There is an option or three for doing this, though they all join together at the roundabout on the A-89 under the canal rail bridge in Coatbridge centre. No matter which way you choose, you will be sampling the quiet high moor roads of Slamannan Muir, and this sort of terrain – as you know by now – finds me in my element.

Shortly after entering Slamannan, a T-junction is reached, and a decision has to be made about which way to reach Coatbridge. All are good, and I use all of them from time to time. It is more direct to turn right and head straight for Greengairs and then Glenmavis, to get to Coatbridge that way, or you can turn left onto the B-8022 and go via Limerigg. The Limerigg option requires a bit more climbing and keeps you up on the higher ground for longer, with a further choice to be made about whether to return via Longriggend or Caldercruix. It all boils down to personal choice.

The most direct way is to simply turn right and stay on the B-803, making a B-line for Glenmavis enroute. Or you can go a slightly more circuitous route, which will re-join the B-803, but will take in the villages of Longriggend and Upperton, after going via Limerigg. Finally, you can also, after taking the Limerigg road, return to Coatbridge via Airdrie.

COATBRIDGE DIRECT B-803

So, no real route-finding difficulties if staying on the B-803; simply turn right at the Slamannan T-junction and away you go. Incidentally, the large ornate light that sits across the road from you at this point is there to commemorate the Boer War no less. Almost immediately when you do make your turn, you pass one of two village war memorials which is a fair bit different from most others. This one, in particular, commemorates two of the town's most famous fighting sons – Alex Penman, who won the Military Medal, and Samuel Frickleton, who went one better and was awarded the Victoria Cross. This was for his bravery on Messine Ridge, an action which was so daring that his CO said could have won him the VC twice over.

From here, start to climb up Bank Street, through the homes and buildings of the town, which is not an inspiring start to be honest, but it soon gets better. The school and grey community hall are passed, and before you finally leave on the Brownrigg Road, you run the full length of the wonderfully named Blinkbonnie Terrace. It lines the left, but nothing does on the right, so uninterrupted views are with you the whole way on this road. The 803 is a rather interesting road in its own right, which more than makes up for the uniform flat and bleakness that it carries you through. It soon falls and rises between an avenue of good old trees the minute you leave Slamannan, which is something that it does from time to time along the way. This takes you past what appears to be a graveyard for old Volvo estates at Middlerigg.

The green fertile rising fields that follow on the left, with their white farm attached, actually show a rich face for a short while, before normal bleakness is resumed either side. Rough, I said rough, that's how the going will be from here on until we lose some height. This is certainly obvious as you pass the dilapidated old barn at Greenhill, with its reed-filled fields; some ponies are their residents hereabouts. More scatty old buildings are passed, and scatty rather sums up the surroundings. The road, though, undulates slightly, bends a little, and therefore isn't demanding at any point, and entertains enough all the way. Soon, you re-enter North Lanarkshire, just as a wind turbine or two appears on the horizon.

You seem to be constantly passing rickety old fences, more than your fair share of dilapidated old gates, scatty old hedgerows, and enough conifers to service Ikea for a decade. The road straightens out on the way to Easter Glentore Farm, but just after that the fun begins again, with more wood-lined twists and turns. At the point they begin, up among the fields on the left, can be seen rows of isolated tenements. These, which now look totally out of place, once housed the prison staff for Longriggend remand centre. This has now been razed to the ground, and only the perimeter fence of barbed wire remains for some reason[9]. The first time I came this way on the bike, I thought I would pay the old place a visit for old times' sake.

Now, although by taking the B-803 you make for Coatbridge direct and therefore it is the fastest route, I have to say that in my opinion it isn't the best one. I much prefer to reach this same point on the 803 by taking a more circuitous route through Limerigg and then Longriggend itself. This does involve a fair bit more climbing, but it is worth all the effort nonetheless. To go via Limerigg, we have to return to the T-junction back in Slamannan.

COATBRIDGE VIA LIMERIGG

To return via another even higher mining village, in this case the very highly perched Limerigg, turn left at the T-junction and then swerve almost immediate right (well signposted) to take you onto the B-8022. You pass the other war memorial right on the bend, and also the rest of the town's houses on the right as you run out of the main part of town. I say the main part, because there are a few houses that sit higher up, which will be reached shortly. But before them is a most interesting wee climb that looks as good as it is. You catch sight of it right away and that's because of its sway – a wood and wall-lined wonder – rising up on what is known as Station Road.

It leads to the upper houses, which is an area known as Binniehill, I think, and the first road on the right, Binniehill Road, goes directly to Longriggend. I don't usually take that one, but carry straight on and leave Slamannan when the last of the houses are passed. The Binniehill, incidentally, is often used by local riders I believe to make a good short training circuit, and is a great wee single-track road in its own right. It leads long, straight, and very solitary west, till it seamlessly becomes Longriggend Road and then runs into the village itself. Great swathes of conifer trees keep you company as you go, particularly on the left-hand side. There is a good reason for this. This is a very quiet option, and fine if you want to explore it. I still prefer to head for Limerigg first. So, after leaving Slamannan, a little more gentle rising is encountered before the first gable ends of the Limerigg houses are spied.

These sit at the top of a very steep, ramp-like climb, one which gets the old thigh muscles screaming at you as you pull up. The pain and gradient only cease when you pass the village name sign. The village is characterised with yet more similar rises, with the council homes running up the hillside – very miners' row-like – beside the road. These carry you near to the very top of the village. Miners' rows indeed, which is hardly surprising, because I was informed by a very knowledgeable elderly female resident that the place was solely built as a mining village and nothing more. She also told me, by rhyming off machine gun-style, the names of all the pits this little place once served. It was quite a list. Although the last pit didn't close till the 1950s, most of the coal seams were exhausted by the turn of the century.

With the loss of old king coal, most miners abandoned ship and went to work elsewhere, though some stayed and commuted to nearby collieries. It was local Minister, Councillor, and Big Man, the Reverend Alex Cameron, who had the old miners' cottages demolished and better housing put in their place. He was also responsible for persuading the Forestry Commission to plant so many of their trees on the muir round about. Hence the reason that forestry is so extensive here. And it is Alex's houses that guide you up the next brae – in rather dramatic fashion, it has to be said – and after just a little bit of respite, the climbing starts again and takes you, just as it did in Slamannan, to an important T-junction. This one abuts you with the Lochside Road.

If you decide to turn left in Slamannan, then you're on the road to Limerigg and a tough wee ramp-like climb is needed just before you enter the village. This is followed by a main street that rises much more easily to the T-junction with the Caldercruix Road. The village itself sprouted up to provide homes for the miners who worked in numerous pits around here.

9 - This has finally been removed.

FALKIRK & SLAMMANAN RUN

The B-803 going directly from Slamannan to Greengairs carries you through rough, harsh-looking ground, as the above photo of a sheep field shows. We are approaching the site of the former remand centre of Longriggend, and it couldn't have been much of a view through the bars of the window for the inmates.

And so it is with a right turn that we bid farewell to lonely Limerigg. It more than punches above its weight in entertainment terms, what with its sloping gait and high position. You run onto the Caldercruix Road, which will lead you west by first bending through the conifers, before passing an access road for the Black Loch. You don't actually see the water itself, as it's on the other side of the hill, but that's not a problem, for the road you are now on (the B-825) is about to steal the show anyway. It does so with the aid of its sweeping, shining, crash barriers that bend you grandly round and onto a long, long draw of a pull-up, through magnificent heather-clad moorland. To add to the brilliant bleak eeriness, on the hillside above the loch sits a rather ominous-looking, large grey building, whose profile seems to bring a feeling of menace.

This is as stunning and as drama-filled a stretch of road as you're ever likely to ride. This is especially so on a wild winter's day, when strong winds and dark, leaden rain clouds challenge your commitment to the full. Fear nothing as you pull up towards that horizon, with the white lines of the road stabbing through the brown blanket of heather carpeting the earth all around. Wonderful, it's simply wonderful. You will feel on top of the world as you level out into more muir than you could ever shake a Claymore at. It's a high lonely road into the bargain, and you will feel that there ain't anybody here but us chickens. Long and straight and undulating goes the road in front of you, and continues to do so for a mile or so, until meeting an isolated cluster of houses.

At this point, another choice has to be made as to the best way home. For it is now possible to continue straight on and get to Coatbridge through Airdrie on the A-89; or turn right and head for Longriggend, rejoin the B-803 again, and then return via Glenmavis. I will cover the latter option first. Distance-wise there isn't a lot in it. The Airdrie route is a couple of miles shorter, but it gets you off the high muir quicker, so if the weather's really bad, then it's probably your best option. Longriggend and Upperton are well sign posted from here.

COATBRIDGE VIA LONGRIGGEND-B-803

Turn right at the houses and again head up, long straight and true, in a northerly direction this time, towards Longriggend. The village sits directly at the end of this road, and the landscape here is so flat that it allowed the road builders of old to lay their tar in a dead straight line. No need for bends or curves to avoid natural obstacles, not in this part of the world. All is flat and easy. Well, perhaps not that flat on this particular road, which is the Telegraph, but certainly easy enough. For it is a long, gentle, angled draw again that will find you pulling up through fields that are being stripped of their peat. I assume it is destined for numerous garden centres nationwide. This unethical practice caused some unrest in Ireland a few years back, if I remember rightly.

If you look to your right as you gain a bit of height, you will notice a rare blast from the past – on this muir anyway – and that is the one and only pit bing still remaining. It's quite a striking one at that, due to its shape, which has earned it the local nickname of the "Mexican hat". The bing, incidentally, came from Lochend Colliery No 5. No other bings seem to have survived, as far as I can tell. In fact, if you want to find anything to do with the old mine workings up here, you have to look very hard indeed amongst all the forestry plantations. On the horizon up ahead will be the silhouette of the old Longriggend Kirk, which pulls you

Low winter sunlight lights up the bends and crash barriers of the B-825 Caldercruix Road which carries us high and westward back in the direction of Airdrie. We are in for a treat on this road, as it rises long and barren ahead of us and can be a fabulous sight on a wet, wild day with ever-changing light and clouds.

FALKIRK & SLAMMANAN RUN

Barren, brown, bleak moors are either side of us as we continue our return on the B-825 Caldercruix Road, but we don't have to go that far, as the cut-off for Longriggend is coming up shortly on the right.

along to the west end of the village and then begin the dive down and out north into the fields.

Now, your perception of it will depend what time of year it is and what the weather is like when you come down this road. On a warm summer's day, yes, it a pleasant, fun-filled jaunt. On a cold, wet, windy winter's one, my God, the bleakness will surpass everything that you have encountered up until now, and that is bloody saying something. Recently, some very high imposing big wind turbines have been built here, very close to the road. They are, in a way, quite impressive in their size and formidability.

So, regardless if you are on warm, sunny or cold, wet tar, when you bottom out through all the bends and drops, you run into Upperton and its unlikely cluster of

up towards it. It sits right at the junction of the Telegraph Road and Main Street. Nowadays it lies empty and slightly derelict, though is not beyond saving.

Three things will hit you on your arrival in the village. One will be the view, because you have now gained a fair bit of height in reaching it. Two will be that nearly every house in the place is very modern; this is opposed to the old Lanarkshire council jobs we have always met thus far. And three, there is no prison in site. So, where the hell is it? Quite a wee bit away, you'll be surprised to learn. To get there, however, is a thrill a minute, so hold onto the old tit for tat (hat), because the road down to Upperton is a helter-skelter ride-and-a-half. It begins when you roll

As Longriggend village sits quite high, there follows a great swerving drop down to Upperton village that was the site of the old remand centre. This is a fantastic, fun-filled fall, and has Highland views thrown in for good measure.

If the cut-off for Longriggend is taken, you will find yourself climbing gently on the Telegraph Road leading up to the old kirk in the village. It is a road that has a most desolate look to it, because a lot of the peat has been lifted – for garden centres, I presume. It makes the area look like a wasteland.

homes. Soon you reach a bus stop and terminus, which – just like the nearby tenements – also look totally out of place nowadays. Even the post box across the road seems to have been put in the wrong spot. However, a quick look to the right will explain their existence. Still standing to this day is the high perimeter wire fence erected to ensure the continued incarceration of about 150 young men, who at any given time fell foul of the law at an early age. This was the last line of defence of HMP Longriggend. The first time I ever did this run, I decided to come via the prison, just to remind myself what it looked like. I'd no idea it had been closed since 2000[10], as I hadn't been up visiting since round about 1982.

---

10 - I first did the run in 2003, I think.

The perimeter fence was all that was left of the former HMP Longriggend, but even that has gone now. No sentiment here, as the place will be missed by none.

The eagle-eyed among you will have spotted that it is Upperton Village and not Longriggend Village that contained the prison. I read somewhere, however, that the present-day residents of the place changed the name to Upperton – this part was also called Longriggend at one time – to disassociate themselves with the place's past. I don't know if that is true or not, but I do know it was a difficult place to get to for a lot of the relatives of the boys who were "banged up" there, and the prison itself had a bad reputation for how it was run for a time. Young men, many from troubled backgrounds, though not all, were getting their first taste of the Scottish penal system at a really impressionable and crucial stage in their lives. It wasn't a good experience.

A few of the gentlemen who I grew up with in Foxbar had the misfortune to be there for a stay, mostly three-week remands, but that was long enough. It was in this very nick that a young Paul Ferris[11] met a young William (Tootsie) Lobban. You may have heard of them. As I said in the intro, it will be missed by none. And so, for me at least, it's nostalgia time over and on with the show. A show in which we will shortly be passing through another couple of old mining villages on our way to Glenmavis, and once again the tree-lined B-803 does a grand job in taking us there. We rejoin it with a rise and a dip after the old remand camp is left behind.

The first village is Greengairs, whose rooftops and chimneys let you know you're getting close. It's a great long batter down through and along its main road, which is Greengairs Road, where the local social club insists on flying the Union Flag. The down slope hastes our progress through, and its assistance is greatly appreciated on this fairly arduous stage of the run. So, too, does the initial dip that follows our leaving the village, and then the following rise sees an almost identical entry into the next village of Wattston. By that I mean it's once again rooftops and chimney pots on top of solid-built council houses that signal you're getting near. Wattston seems to be even more battleship grey-looking than Greengairs, perhaps because of the paint job on a lot of the homes.

The open cast mine, once active here, has also closed. I imagine things must get really harsh and tough up here during wintertime, but the houses look more than fit for the job of keeping their inhabitants cosy and warm. A swerve past more modern houses takes us out of Wattston and on towards the A-73. There is only a slight angled, though long downhill[12] approach to it, and it will dawn on you then that the 73 must sit quite high, as there has been no appreciable drop in height since we climbed up from Falkirk. This is exactly the case. You are still up at about 180 metres here, even though you are now approaching a major A-road. There is flatness and a gentle calm feeling to this long glide down, as you steel yourself for the busy road ahead.

You're not on it for long, though. After turning left onto it, in just over ½ a mile, you come off it again. This you'll be glad of, as it's normally flowing with traffic, and a lot of heavy stuff at that. First of all, you ride through the tiny hamlet of Stand, before reaching the big roundabout that will throw you off to the right in the direction of Glenmavis. All around in the fields it's still rough and gruff as you spin along the Raebog Road (still the B-803), which shortly carries you into the village. When you do get into Glenmavis, get ready for some seriously good descending, for it's in this former mining town that the drop down finally begins. Glenmavis, incidentally, is really two former mining villages joined together.

This took place just after the war, when New Monkland Village simply joined with and became encompassed by Glenmavis itself. And so now you find yourself in among the surrounds of this sprightly-looking wee place. One that is quite markedly more modern and upbeat-looking than what we have ridden through of late (for the most part).

---

11 - I've enjoyed the Wee Man's writing, and wish him all the best. I wish I had his strength.

12 - There is a great wee snack bar that sits in a layby on the right.

FALKIRK & SLAMMANAN RUN

Shortly after leaving Upperton, you meet the B-803 and you join up with the direct route from Slamannan. Greengairs is the first village you come to as you head back, and will be followed by Wattston, and then the fantastically flowing Glenmavis.

The Raebog sits high in the village and leads, through various housing styles, to the Coatbridge Road. This runs up from the village centre, and where the two meet at a mini roundabout, the fun begins big-time. A screamer, and I do mean screamer, of a dive fires you down through the middle of town, which only has another mini roundabout at the bottom to cause you any concerns.

Glenmavis is taken at speed – welcome, easy speed at that – and the payback for all the climbing out of Falkirk has been a long time in coming. It's a whoosh down and through the wee mini, before the level section ahead through the last of the houses provides just a little bit of respite, then the good stuff kicks in again. This time it does so in dramatic fashion, not only by the road's sway, but by the views beyond as well. As the last house is cleared, a wonderful panorama of Coatbridge and Glasgow greets your gaze, and not even a most inappropriately positioned, enormous wind turbine can ruin it too much. This ugly monster, with its flapping wings, sits slap-bang in the middle of the view.

The view accompanies a series of fantastic, flowing, falling bends, down through which you manoeuvre your machine with carefree abandon. It's Coatbridge here we come – in some style, I might add. What a stretch of road it is that takes you into the back end of this most infamous of industrial towns. Infamous indeed; it more than any other epitomised all the ills that the working

The town of Coatbridge from Glenmavis, and what a sight it is. What a road down to it, too, for there now follows a roller-coaster descent round bends and banks that drops you into the Daddy of all of West Central Scotland's industrial towns. If you think that you've got a lot on your plate and that life is tough, wait till you find out what life was like for the foundry workers here and you'll soon change your tune. It was grim, take it from me. The Summerlee Museum is well worth a visit to find out.

class of this country had to suffer. But there's no hint of that yet on the approach road. Still the steeples and high-rise flats on the horizon keep you transfixed, while the B-803 keeps you occupied and entertained with its swerving, dropping, and even occasional rising bends.

You enter the town by a tight right-hand bend at the bottom of the last descent, which is a fitting end to the great stretch of road that carried you down from Glenmavis. It's here that you do get a taste of what has gone before, as it's a heavy industrial landscape of sorts that greets your arrival. Things resembling scrap yards and goods yards are met immediately, and then on the long straight run-in on Burnbank Street, the gas works is passed. Full of character, I must admit, but a legacy of a dismal past.

Coatbridge centre finds rail bridges aplenty, as the town still has no fewer than 6 stations in it, which is testament to its huge importance as a major player in the British Empire and to its industrial might. The Monklands canal is also close by; it was used to shift raw materials to the Parkhead Forge in Glasgow. This is the A-89, which we have now joined after coming down from Glenmavis, but it can be picked up much earlier than this, before Plains, if you don't take the Longriggend cut-off when coming from Limerigg on the B-825, and carry straight on for Caldercruix.

Coatbridge was the real McCoy for iron production in this country, and that is saying something. The iron industry flourished here, with the hot blast process being its particular forte.

That, along with coal and steel, brought in countless Irish immigrants – mostly from Donegal – to provide the labour. The Baird brothers, all six of them, built most of the iron foundries in the town, the Gartsherrie Works being the pride of the fleet. The employers also provided the housing, which was appalling. Mining families and foundry families literally lived in one room, with the coal kept under the bed. Water was collected from a standpipe in the street. And the less said about the outside cludgies the better. All the old diseases and illnesses, like TB, were rife, and if a man was killed whilst working, his wife and kids were then put out of the company house and rendered homeless.

Work went on day and night, night and day, seven days a week. When the heavy industry declined here, as it did elsewhere, living conditions for those who remained didn't improve by any great measure, if at all.

It is with this rather depressing thought that we reach the two mini roundabouts at the bottom of Burnbank Street, where a left/right shimmy through them keeps us on the B-803 and heading for the town centre. If in doubt at this point, simply follow the direction signs for the town centre and you can't go wrong. As you approach the centre on Sunnyside Road, you pass the first train station since Falkirk, which is Coatbridge Sunnyside. I mention it in case you require Scotrail's services for any reason.

This is one of six stations in the town – an incredible number for such a small place. This is due to the fact that no fewer than four rail lines all cut through here, which again gives some idea of the industrial importance it once enjoyed. At the bottom of Sunnyside Road, you come into the centre and meet with the A-89 at the big roundabout below the canal rail bridge. This also just happens to be right beside that Scottish bastion of finance, the Airdrie Savings Bank.

Talking of Airdrie, but only if we must, it is also possible to reach this point from Slamannan Muir by going via that town as opposed to Glenmavis. This, as I said earlier, would avoid cutting back up and through Longriggend, and would get you off the higher ground faster.

COATBRIDGE VIA AIRDRIE A-89

So, if you it suits your needs, when you are on the B-825 coming from Limerigg, ignore the right turn for Longriggend and carry straight on for Caldercruix. This isn't long in coming, and neither too is the junction with the A-89. In fact, you don't actually go through Caldercruix, but merely skirt the edge of it. The town's name comes from not only the nearby river, the North Calder, but also its bends or crooks. It will, of course, be the overall lie of the land that forms these bends, and it's this terrain that has a similar effect on the road that takes you past the place. It is a rather interesting one, I must say, what with its crash barriers and wood-lined curves.

This in turn is followed by a great dip down under a

FALKIRK & SLAMMANAN RUN

This is the A-89 just after joining it from the B-825 at Caldercruix, and the old lampposts with telephone wires attached give it a look of the 1970s. That's just fine by me, as is the ride through Plains to come and the great long drop down through Airdrie into Coatbridge on the 89 which follows that.

magnificent railway bridge, which has just had its service reinstated in 2010, after previously closing in 1956. After this, you roll up to the junction with the A-89. Again, when you turn right and head for Airdrie, it is the lie of the land that brings a surprising amount of interest, even to this major A-road. Steep embankments falling down from the rough hillside above force the road to swerve and curve to avoid them, while across the valley on the right, the roof tops and church steeple of Caldercruix make a fine view.

Great, old, rusted-to-hell lampposts, with telephone wires running between them, are shortly picked up and, boy, do these look like they belong in the sixties. Round about the same time, you pass an old kirk and other isolated old houses, one of which contains a sort of scrapyard for horse boxes, and you could be forgiven for wondering what decade it is. The road now fires you long, straight, and down, towards the village of Plains, and as you make your way there, the railway will increasingly encroach from the right. This is all very modern-looking and sprightly, as you'd expect from this new line. You pass underneath its steel green bridge by a delightful double bend, after which a slight rise in the road brings you into Plains.

Now you may notice, just after the bridge, a sign for a cycle track. This seems to start and end here (for Plains, that is), and will not only take you up to Caldercruix, but beyond to Bathgate and Edinburgh as well, apparently. This track, I think, used to run the length of Plains in its day, and I believe it followed the course of the disused rail line before it was brought back into service again. You can, of course, use the track to get to Plains from Caldercruix, but it doesn't begin in earnest again until the beginning of Airdrie. I only initially discovered this cycle track by accident a few years back, when I was riding up the A-89 from Airdrie and stopped at a small store in Plains. The 89 was busy and unpleasant that day and the storekeeper said to me, "Did you come up on the cycle path, mate?" I replied, "I didn't know there was one, mate." So, he duly took me out of his store and pointed me in the right direction for it.

One thing I will say about the A-89 is that it is a brilliant slow burner of a descent, making for a long and easy passage all the way into the heart of Coatbridge from just after Plains. This is opposed to the descent on the B-803, which puts all its eggs in the one basket, with its great dramatic drop down after Glenmavis.

So, we ride the mile-long Main Street of Plains, which once was – surprise, surprise – yet another mining village. Most of the houses sit on the north, right-hand side, with the railway and a fair few works and the like on the left. The descent into the rest of Monklands begins just when we leave Plains and ride the short distance through the fields to Airdrie.

This area is known as Monklands and has been for centuries, ever since the land was given to the Cistercian Monks of Newbattle Abbey by King Malcolm IV in the 12th century. They worked the land, built the roads, and were true grafters; the old monks didn't just sit on their arse all day and pray. This is in contrast to some of the modern-day clergy, of course. The easy roll down from Plains to Airdrie will continue in a similar vein right till we reach the Canal Bridge roundabout in Coatbridge centre. Now, the initial stretch has much going for it, just the way the road curves down between two old stone walls and enters Airdrie beside the old parish kirk.

However, just over one of the walls, to the left, is a road tarmac removal yard. It's full of old broken bits of macadam and debris, along with all the heavy machinery to do the job. In a way this just sums up the whole of North Lanarkshire for me. For despite all the coal mines closing a long time ago, with even Coatbridge's flagship iron foundry, Gartsherrie, closing in 1967, I feel there is still a grey, industrial grittiness about the whole place. As much as I like coming east for a run from time to time, and as much as the Slamannan Muir is my type of riding, it is no picture postcard pretty run, that's for sure.

This is not Arran west coast here. Not that that's a problem; far from it. Just don't expect the same views you get when rounding Rothesay, that's all I'm saying. If you're over this way and it starts raining, especially if it's winter time, then fully expect to have to clean your machine before your next ride. The stour from the past just seems to refuse to leave the place and is still clinging on, ready to come out and cover you and your bike at a rain moment's notice. It is totally different riding from the scenic west coast, but the variety is what I like about it.

I also like the next stretch of road – the long, long, easy downhill through Airdrie Town. It's not a bad looking wee place, despite the grey picture I just painted of it and its surrounds. Not a bad looking wee place at all. It's open and airy, providing a pleasant channel to funnel you down through all the houses sitting at the top end of the town. You pass the cycle lane on the left, just after re-entering, and the signs say it will take you to Coatbridge and Uddingston. Now, I admit I never use it, because the ease of the road to come is just too good to miss. Get ready to enjoy the next mile or three, for they are all energy-free ones, with no effort being required to propel us ever closer homeward.

You will shortly go through several well named roundabouts; the first one's the Terminus, on the road down, running past many splendid homes. Some are even fine-looking fellows of sandstone garb. The road takes a slightly more profound dip as the town centre is neared, and that will be the name of the next roundabout you meet, too. Now begins a slight detour as you veer left and avoid the old centre via a big sweeping move. It takes you past the very modern-looking rail station by the aforementioned series of roundabouts that drop you down like a flight of canal locks. Not for long are you off the beaten track, however, and you soon rejoin the main A-89 at the Stirling roundabout and start to head out of Airdrie by another slightly more profound dip in the road.

Now, it isn't that easy to tell when you go from Airdrie into Coatbridge, though I suppose it's purely academic when you do. The only relevant sign that I have seen is one just after the Stirling roundabout, saying that there are 2 miles to go to Coatbridge, though I assume that is to the centre. I think, though I could be wrong here, that the boundary is right at the big cenotaph you pass as you fire down the slope. Monklands General Hospital sits grandly behind at this point. Ahead, you see a great steel girder rail bridge that you pass under, and then glide onto the delightfully named Deedes Street (nice one). Not far now to the centre, with just the little bit of hustle and bustle to get through on Deedes.

Things do get quieter when you go through the roundabout onto Main Street, but that only lasts, visually at least, till you round the bend. Then you get hit full in the face by more colour than the Notting Hill Carnival. For behold Cliftonhill, home to Albion Rovers Football Club. This is a spectrum of brightness in an otherwise grey landscape, because the main stand is banded black, red, and yellow, and perhaps this was intentional to make a statement and bring some colour to the town. It certainly does that all right, no doubt about it. Good luck to the "Wee Rovers", that's what I say. I don't know if Paolo Maldini is still the manager?

So now, here we are, coming into Coatbridge centre from this direction, and it's more modern big roundabouts and the Asda store, along with its filling station, that now holds the centre ground. No getting away from all that stuff nowadays as it's just so ubiquitous. The roundabout by the Canal Bridge means we have come together with our brethren on the B-803, and now that we are all together again our thoughts turn to home. The going over the high ground from Falkirk to Coatbridge I regard as stage three of the run, and that only leaves the final stage four – the home run – to be tackled. Incidentally, the Canal Bridge takes its name from the Monklands Canal that ran for 12½ miles from Calderbank to Townhead in Glasgow, more of which later.

We go under this bridge, heading west on the A-89 that will carry us Glasgow-bound. Even before we do that, you see a sign for the Summerlee Industrial Museum, which shows off the machinery and heritage of the area's heavy industrial past[13]. We are now running long, flat, and straight through the west of the town, past the houses belonging to the Langloan area, and skipping along nicely as we go. A couple of big, white, high rise flats bid us *adieu* as we fly past the red/brown tenements and flats that line Bank Street. On passing the town's last watering hole, the Eagle Inn, we take our leave of this rather hard-done-to place, one that has not had its woes to seek in the past or even present day, so I wish all the residents well.

We now find ourselves riding into no man's land, and that is the space of green belt between North Lanarkshire and Glasgow. This stretch is done on dual carriageway, fairly devoid of charm, although the sunset on some of the fields can be pleasant enough in the evening. We are in the vicinity of Bargeddie, which is a rather unusual village in as much as it didn't really exist until development of the area in the 1930s. So this place arrived rather late on the scene, compared to all the others round about it. When you drive along the A-89 here, you hardly notice Bargeddie, which is mostly on your right-hand side at first, and is comprised of pretty, middle class bungalows. But once through the second roundabout, it's the big council estate of Dykehead on the left that takes over.

It's only when you are going a lot slower on the bike that you really appreciate just how much housing there is on that side, and it almost runs right up to the motorway. Next, it's under the M-73, before breaking off left to take us over the big bad M-8. It is quite a sight and feat of modern civil engineering, it has to be said. Just how did they build, then manoeuvre, those big concrete pillars into place? Then the massive bridge sections had to be manoeuvred on top of the pillars – all inch perfect, of course. I am in awe of it all every time I pass this way.

I often stop and just wonder in amazement at the speed and smoothness of the modern automobile as the vehicles fly beneath me. It's so easy to take it all for granted. Don't forget, it wasn't that long ago that cars were still pretty unreliable – which is now mostly a thing of the past – or that horses used to be the mainstay of transport, even in war.

It's a thought I carry with me as I make my way along the last section of green-lined dual carriageway taking me to the door of dear old Mother Glasgow. We arrive at a very busy, complex-looking junction that criss-crosses the A-89 with the A-8 Edinburgh Rd. There are a couple of side streets thrown in for good measure. Not to worry, just keep it simple by staying on the 89 and heading directly across for Garrowhill and Shettleston. This is you finally back in the city, in the east end this time.

This is a part of Glasgow that has a character all of its own, no doubt about it. Right away, you find yourself into some serious buzz, as you try to make your way down Main Street, Baillieston. I say try, because sure as hell you'll get stuck at the traffic lights early doors, and just to get up through the traffic to give yourself a chance of getting your nose in front won't be easy. Now, the overall plan here is a simple one, for me at least. This is despite the fact that on most occasions I chop and change the exact way I negotiate the east end's long corridors to get me back home to Paisley. No matter which route I choose, and there are numerous, the general plan is always the same.

---

13 - I usually don't like museums as I think they are dead places. This one's worth a visit, however, and the entry is free.

Coming down the A-89 between Airdrie and Coatbridge, and just about to pass under yet another rail bridge. This road can often be a bit busy at times, but that is the only thing against it as it a wonderfully long descent down.

I simply want to head in a west/south west direction to get me onto Paisley Road West. For the purposes of describing this route, I will stick to the most direct way into the city centre by staying on the A-89 all the way this time. Normally, I would slowly but surely, move left and across, usually round about Celtic Park. But to be honest, it doesn't really matter, and it's nice to vary the route from time to time, of course. So, this time it's on down the 89 we continue, shortly passing the fine old looking Barrachnie Inn, at what is another small east end enclave that looks like a village within the town.

It's mostly houses, schools, and other urban block that we meet enroute, but not always, as there is the occasional leafy stretch. This is only on the very outskirts, however, for as we near Shettleston, things become very built-up indeed. It's here on the Shettleston Road itself that the first of those great, big, red sandstone tenements of Glasgow are met. There are plenty more of them to come, of course, and now it also starts to get very busy and tight with traffic and all. On a public/bank holiday, or even a Sunday, things might be quiet enough to allow you a pretty good free run down the Shettleston. But I have found it very hectic a lot of the time, and usually try to dive left down a side street to get onto Tollcross Road.

It can seem a bit quieter for the most part, but as we're sticking to the direct route this time, then the best thing to do is to take the right fork every time a split in the road appears. One is soon met up ahead, and by going right down the Old Shettleston Road – as opposed to left and staying on Shettleston itself – you will avoid the worst of the hustle. Both roads meet up ahead fairly soon anyway, so either can be taken. But the Old option has housing only, with no shops or stores to attract additional traffic, and therefore is less busy and hopefully quicker.

No sooner have both roads rejoined when another sort of split in the road appears. The left turn, Westmuir Street, runs you up to Tollcross itself, which again I have used often in the past. But once more I can also recommend going straight on and sampling some more of old industrial Glasgow. Just to get you in the mood for that, you will see a big, blue-painted piece of iron work standing in the apex of the Y-junction. This is a former steam hammer. It's a smaller version of the two that were used in the biggest, baddest, blackest forge there ever was, the Parkhead Forge, and was once the pride of Glasgow with regard to steel production.

The two big hammers that the replica represents were the Samson (100 tons) and the Goliath (500 tons). The monument plaque will inform you that Goliath was the largest in the world at the time. The Forge was the pride of the fleet for the Beardmore Group, and the diversity and amount that the place produced was simply incredible. Shipping was their big game, turning out the plates for things as big as oil tankers, but they tried their hand at diesel engines, locomotives, aeroplanes, and in fact any form of transport.

This area was linked to that other great industrial zone of Monklands, the one we've just ridden through, by the Monklands Canal. This 12 miles-plus of waterway originally brought the coal from the Monklands coalfields into the town, but latterly also brought in other raw materials for the forge and the likes. The canal was actually started off by that biggest of big hitters, the great James Watt, in 1771, but even he didn't stick around to see its completion, such was the length of time it took to finish the job. It finally reached its intended destination of Townhead in 1794.

Again, like a lot of our former heavy industrial areas,

FALKIRK & SLAMMANAN RUN

One of the few splashes of colour in the area is Cliftonhill, home to Albion Rovers FC, known as the Wee Rovers. Their ground really does jump out at you as you come round the corner, and fair brightens up even the greyest of days.

it's all gone now and it's very difficult to imagine what it must have been like. What a sight the Parkhead Forge must have made as it worked round the clock, day and night, every night. So, as I was saying with regard to the road home, once again it will probably be faster to go straight on at the monument and stay on the A-89. Ahead, in the distance, those two tall grey sentinels that are the Whitevale Street high flats will act as your target to guide you correctly back. There is not any real navigation to do *per se*, for this one great road that you are on will take you right to Glasgow Cross, by carrying you and your machine right on down the famous Gallowgate.

First, you must ride past old factory buildings on the right, and a real rough, industrial-looking area it is, too. It contains old factory buildings, along with a cement factory and scrapyards, making for as ugly a front as is possible. To add to the feeling of real old, there are very lengthy stretches of brick walls that belong to an earlier time, and these must have surrounded and protected factories from the forge's era. Just at that point, the road makes a slight rise as it passes through a couple of roundabouts, which feed the Forge shopping centre's car parks. This means you have finally left the Shettleston Road and are now on Biggar Street.

This, you will notice, with the added elevation throws you into a totally different landscape entirely. Celtic Park will now be over your left shoulder, and ahead will be the new era. You have now left all the old industrial stuff behind. It's the brilliance of colour from the ultra-modern retail park that hits you full in the face.

The difference from what has gone before, which is just a few hundred yards behind you now, is astounding. All the usual suspects (shops) are in the retail park, and I hurry past as fast as I can. Then it's the residential that takes over from here on in, and that will start with the open and airy new road set-up and some very modern flats. The Whitevale flats have done their job and guided you thus far; you will shortly pass and leave them behind, too. If you're new to an area, it can be a great help to have a distant target to aim for, and the Whitevale fellas do a good job in that respect.

All the way into the city the new stuff continues unabated on the Gallowgate now, and this is something that I find strange. If ever there was a road that typified the old east end of Glasgow at one time for me, it was the Gallowgate. Now it's only when you get near to Glasgow Cross and you hit the almost carnival-like colours and flags belonging to the buildings and numerous Celtic pubs there, that you get a feel of 1970s Glasgow. Pride of place here goes to the famous Barras, of course, with all the bright greens and whites belonging to the Hoops'

As this has been a run that has carried us for the most part through the areas of our old heavy industry, then this photograph taken in Glasgow's east end is a fitting finish. It shows a replica of one of the giant steam hammers that was used in the Parkhead Forge. I'm glad I missed the industrial revolution.

watering holes (Tim Land et al), adding to the spectacle. Then there's the Barrowland Ballroom – another stalwart of this area, as infamous as it is famous.

Famous, too, is the Saracen Head pub – or Sarry Heid, as it is known – one of the oldest, if not the oldest, pub in the town. Handwritten notes by Robert Burns exist in the place, along with the skull of the last witch to be executed; I wonder what she did to deserve such an ending.

And so we roll through this jamboree of pubs, clubs, shops, and stalls, then under the rail bridge of the old St Enoch line, and onto the Saltmarket at the famous Glasgow (Mercat) Cross. It's a place we have come through a few times before, but I feel it's always a pleasure to sample the oldest part of the city, so I never tire of coming this way.

Now, all I have to do is cross the Clyde by the Albert Bridge, turn right at the end of Crown Street, and steer straight ahead. This will, of course, run me onto the Paisley Road and I'm soon in the old home town again.

Returning home from the Saltmarket is something we have done before, so I won't go into any great detail about it this time. Suffice to say that on this occasion it will provide an easy, though fairly busy, fairly flattish wind down from this great 70 mile-plus run. There are only the slight rises around Corkerhill and Barshaw Park which will require a bit more oomph to get over. The rest is more or less a purr home, till the Munt on the way up to Glenburn has to be taken. And then, boy oh boy, does the flat that follows feel good.

That's it for this run. Something a bit different from our usual stunning, scenic runs, but one I hope you enjoyed for the contrast. The reason I say that is because we haven't entirely finished with Lanarkshire and all its industrial history, far from it. The next run is going that way, too. Hope you can join me on it, and till then take care.

FALKIRK VIA KILLEARN
83.9 MILES
6.12 HOURS
ASCENT 2680 FT
4162 CALORIES BURNED

(VIA MUGDOCK, HIGH BONNYBRIDGE, LIMERIGG & AIRDRIE)

O'S LANDRANGER MAPS 64, 57, 65.

I mentioned in the text that it is possible, when doing the Falkirk run, to go over the Campsies and make a real day of it by either taking the Tak Ma Doon Road, or the Crow Road from Lennoxtown, or even by a big loop round through Killearn. In my opinion, going via Killearn makes for a wonderful day out, and I thoroughly recommend it as the best option. Where you stay, of course, will determine whether or not this is a viable option for you, but if it is, I cannot commend it highly enough. It gives you the best of both worlds in the one run. You have the pastoral scenery of the Campsies and Fintry Hills first of all, before flipping over into the old industrial landscape of Falkirk and North Lanarkshire.

Distance-wise, it will only add on an extra 13 to 15 miles or so, depending on what option you take, but if you're in the mood for some serious climbing, then by including Mugdock going via High Bonnybridge and then Limerigg, you get plenty of ascent for your money. You will enjoy this run no matter which option you choose, but I would say that to get the best out of it, making the big loop via Mugdock, Killearn, High Bonnybridge, High Falkirk, Limerigg, and Airdrie is the most satisfying way of all the choices… Give it a go.

Liam Boy.

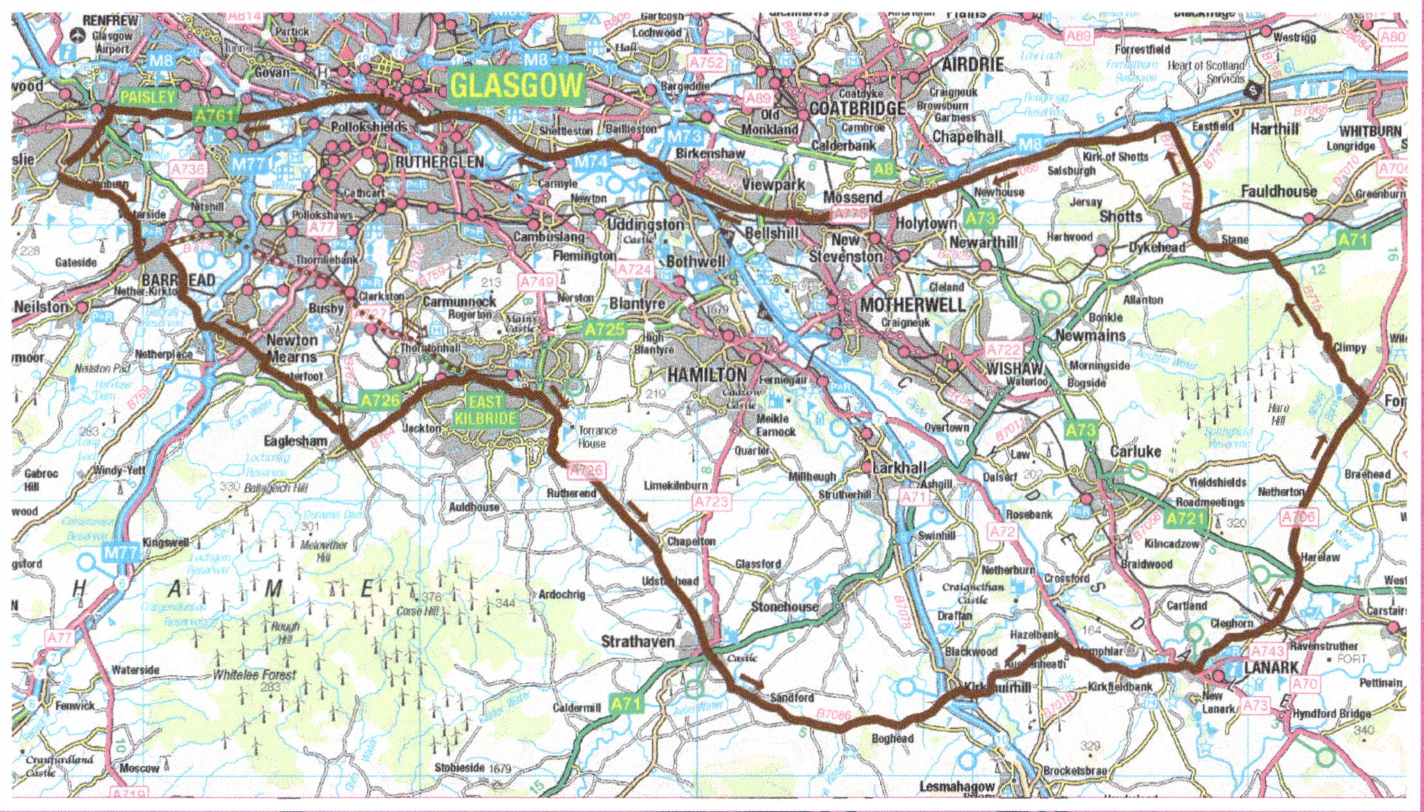

THE FORTH RUN

VIA JACKTON

80.1 MILES

4.58 HOURS

ASCENT 3540 FEET

2888 CALORIES BURNED

OS LANDRANGER MAPS 64, 71, 65

ROUTE SUMMARY

	ALTERNATIVE START	ALTERNATIVE ROUTE
Barrhead	A-726	
Aurs Rd	East Kilbride Rd	
(Barrhead Dams)	Eastwood Toll	
Mearns Cross	Clarkston Toll	
Mearnskirk	East Kilbride	
Humbie Rd		
Eaglesham		Auldhouse
Jackton		Leaburn
East Kilbride		A-726
Chapelton		Chapelton
Strathaven		
Kirkmuirhill		
Lanark		
Forth		
Shotts		
Kirk O Shotts		
Salsburgh		
Holytown		
Bellshill		
A-721		
London Rd (Glasgow)		
Paisley Rd West		
Paisley		

THE FORTH RUN

CONTRASTS

Now, when you looked at the title for this one, if you said, "Where the hell is Forth?" then join the club. For believe it or not, it wasn't until the very morning of my first run to this South Lanarkshire mining town that I became aware of its existence. It all came about when I was planning to go out for a run somewhere, and the weather report was for a sunny day accompanied by an east wind. So I thought, I'll head out east and get a nice tailwind on the way home. The question was: where?

After a quick once-over of the old 65 Landranger map, I spotted Forth. This looked to be about the right distance away, and also had potential. That was because of the way the road system ran towards and away from the town, and I realised that if I approached it via Strathaven and Lanark and then returned via Kirk o' Shotts, it would make for a great circular run and day out.

I was not in the slightest bit disappointed, for it's a run that has it all and is very much a mirror image of the Falkirk run when going via Killearn. First of all, there are the beautiful, green, pastoral scenes when going between Strathaven and Lanark – just like there are around Killearn and Fintry – before you arrive into those tough-looking, old, mining muirs again, this time between Forth and Shotts.

Then, after taking the road over to that great old landmark which is the Kirk o' Shotts itself, the return is by Salsburgh and Bellshill, running you directly down and onto London Road in Glasgow. This gives a really fantastic day out, coming in at around the 80 miles mark. And this run's existence, more than any other, shows the advantage of owning and possessing a good selection of OS maps.

This is not an easy run in its early stages, as there is a fair bit of climbing, for me at least, to get to Strathaven, which is followed by a lot of uppin and doonin to Lanark. From there to Forth and Shotts is fairly easy going, though, but it then requires a tough wee back road climb to get you over to the kirk.

Now, this run is best done on a day when an easterly or south easterly breeze is blowing, because when you clear the long draw-up through Salsburgh, just after Kirk o' Shotts, then boy, oh boy, do you have a long, no-holds-barred flyer of a straight road back to the Toon. You will be amazed at just how quick will be your return home on this one, especially after all the time and effort it took to get out there in the first place. The scenery is particularly pleasing across the Clyde Valley, and the road just seems to have a meandering style all of its own, as it makes its way to there from Strathaven. That's what we've got to look forward to this time, and if you're up for it, I'm ready when you are.

So, all the usual checks are made, as always. Tyres pumped, well grubbed, food for the road, tabs in the drinks bottles, et al. And if you have been doing a lot more miles than usual recently, then it is a good idea to buy and use a chain checker from time to time, as this wee tool can save you a lot of dough in the long run. This will tell you if your chain has stretched too much, which they all do after a period of time. Now, if you change the chain early enough, you won't need to change the rear sprockets (back block) as well. If you don't change the chain before it stretches too much, then the rear sprocket must also be changed, otherwise the gears will slip on a hill when you apply force.

Worse still, if you continue to run on a stretched chain, then eventually you will need to replace one or more of your front chainrings as well. This is usually the inner ring on a double chainring set-up, and the middle chainring on a triple set-up. So get wise to that potential problem early doors and save yourself some cash. It is not, incidentally, beyond the scope of most competent individuals to be able to do their own bike maintenance, which can also save money and a lot of hassle. Most bikes aren't as scary or as complex as cars, and so with a good maintenance book and some basic tools, you can start looking after your own machine.

Don't forget that this will at some stage in the future be out on the road, most likely starting with the dreaded puncture, which may be a while in coming but is a certainty to do so. It gives a rider confidence to go into the middle of nowhere, knowing that if a brake needs adjusting or a gear cable works loose, or the gears aren't shifting just right, then the problem can be sorted out on the spot. After a while, more specialised tools can be bought, and there's no need to go running to the bike store to fix every small ailment. This may lead onto truing your own wheels, so just remember that no other tool in the box can do as much damage in the hands of a novice as the spoke key. So, get some knowledge before you wreck a rim.[1]

Right, with that lecture now over, we had better get going on this run, for it is no 10 minute jaunt, that's for sure. OK, we're off and running and it's Strathaven here we come. This means heading for Barrhead first of all, and this will be our first time heading out in a south east direction. I must start climbing the very second I leave my street and will have to do so, on and off, till I am on the final approach to Strathaven itself. I can either use Glenburn Road or Glenfield Road to gain access onto the Capelthill Road (the B-774) which will carry me towards and into Barrhead, entering East Renfrewshire District into the bargain.

It is a most fine, field-lined, big, swerving bit of tar, the old Capelthill, and with its rises and dips, coming in equal amounts, it's a great way to warm up for any run. Especially this one, as it mirrors a lot of the terrain and riding that we are going to do today. Away to the right, above the rich meadows, sits the Brownside Braes, which are the bracken-lined, eastern extension of the Gleniffer Braes. Fine, too, to have as company the high Brownsides, giving a grand backdrop to your first patchwork of green squares. Already, at this early point, I'm in the mood for more of the same, and that's just as well as there is plenty more of the same to come.

The fairly long pull-up past the lengthy entry road to Brownside Farm, giving an early view of Glasgow's south side Kennishead flats, is cancelled out by the plummet down into the Barrhead bungalows. The black and white attire of the Cross Stobs Inn, sitting at the top of Grahamston Road and guarding the entrance to the town, welcomes you onto long, straight Paisley Road. This guides you eventually under the rail bridge and up to the big roundabout, known as Allan's Corner. When you turn left onto the Main Street, you will soon be faced with your first decision of the day.

This comes when you run up to the first set of lights just at the Arthurlie Club, because the plan here is to make our way to Strathaven, and two routes now present themselves to allow us to do that. One is to carry straight on and access the main East Kilbride Road (the A-726)

---

1 - I'm talking from bitter personal experience here.

via the (B-773) Darnley/Parkhouse Road. This is the easier, though much busier of the two options you have, and isn't my first choice. I prefer to make for the village of Eaglesham via the Humbie Road, which is quieter and much more scenic. Tougher with more climbing? Eh yes, but still the best route by far. So, let's go that way first, whadda ya say?

BARRHEAD TO EAGLESHAM

From the lights on Main Street at the junction with Ralston Road (Arthurlie Club), turn right then first left, just as you pass the club and head up Arthurlie Avenue. Now, so far we have come across certain local names since we entered Barrhead. Names like Grahamston, Gateside, Arthurlie, and Barrhead itself, of course. These originally were four different textile-producing villages that all came together to make the one town. You can really only appreciate just how much of a textile town Barrhead once was, when you view it from above on the Fereneze Hills, where it does still retain a mill town look. These mills, like all its other factories – and there were many – have now closed for good.

A tremendous view of Glasgow is to be had from the climb up Newton Avenue in Auchenback, Barrhead, as height is gained enroute to the Aurs Road and the Barrhead Dams.

Last to go were Spillers and the Armitage Shanks Porcelain Works. They actually did very well to last as long as they did, but alas, they finally went the way of the others. Now, as you ride up Arthurlie Avenue, you enter the massive, sprawling Auchenback scheme. No more bungalows or villas here; this is you into the council houses, though there have been new developments up here recently as well, as you are just about to discover.

Balgray Reservoir is the largest of the Barrhead Dams, and it often pleases with the views it provides as you make your way round its stone walls on the Aurs Road. The gate we are passing here actually has a plate in its top right hand corner that says "Please shut the gate". How very quaint.

These have mostly been on Fenwick Drive, which you reach when you round the bend at the end of Arthurlie and roll up beside the school on Roebank Drive. First left finds you on Fenwick, but it's only one of three roads running parallel with each other that will do the job of taking us up towards Aurs Road and the Barrhead Dams.

You started climbing as the primary school was met, and continue to do so on Fenwick, which opens up fantastic views away to the north when you level out. The Fereneze Hills, away to the left, start the sweep, but it's dear old Mother Glasgow, with its uncountable number of high rise flats, that will be hogging the main ground. What a sight to get from a housing scheme. If this was the view from a private estate, it would easily add 5 to 10 grand onto your house price.

So, feeling well buoyed-up when we get to the end of Fenwick Dr, we meet the great Aurs Rd. Great indeed is the road that carries us first up and then under the solid, old, arch-backed, bugger of a railway bridge, a rare one that still carries trains over it.

And then by water and walled curves, it leads us through the magical world of the Barrhead Dams. Scenic is a word that doesn't do this stretch justice, especially when a mist lingers on the water. This is the water contained within the Balgray Reservoir, which is the big dam that sits on your right and will be the most visible of the three. The others sit hidden down to your left. It can be a bit tight and a bit busy on the old dam's road, but I've never had any bother on it and always enjoy the delight and the dance round the water's edge that the Aurs fellow provides. It ends all too soon, unfortunately, with a series of curves and then a rise up and over the M-77, as you make your way into the Mearns.

The unnecessary set of traffic lights you meet at the top of the rise guards the entrance to the great Stewarton Road, but we carry straight on this time, where there now follows a long dip down and up from here to Mearns Cross. The pull-up on this one overstays its welcome a bit, so the cross itself, along with its flat terrain, is always, always met with glee. So, too, is the hurl along the Eaglesham Road that is gained by a quick left/right turn on the old Ayr Road at the cross. This road dips and dances through the bungalows of middle income earners in a most easy, delightful fashion

It ends rather grandly at that white-walled old stalwart of Mearns Kirk itself, after which this area is named. This is you now at the junction of Eaglesham Road and Mearns Road, and just another quick one-two, right then left this time, and we meet the Humbie. Now, here is a road-and-a-half. God knows where the name came from, but it's not one to forget easily and neither is the road itself. It packs plenty of punch and excitement, with one or two flying descents and one or two wee peckers of climbs. The road sign is extremely accurate in its distances, telling you, you have 2¾ miles to go to the village of Eaglesham. It is a very pretty 2¾ miles of agricultural landscape at that.

The action isn't long in coming, for you immediately plummet down from the early height and twist and turn wildly at the bottom, ensuring you don't clip the edge of the bonny, wee stone bridge that takes you over the Earn Water. But just to slow you right down, it leads straight onto a tough, but short, hard wee climb – the hardest the Humbie gets, and although it isn't easy, it restores your altitude and views. Now, coming up is the first roundabout, just before you go under the new bypass, which has a side road shooting off to the left, called Floors Road[2]. Floors Farm will be the first farm on the left on this road, and it was the scene of one of the most bizarre episodes in the whole of the Second World War.

It was by this farm, on Bonnyton Moor[3], on the night of the 10th of May, 1941, that Deputy Reichsfurher (Adolf

---

2 - It's signposted for Waterfoot.

3 - The exact spot of his landing was where the new road is, and at one time was marked by a plaque. However, due to continual protests, the plaque was removed.

After the rollercoaster ride on the Humbie Road is over, it's into Eaglesham you trundle, and expect to be charmed by this pretty, white-walled village every time you ride through it.

Hitler's right-hand man) Rudolph Hess parachuted out of his Messerschmitt Bf110 and floated down to earth. He subsequently demanded to speak to the Duke of Hamilton. It was the ploughman from Floors Farm itself, a bloke called Dave McLean, who came out and escorted the German airman into his home. At first, Hess pretended to be Hauptmann (Captain) Alfred Horn, but soon revealed his true identity when he was taken into custody by the Busby Home Guard. Although he did get to speak to the Duke and other senior British officials, the reason for Hess's flight still remains a mystery, even to this day.

He was a bit of an enigmatic figure to the German people and also to fellow Nazi Party members. He often pleaded amnesia during his long incarceration. However, his secret flight over that night may not have been as secret as was supposed. In the British Cabinet during the war was Ernie Bevan, the strong man of the TUC. A big, domineering man, who Churchill realised was a good man to have on board. Bevan's favourite saying, whilst having his thumbs stuck firmly in his lapels, was:

"I said I'd do it and I did it." A very conceited but likeable individual, big Ernie had industrial contacts all over Europe, including Nazi Germany.

"Don't you question me, don't you challenge me"; that was the big man's attitude. Needless to say, he was often at odds with that other big ego in the cabinet at the time, Lord Beaverbrook. Beaverbrook was in and out, in and out of the cabinet, whereas Bevan was a permanent fixture. Churchill realised that it was good to have the workers on his side, and so backed Ernie. It seems that Bevan was aware that Hess was going to make his flight over that night, as he had been tipped off in advance by a leading German industrialist about the whole escapade. But just who was his highly placed industrial informant? It was strongly believed to be Billy Messerschmitt, no less.

As you all know, Hess's efforts came to nothing, as the war carried on much as before. Whatever the senior ranking German had in mind, whatever was planned, real or imaginary, we will never know. He spent the rest of his life in incarceration, becoming the one and only inmate in Spandau Prison, right up until his death in 1987, aged 93, when he apparently committed suicide. However, even this is a contentious issue, as some claim he was far too frail to be able to hang himself, as it appeared he did. A book out in 2014 attempted to clear up the mystery of his flight, claiming the British had conned the Germans into thinking they would do a deal and so Hitler sent over Hess to handle it. I've not read the book yet, so can't comment.

Battering along the Queensway (A-726), East Kilbride, and I do mean battering, as pretty it ain't. Creating the Scottish new town was an idea that was dreamt up in the 1950s and I'm sure it looked good on paper, but they all turned out to be concrete eyesores. Therefore, I try and get through them just as quickly as I can.

THE FORTH RUN

And so with another history lesson under our belts, we continue on down the Humbie, and pass under the modern slab of concrete which is the Eaglesham bypass. Not pretty the A-726, but a necessary evil, as it takes all the traffic away from the village itself and especially the Eaglesham Moor Road, which opens up a great training run for our benefit. Another small roundabout and wee climb are needed to finally leave the big, traffic-flowing river behind, and then we can get on with our serene jaunt through lovely, rural Renfrewshire again. Lovely indeed it is, sitting up high between the fields, but the village is approaching fast and we must drop down to meet its acquaintance.

On the A-726 here between East Kilbride and Chapelton, and it is a fine road to ride. The rise in the distance is the only tough part of the road if you're Strathaven-bound, and after the initial rough pastures that are encountered soon after leaving East Kilbride, they get replaced by a broad, prairie-like landscape of clipped green fields. It's quite an unusual setting.

It's a straight, screaming dive down, and in no time you are passing the first homes of Eaglesham on your right. And now that you're on the level, it's a short roll up to the junction with Glasgow Road. Turn right into the village and expect to be charmed. At first, it's nothing too special, just pretty homes that you would expect to find in any small village, but as the crossroads is neared on Gilmour Street, then it does get seriously quaint. It starts with the white and black walls of the Eglington Arms Hotel, which introduces you to the rest of this 1769-planned village. Planned by Alexander Montgomerie, the 10th Earl of Eglington, whose family owned the land hereabouts for about 700 years.

Eaglesham, originally a 17th century small market town, was a place that flourished during agricultural and

Street crossroads is a major junction for us, because not only does it provide us with a couple of options to get to Strathaven, but by turning right and climbing up Montgomery Street, you will run onto the Eaglesham Moor Road, which is another very popular training run done by myself and many others.

However, we are concerned at the moment with going either straight ahead or turning left. If we go straight on, then we can, by turning second left, follow a multitude of twisting and turning back roads all the way to Strathaven. The only problem is that it is 10 miles of tight, single-track, back-road riding. Now there is nothing wrong with going this way ordinarily; in fact, these very back roads are all part of the national cycle route. It is just that when faced with such a long run in front of you, it may be preferable to stick to the main roads, as a faster cadence is usually easier to maintain. These back roads, which carry us close to Auldhouse Village (though not actually through it), can be a little too time-consuming for my liking, especially for as long a distance as 10 miles.

That said, if you do decide to go via them, then there is an early opt-out option that will take you onto the A-726 before Chapelton, and is often my preferred choice. This way avoids East Kilbride entirely, but allows me to enjoy the majority of the road between East Kilbride and Strathaven, which is one of my favourites. The alternative from the centre of Eaglesham is to turn left onto the B-764 and head for the village of Jackton, which will lead into the Peel Park area of early East Kilbride. As it is the more straightforward option, it's probably best to cover that way first. Just for the record, Gilmour Street was named after the Gilmour Brothers, Allan and James, who bought the land here in 1844 after the Montgomery's fortunes declined dramatically.

Dropping down the Glasgow Road in Strathaven, which is a lovely, free-flowing brae and a nice start to the village, but it gets even better, quainter, and prettier the closer you get to the centre.

industrial reform, and what you see round about you now was constructed to take advantage of the period. All is pleasing to the eye, there is no doubt about that, with solidness in the buildings, which are all colour co-ordinated to add to the attraction. The Gilmour

EAGLESHAM TO PEEL PARK VIA JACKTON

So turn left from Gilmour Street onto Cheapside Street (the B-764) and make your way past more stone-built stunners on your right, and more parkland on the left. The 10th Earl made a helluva job of the town, all credit to him. Ahead now is a long, and I do mean long, stretch of road that carries you due east through some flat, rich, lush, dairy fields. A gentle, undulating straight stretch of tar is what you will find yourself on at this point, where large numbers of big, black and white munchers (Heifers) or perhaps even small, white woolly ones, moo and baa

Strathaven isn't only pretty but it's colourful as well, with a lot of the buildings painted in either a mint green colour or, as here, in a pale orange. I assume this is compulsory, perhaps for some traditional conservation reasons, though I could be wrong there. It makes it all most pleasant, however, and this shot is taken right below the castle just before we head out on the B-7086 bound for Kirkmuirhill.

in support of your efforts from the sidelines. Unless I am imagining that, of course.

Unlike on the Humbie, all is flat and fertile, and by now you are firing fast along with gay abandon; well, you are until the pull-up just before Jackton is reached. This is a considerable wee climb, but nothing that will stop you in your tracks. When you level out, the countdown markers for the village begin. Not a lot in Jackton, just a few old houses as reminders that this was a wee ferm toon at one time, with just the side of a white-painted, old barn with a rusty, corrugated iron roof attached, to see you on your way just as you slip out the other side. And what a contrast when you do; even before you leave Jackton, already the new houses of the ever- encroaching East Kilbride can be seen.

Within about two fields' lengths, the green stops abruptly when you slam into a new stripy roundabout, whose tentacles radiate into shiny new estates that add even more housing muscle onto EK's already considerable repertoire. You are about to go from one extreme to the other here, because from the 16th century charm of Eaglesham, you suddenly find yourself in the 20th century concrete of that most hideous of creatures, the Scottish new town. This is not our first trip through such terrain, as we sampled Irvine's delights on our very first jaunt in the book. But I must say I was a bit hard on poor old Irvine, as it's only its fringe schemes that look bloody awful. The old centre is a totally different animal and retains a lot of its dignity and charm from an earlier era.

As for East Kilbride? Well, it does have an original village and, yes, that is very pretty, but it's very small and almost totally hidden from view. Bear in mind that in 1930, the place had a total population of 900[4]. This was before it got the nod for redevelopment in 1947, and I think building started in earnest in the1950s. Other than the tiny village, I must say that the place doesn't have a saving grace, and when you consider some of the people who have hailed from the town, including amongst others, Coisty, Muriel Gray, Kirsty Young, and Liam Fox, you can't help but think, could it get any worse?

That's difficult to say, but the place certainly tries. As it's a new town, you now start to plough into roundabout, after roundabout, after… you get the picture. I think there are nine of them between Jackton and the A-726, but you can count them yourself, just in case I've missed one. So, after mucho swerving round the circular ones, firstly between overpriced flashy housing, you then reach the Hairmyres roundabout and begin swerving round the circular ones between a couple of heavyweights. These are the massive DFIA[5] building and Hairmyres Hospital itself. Hairmyres station throws in its tuppenceworth for good measure.

The finale is through the car dealerships that seem to actually breed here, or again is that my imagination? They very colourfully and flag-flyingly herald your arrival at the main road through the town, this being the A-726 at Peel Park, and so far so good. We've had a pretty and history-filled jaunt thus far, but that route was not the easiest or shortest way to reach here from Barrhead. If you want that way, then the A-726 is your baby, all the way from Nitshill.

BARRHEAD TO PEEL PARK VIA THE A-726

Now, this is a fairly straightforward route, one that poses no great strain on your navigation skills and probably needs no introduction to you either. The A-726, which despite several name changes along the way, is to all intents and purposes the main East Kilbride Road, and is one you have probably driven up more times than you care to remember. Unless you are still a nipper, who hasn't passed their driving test yet. But just in case you don't know it, I will give a description of it to you, just to be on the safe side. From Main Street, Barrhead, at the Arthurlie Club lights, carry straight on and run down the Main Street, past all the shops, till you can ease up on the slight slope down to the Dovecoathall roundabout. We want the second exit, taking us onto the Darnley then Parkhouse Road (the B-773), that runs us through what is now more new modern housing estates, which is a great improvement on the old tenements of South Nitshill.

They were a terrible, hard-looking sight, a real eyesore, and the place is all the better for their removal. I think the paint was still wet on some of the new houses the last time I rode past. The Parkhouse Road drops down to the lights where it meets Nitshill Road. This is the A-726 and this will run us all the way to Strathaven.

It will be apparent right from the word go that this road has a major drawback for the cyclist, and that is its busyness. This is the reason I use it as little as possible. It is dual carriageway, yes, with a low speed limit which

---

4 - At the last count there was over 74000

5 - It stands for Department for International Development.

helps. But, boy, is it still a busy one. Keep well tucked in and your wits about you when on it, and make your way along past Darnley and begin the long draw up and under the M-77 motorway.

Now, in the old days the road all the way was the 726, but because that number has now been allocated to the new Eaglesham bypass, from here until the start of East Kilbride it is the A-727[6], before it reverts back to its old number. That is academic to us, of course, as we level out past the entrance to Arden and then fire straight through the Spiersbridge roundabout. It's more busy, busy dual carriageway here, beside Rouken Glen Park, and only when we make the short hop through Eastwood Toll up ahead, does it become single carriageway. And along it we ride, into one of Glasgow's well-heeled suburbs, that being Giffnock.

It's a procession of beautiful villas and cottages that take us slightly round the corner, and then it's under the two big, beautiful, red, railway bridges at Williamwood. From there, we rise slightly up to Clarkston Toll itself, which is always – and I do mean always – teeming with traffic. The cars come at you from all angles and directions, as you, in a desperate dash, dive across and attempt to reach the safety of the Sheddens roundabout, ¼ of a mile away up the road. Watch out for cabs, buses, buggies, babies, pizza delivery guys, shoppers, other cyclists, and everything else that middle class Glasgow can throw at you. Mark my words here; you will never find Clarkston Toll quiet[7].

A left turn at the Sheddens takes us, undulating fairly wildly, through Busby. Up then down, crossing the River Cart, back up again after going under the railway, and then we're on our way out. Out of the city and into the green belt at the beginning of South Lanarkshire. Quite a wee pull-up it takes, too, just to get us finally clear, and then we fall to the Thorntonhall roundabout. The Castlemilk high flats are about the last bit of Glasgow you see before encountering the delights of the new town's roads.

The stretch from Thorntonhall to Peel Park is not one I relish, far from it. I always get along and over it as fast as I can. That's because the road here becomes fast, open dual carriageway, which not only supports racy motorists, but being open, there is no protection from any headwind. If that wasn't enough, an awkward angled and fairly long climb is encountered, taking you above the main Stewartfield roundabout below[8] and, just for good measure, the only scenery is factories and the bloody Tax Office.

The road starts to lie back as it runs past even more industry, but it isn't long till you join up with the Eaglesham route at Peel Park, when you meet your second roundabout. This way is about 2 miles shorter and involves about 140 feet less climbing than going via Eaglesham[9].

The good news is that all the climbing is over, for now at least, as the road through the remainder of East Kilbride is full flat and bolt straight. Save, that is, for the main roundabouts you will need to negotiate enroute, of course. Each one is named after some adjacent area, and each one met in turn as you ride along what is known as the Queensway. The Queensway itself would make a great time trial route, and I'm surprised it isn't used for such a thing. It isn't a scenic stretch, the old Queensway, but you're not long in battering along and through its roundabouts, before you find yourself passing the last of EK's schemes, St Leonards, and making your way out of town.

What with the massive concrete block that the town has for a centre and a main road that resembles a dried-out canal, which is surrounded by more concrete than the New York Mob could supply, it's certainly not an advert for visitscotland.com.[10] But the road that follows to Chapelton then Strathaven more than makes up for EK's shortcomings. The sign says 7 miles to Strathaven as you approach the town's last roundabout called Torrance, which follows on from its much larger brethren in the heart of the town – roundabouts like Rigghead, The Murray, and Birniehill. So 7 miles it is, and it is 7 miles to savour.

This is another favourite stretch of mine. Particularly so when I am returning from Strathaven on a cold winter's day and, with the aid of the frost, there is a stillness and clipped hardness about the fields all around. That is the very flat band of fertile fields closer to Strathaven than

---

6 - You would have thought it would have made more sense to give the bypass a new number.

7 - The place is still best remembered for a gas explosion that took place there in October 1971 killing 21 people and injuring about another 100.

8 - As the Eaglesham bypass starts and ends at the roundabout below, we officially are back on the A-726 at this point.

9 - It is exactly 11.7 miles from my front door.

10 - The new name for the Scottish Tourist Board.

EK, because the ones you meet as you leave the new town are much more rugged and scatty. Hardly surprising, as you are up at a good height here, round about the 200 metres mark.

The road entertains with sweeping curves up into the windswept rough. These rise gently at first, but just after another particularly big sweep in the road, you come to a much steeper rise.

At the bottom of this sits an isolated white cottage, beside which a side road feeds in from the direction of Auldhouse, which the sign says is 2½ miles away. This road can also be used to gain the A-726 from Eaglesham.

EAGLESHAM TO THE A-726 VIA AULDHOUSE

From the crossroads on Gilmour Street, carry straight on and over the brow of the hill, and head out the south end of the village. Ahead will be very barren moorland of conifers and turbines. The plan here will be to use the back roads, which are also part of the national cycle route, to take us on a windy route to Strathaven. This is well signposted and takes you firing down into Millhall, which begins a series of twists and turns over burns, along hedgerows, and through a rabbit warren of roads. The correct route will be well signed whenever it is required, and the road surface in general is in good nick.

In my experience, only occasionally will tractor tyres leave a very muddy surface, but there are enough short, steep climbs, sharp bends, and junctions to slow you down just a little too much for my liking. Eventually you will get onto a long straight[11] that takes you past Laigh Cleughearn Farm, where the sign says take a sharp right to stay on the cycle route. I prefer to go straight on here instead, and run long, straight, and fast onto the A-726, at the aforementioned white cottage, just over a mile short of Chapelton. I do this because it seems faster and I enjoy the run into Strathaven on the A-road so much. If you stay on the back roads (cycle route) instead, it will take you into the top end of Strathaven that way.

Just after Laigh Cleughearn, you will see on the left, two modern houses, white in colour and large in spread. In the second one resides the great Frank Coll. A plumber to trade, who came from the Gorbals, and is the funniest guy I've ever known. He was also an endurance man of repute, and now only a dodgy knee and family commitments prevent him from going as strong as ever.

---

11 - This is the Millwell Road.

If you're passing this way and want some entertainment, drop in and see the Frank boy; tell him I sent you, and that I was asking for him.

A short distance past Frank's drum will see you reach Leaburn Hamlet and then shortly comes the drop onto the 726.

When you hit it, you unfortunately have to take the tough, wee climb ahead of you immediately, but once over, be prepared to enjoy the rest of the run in. The funny thing here is that the higher you get, the more cultivated the fields become. On the run into Chapelton, you will begin to get your first taste of the great, broad plain that will accompany us from here all the way over to the Clyde Valley and beyond. Chapelton is a very small, isolated, high village that you batter straight through in seconds, on a road that has been running straight for a mile or so already. And once through the village, the road climbs and curves a bit more interestingly for the next 3 miles or so.

On this stretch, you really do get a sense of the vast flatness that balances out either side of you. It is a landscape that is rare hereabouts, and it makes it oh so special to ride this road and also the one that follows on from it, when we go over to Kirkmuirhill from Strathaven. The final drop into Strathaven has quaintly got houses on one side and sheep on the other.

Now, if you thought Eaglesham was cute, just wait till you get a load of Strathaven. The road in is good, with its offering of old, but the small centre is just something else entirely. When you meet the big church, slip down the colourful lane to its left-hand side[12] and run right down to the bottom, meeting Boo Backit Brig (Bow Backed Bridge) going over the Powmillon Burn.

Colourful indeed, as the shops and pubs are painted a multitude of bright hues, including orange and mint green[13]. Then just a short hop up and across the busy A-71, takes us below Gavlers Castle,[14] which still has an impressive front, though not much else. A plaque on the wall tells you it was built by Sir Andrew Stuart and resided in for centuries by the Hamiltons. It also tells of

---

12 - You can take the left turn after the church and go through the very centre, which is Common Green, and it's just as quaint.

13 - This is the colour of the baker's shop at the bottom of the lane. I recommend their croissants.

14 - Also known as Avondale Castle

Crossing the Avon Water on the B-7086 when enroute from Strathaven to Kirkmuirhill. This requires a steep drop down and then an equally steep pull-up the other side to get over it. But once that's behind you, the rest is much easier going on a delightful bending and dipping country road all the way over to Kirkmuirhill. This scene, incidentally, looks like it should belong in Cumbria.

its Covenanter connections. An information board tells you a bit about the town, how it goes way back to Roman times and was previously a market and weaving town. Hence its prettiness, I suppose. To continue on our way to Lanark, we run down the right-hand side of the castle.

As you do so, you will pass the cutest and cosiest-looking wee boozer you ever did see, in the shape of the Drumclog Inn. The initial tight, one-way lane spits you out onto the Lesmahagow Road, where the charm stops almost immediately; for the time being anyway. Surprisingly, the B-7086 initially takes on a modern look about it, as it plummets you down, well down, over the Avon Water. However, a look upstream to the left, at the old bridge and house that sit there, restores the rural charm, as this resembles a scene from the Lake District. There now follows an equally long pull-up on the other side, where the B-road now starts to entertain and charm on the remainder of the 7 miles over to Kirkmuirhill.

It slips past the side of Sandford, whose red, corrugated iron-roofed village hall is as bright as a button, and then continues to rise a bit till it passes the red, corrugated iron barns of Castlebrocket Farm. After this, the road will twist and turn in joyous fashion, seeming to act in concert with the meandering Kype Water, flowing in the fields beside. Then the 7086 becomes a bit more business-like in the run over to Kirkmuirhill, as it carries you again through a vast, broad, and flat agricultural landscape. Agricultural indeed, for several farms are passed enroute, which is surprising considering the height you are up.

It's only when you near tiny Boghead[15] on the approach to Kirkmuirhill itself, do you get an idea of the height you are presently riding at. It's a good bit above the 200 metre mark, and this will be obvious for the first time as you look across the valley ahead that carries the River

---

15 - Its houses were inhabited by the workers from the nearby Blackwood Estate.

THE FORTH RUN

After pulling up from the Avon Water, you pass by Sandford Village, and despite the fact that you only skirt the edge of it, you will still notice quite clearly its brightly coloured village hall. It fair brightens the place up.

Nethan, and it's quite a wee treat to cross this one. First, you must drop down into Kirkmuirhill, and as you do, a quick look to the right on a clear day gives a view of Tinto Hill. Fire down and under the M-74 – that lifeline to the Sassenach Kingdom to the south – and then you're into the shops and houses of this struggling village.

At the bottom of the drop is the Carlisle Road and I assume this must have been the main artery south, way back in the golden days of motoring. God knows how long it must have taken back then to get to England in a Morris Minor.

We've turned right onto it and run past the Esso station, and even that has a look of the land that time forgot. There is a very dull and tired look about

After a lot of enjoyable road riding, the drop down into rough Kirkmuirhill is made, taking you under the M-74 on the way in. It's been a high level ride over from Strathaven, but nothing too taxing once the Avon Water has been cleared. We both enter and leave Kirkmuirhill on the B-7086 in quite fast fashion.

Kirkmuirhill and here, as well as in other old mining communities we pass through along the way, the demise of old king coal has been replaced by the growth of the modern narcotics industry. As you roll along Carlisle Road, a fine, solid, big railway embankment keeps you company, as it runs parallel with the road on the left.

We are just about to crash through it in very dramatic fashion after we turn left onto the Lanark Road up ahead. This we do when we reach the local parish church – a big, grey sentinel that stands rather appropriately in the middle of a very pronounced Y-junction. As soon as you make the turn, the drop down towards the Nethan begins. As stated previously, it is done in rather dramatic fashion, because between the walls that once supported the now removed rail

It's a left turn at the Kirkmuirhill Parish Church that will put you on the right road to Lanark, and that shouldn't be a problem, as you can't miss it.

bridge, we find our door to the beginning of a very steep and thrilling fall down to this shy, retiring river. It's a very tight and technical fall at that, curving viciously round bends and bungalows. So, be ready for the first one, or dire consequences may result!

Swish and swoosh, round and back, on the way down to the great bridge that takes you over to the other side. Immediately begins an equally delightful climb, bending none-too-steeply up and away from the meandering river below, and leading into the village of Auchenheath. We're not in it for long – just a street's length – and when we exit the other side, we find ourselves about to do an action replay of the road we were on between Sandford and the Nethan. Because initially, this will be another great ride, more of long, sweeping curves into the

After turning left onto the Lanark Road (B-7086) at the prominent Kirkmuirhill Parish Church, you leave the village in some dramatic style as you plummet down between the stanchions of the now gone railway bridge and begin the descent down to the River Nethan. It's a belter.

Falling fast on the B-7086 Lanark Road out of Kirkmuirhill and heading down and over the River Nethan. This is a most pleasant corner with a very tight, technical descent and an equally twisty climb up the other side of the valley to Auchenheath. It is very, very pretty and pleasant all the way, and even the climb away from the river will be enjoyed despite the effort required.

distance this time, again through a broad, green, plain landscape. This before beginning another steep, river-bound drop, down towards the mighty River Clyde.

As you make your way over the 2 or so miles, ahead for the first time will be spied the multitude of wind turbines that reside up on the Blacklaw Moor. That is exactly where we are heading. In the meantime, we are about to encounter another real deal descent, as we unwittingly roll onto a belter of a drop, that's not as technical as the Nethan one, but longer and faster. Across the tight upper Clyde Valley, the steepness with which the fields opposite drop down to the floor will give you some idea about what is to come. This is definitely a Geronimo job, and as the fun begins, a quick look up will reveal the church spires of Lanark. We're getting close alright. Get low on the hooks for some stability, as you fire straight down among the beech hedgerows.

It's a pretty and leafy fall through the woods, and thrilling into the bargain; just brilliant. It ends when we meet the much more horizontal A-72 tootling up the valley floor, which must get a fright at the speed with which we arrive. We now find ourselves right on the bonnie, bonnie banks of the Clyde and soon begins a steepish wee curve and climb up to the Kirkfieldbank welcome sign. The height this gives allows not only a nice view down onto the river, but also the opportunity to gleefully fly past the early houses of the village. That is, till the level is found again, right on the valley floor this

A view of Lanark Town from high on the B-7086 just before it drops down long and fast to the floor of the Clyde Valley. The road from Auchenheath to here is almost an identical rerun of the Strathaven to Kirkmuirhill stretch, and is enjoyed just as much. The long descent down to the Clyde is very fast but mostly straight.

THE FORTH RUN

The River Clyde from the Kirkfieldbank Bridge looking downstream. This one was opened in 1959, and replaced the older one which still sits slightly upstream to this very day. The ride through Kirkfieldbank itself feels like a trip down memory lane, so old-looking are some of its buildings. You're now on the A-72.

time. A look of ye olde has Kirkfieldbank, not that that is a problem, far from it. It makes the riverbank plouter all the more pleasant.

A swing round left and it's across we go. On not a bad-looking bridge built in 1959, I might add, but a look over the upstream parapet will reveal the original, which even today still looks brilliant[16]. And now here cometh the main fly in the ointment of today's run. That would be the climb up from the Clyde into the town of Lanark itself. Get ready for an ouch! No, make that a double ouch!! I've got about 30 miles in my legs already at this point, which is not a helluva lot of miles, but there's been a fair bit of climbing along the way and this one we could probably well do without. But there's no way round the bugger, so up we go.

Someone has strategically placed the Welcome to Lanark sign at the bottom of the hill, perhaps for the benefit of us cyclists, who they figured would be too knackered to read it at the top. How thoughtful. A date on the sign says 1409, since when this Royal Burgh has existed.

As you pass the sign, dig in deep, deep, deep. Steep, sustained, and snaking is how it goes. So it's best to sit and dour out a rhythm, if you can. But even if you have to stand for a bit, which may be more than likely, what the hell? Just get up it. The real sting in the tail with this one is how time and time again you think the end must be round this corner, only to round the corner and still see it snake steeply away upward.

But all bad things must come to an end, and this one does when you abut with the A-73 at the top of the rise; it joins at an acute angle from the left. This before it carries you a lot more gently into the town itself. Still rising a little, yes, but nowhere near as steep as the ramp you were on.

So, here we find ourselves, tongue still hanging out and wondering just what the hell hit us, as we trundle up the West Port. All is as you'd expect from such an aged market town, one going back to medieval times, no less. Small, stocky homes with small, square windows lead you in towards solid church spires.

Immediately once you cross the Clyde, the pull-up to Lanark begins and it is the hardest part of today's run. It's never easy this one, and although higher bends keep it interesting when the going gets tough, the gradient overstays its welcome a fair bit, and you're always glad when you reach the top. Just pace yourself nice and easy if you can here, especially at the start, for you'll need the extra energy near the top.

---

16 - It was built in 1699 by James Lockhart.

Welcome to Lanark, and what a relief it is to get off that bloody brae. You've just joined the A-73 but only briefly, because we are about to take a left turn onto the A-706 and head out of town on the Cleghorn Road. You don't actually get to see too much of Lanark itself, which is a pity; it looks like a real old town of character.

A sign back when you joined the 73 tells you that it is only 2 miles to the New Lanark Mill. This place is well worth a visit, but perhaps not on this run, as we've still got a fair bit to go. Unfortunately, we don't actually get to see much of Lanark Town itself, as we will be taking an early left turn on the A-706, to get us on the Forth Road. The place does have a definite unique sort of Borders look about it, as we are on the edge of that beautiful country. You half expect to see the horses and hounds of the hunt come trotting down the Main Street; well, you did until they banned blood sports.

Well signposted is our road[17], just as you draw level with the bank, passing the magnificent Greyfriars Parish Church before it. When you make the turn, you find yourself on the Cleghorn Road, which starts off rather fittingly as Hope Street. It is a rather splendid street at that, with the Lindsay Institute (whatever the hell that is) and the fine old court building adding some serious grandeur. The rest is quality also, as you begin to leave the town and start to eat into the 8 miles of road, approximately, that is between Lanark and Forth.

I'm sitting on the low 30s with regard to mileage at this point, and will have between 42 to 44 miles on the clock when I reach our destination town. The landscape is still green and fertile round about, with the fields interestingly sloped, as is the road, which has no shortage of interest either at this point, with some great wooded curves coming your way.

---

17 - It's signed for Whitburn and Linlithgow.

These carry us into Cleghorn, which has a couple of great wee treats up its sleeve. The first is a beautiful bridge[18], traffic light-controlled, that requires a serious swerve to take safely, followed by a level crossing soon after. The gates of the crossing rise quickly once the train has passed, but unlike in France, they tend to close the gate well before the train arrives. So, if you do get caught at them, expect a fair wee wait. As you pull gently up and away from the crossing, take a look over your right shoulder and you'll get another great view of Tinto across the sheep fields.

This is just a reminder again, of how close you get to the Southern Uplands on this run. Incidentally, it will not be the last time you get an indication of just how much ground you have covered; there's still one more to come. In the meantime, the road begins to straighten, but is still enclosed and interesting at this point, though only until after about a mile, when you arrive at the big, isolated

The Cleghorn railway crossing is met shortly after leaving Lanark, and there is a very good chance that you will get stopped at this one, as it's a real busy line. They close the gates a good little while before the train arrives, but the second it's passed, up they come.

---

18 - It takes you over the Mouse Water, which joins the Clyde at Kirkfieldbank.

THE FORTH RUN

Once through the Cleghorn crossing, a look behind you will give you a great view of Tinto Hill, and it gives you some idea of just how far south you've come on this run, as you're getting close to the edge of the Borders here.

Harelaw roundabout, which sits open and bare at the intersection between the road you are on, the A-706, and the A-721. From here on, the term open road doesn't even begin to describe the scene you will ride through.

It's a vast, flat plain, way too wide either side for even the sky to reach across. It finds you, your bike, and the slender wee 706, forcing a way through the middle of it all. At the same time, you're constantly looking ahead for your intended target. This will be spotted at quite some distance, because its red rooftops can be easily seen from a long way off, on the long, straight, flat road over. This does seem to have a never-ending quality to it, which can be a mega pain in the bum, for often at this point I'm running low on something or other and can't wait to get to Forth for supplies.

The road, if you're not facing a headwind, is easy going, though, either flat of slightly downhill until the final approach to the town itself. For not only do you find yourself on a slight rise, but also the look of the fields about changes from rich agricultural to more rugged-looking, conifer-filled, sheep jobs. Welcome to mining country. Just like Lanark, we want an early, well-signed, left turn after we enter Forth, to take us onto the Shotts Road (the B-715). Ignore the turn if you need some grub and juice, and carry straight on for the shops, which are

Heading out east to Forth now on the long straight A-706, and just about to reach the big, isolated Harelaw roundabout, which kind of defines the middle of nowhere. Yes, isolated is the word for the houses you see in the photo, and I've absolutely no idea why they were built there.

155

We're getting close to our target town now, and the red rooftops of Forth are seen from quite some distance away as we approach on the long, easy A-706. We are now entering the rough, mining muirs, and the rich agricultural fields will shortly be replaces by rugged-looking sheep fields.

just up the road. The buildings have a hard toughness about them; they would need to have, as this is wild, open country in winter time.

Whilst sitting on the pavement outside one of these shops on my first jaunt through here years ago, I met and spoke with a few interesting locals. It was one of

Looking back at the Lanark Road just as Forth Village is entered, and just before the left turn onto the B-715 Climpy Road is made. This former mining village will be the first of a few former coal mining communities that we will ride through on this stretch, which is just fine as it is the best stretch of the whole run, in my opinion.

these, a bloke who was formerly a plasterer, who told me a bit about the place. He informed me that, yes, Forth had been a mining town, but nowadays what with the lack of employment and all, drugs were now coming in and ruining the area. This is not a problem unique to anywhere, of course. Scratch the surface in any town, city, or village you care to mention, and you'll find that problem lurking just below.

Whether you head for the shops first or not, when you do turn for Shotts, you find yourself on the wonderfully named Climpy Road[19]. A tough-looking housing scheme adorns the Climpy, and the first time I saw the name I wondered why they called the road that. I soon found out it's because that's where it leads to. And it does so in a style that is very much to my liking.

Here we go at last, up into real high moor country, nothing green and pleasant about this land. A wonderful, big, snaking curve in the road leads away north from Forth, and I follow up it in great anticipation.

The barren bleakness will be only background compared to those massive and many big swing'n turbines that have sprouted up on the Blacklaw in recent years. They are already quite visible before you even leave Forth. As you near the crest of the first rise, you pass the Climpy sign and also pass over an old, disused rail line that serviced one of the many mines hereabouts. Climpy is really nothing more than a row of houses – a miners' row, no doubt – and believe it or not, despite their size, number, and close proximity, when the mist comes down, you will not be able to see a single turbine. This is due to the height you are up; 300 metres, that's 900 feet, begads.

Quite an impressive sight the old wind farm makes, I have to concede, but not as impressive as the woodland of Scots pine that you pass next. What can I say? From one extreme to another. This does make for a most unexpected surprise, when all else around is the dreaded sitka spruce. Now we come to a district boundary sign, and if you expected it to say North Lanarkshire, you're in for a bit of a shock. West Lothian's name is displayed, and this is the other indicator of just how far you have come today that I spoke about earlier. Our expedition into Lothian only lasts a mile or so, before we do enter North Lanarkshire, but what a mile it is.

About the best mile in the run, in my opinion. For now, from about the highest point you will be on the

---

19 - The sign says its 6 miles to Shotts.

THE FORTH RUN

Climpy-bound on the B-715.

whole run, you will fire down between broad blankets of conifers. What a swoosh down it is, into a dramatic, almost surreal landscape. If this is a very hot summer's day, and you've been in the saddle for hours, getting dehydrated and thirsty, then you might be forgiven for thinking you are seeing something akin to a desert mirage. For up ahead in the distance appears to be a couple of Egyptian Pyramids. But don't panic, its not Tutankhamun's final resting place, it's just some old pit bings belonging to the former Southfield Colliery near Shotts. Phew! What a scare.

No doubt about it, they are very similar in shape to a pyramid, and what a centrepiece they provide in this bleak, flat canvas. To say this descent and scene lifts your spirits is a total understatement.

You enter North Lanarkshire by the crossing of a small burn known as the kitchen Linn. The next important crossing is almost immediately after, when you carefully

How's this for a contrast? The eyesores that are the wind turbines of Blacklaw Muir right beside that finest of natural occurrences, the Scots pine. Having said that, even the turbines look good when seen in the gorgeous glow of the late evening light here.

This is Climpy. It was a long, easy draw up to here from Forth, and now that you're up the fun can begin. The road ahead is simply magic; despite running through conifer-clad, rough, mining muirs, and therefore not the most picturesque of settings, it's still magic.

dive over the A-71, which seems a rather odd place to find a major A-road. There's just another twist or two along wind-battered lanes, between the bings on a massive, bleak flat, before the Shotts sign and the Springhill Road welcome you into what must have been the Mecca for Scottish mining at one time.

It's a bit of a straggly, disjointed place in a way Shotts, and I think the next part is known as Stane. There are a couple of good wee stores on the Springhill, if you need ought. It has a look of tough, urban edge, this estate, hardly surprising given the setting, and it leads down into the rest of the town by a series of drops and falls, all

The Southfield colliery pit bings of Shotts are first seen when you're still high on the B-715 shortly after leaving Climpy, and you may be surprised to learn that you've crossed into West Lothian District at this point. Despite being mere slag heaps, the pit bings actually make quite a dramatic sight.

The dive through the wild-looking terrain of West Lothian's former coalfields is about to begin here, and it's the best part of the whole run, in my opinion. It's an absolute fire-down screamer of a descent which carries you into North Lanarkshire and over the A-71 as well. Meeting a primary A-road in such a remote place like this, which is full of back roads, does have a strange feel to it.

THE FORTH RUN

Coming into Shotts on the Springhill Road, and boy, does it have a tough and rough look to it. The small general store on the right is handy all the same, and so too is another small store further down on the left. You practically descend all the way down into the town centre from here.

good fun, through the houses and scattered shops, till you arrive at a large roundabout beside a Shell garage. Turn left here, heading for Dykehead, the station, and the prison. In fact, the nick is a very good aid for us here, as that is right in the direction we want to be heading. You know you're on the right road when you pass the station sitting down on the left.

Now, mark my words here and the time if you like, because although I have as near as dammit 50 miles on the clock, with as near as dammit another 30 to go, I can be back home in Paisley in under two hours. This is despite the fact there is a fair wee climb over to Kirk o' Shotts still to come. This is how good and how fast the route back home is, and it starts when we clear the rise through Salsburgh. In the meantime, carry on past the station (if you don't need to jump on the train) and follow the Shottskirk Road round and up, where a left pointing sign keeps you on the right track and also still on the Shottskirk Road.

As we finally clear the last of the houses of Shotts, we pass an enormous factory sporting bright yellow funnels of some sort or another, and then it's a country road climb that takes us up to the junction with the Newmill and Canthill Road. Quite a happening wee road is this one, with a couple of famous residents. The first is right across from you at this point, and that is HMP Shotts. The place caused

On the fall down into Shotts centre, and we want to turn left at the roundabout ahead to take us past the station and onto the Shottskirk Road. Please note another pit bing in the distance.

A view of the modern Shotts Prison is seen here from the climb up and over to Kirk o' Shotts on the Newmill and Canthill Road. You actually come face-to-face with the prison when you reach the end of the Shottskirk Road. What can I say? "Hard luck, lads." Behind, to this day, still sit some pit bings, as I think I am right in saying this used to be the sight of the National Coal Board training centre.

More rough sheep fields are met high up on the Newmill and Canthill Road enroute to Kirk o' Shotts, where a view towards Glasgow can be had on the right day. These are the last of the sheep fields that you meet today, as shortly you drop down into the commercial and urban landscape of North Lanarkshire.

an uproar when the most recent version opened, what with its mod cons (pardon the pun), including heated handrails. People said the regime was too soft and easy on the prisoners. It doesn't have the same hard, old look that Barlinnie does, but at the end of the day it's a nick.

When we turn right, we find ourselves on a toughish wee pull-up through woods and moss-covered walls. It gives a great view back down into the prison, and also shows that there are still a few old pit bings left behind down there as well. 22 mines were sunk in the Shotts area alone, and despite the fact that the last one closed in the 1960s, I'm convinced the old stoor still clings to the landscape courtesy of the bings. From these, it oozes out every chance it gets. If you come this way on a wet winter's day, sure as hell your rims are as black as a chimney sweep's nostrils when you return home.

Not to worry, because you die if you worry and you die if you don't.

Rickety-fenced lined sheep fields are met at the top. The ride through them is high and airy which is just fine. From there we fire down, wary and watchful for lurking potholes, till we are beside the Newmill and Canthill Roads' second famous resident, the Kirk o' Shotts. From 1450, a church has stood on this spot. Originally, it was the Roman Catholic St Catherine's, before it changed hands after the Reformation in 1560. What you see today is the result of the rebuild in 1648. I believe it was under threat of being knocked down a few years back. But, and I'm only guessing here, I think the fact that it was such an important landmark saved the old girl's skin.

And now we turn onto the B-7066. The moment you do you will feel a definite difference in your motion

THE FORTH RUN

It's quite a wee thriller to come after the initial longish and toughish climb up from the prison on the Newmill and Canthill Road. It's a very wooded and pretty climb all the same, and then the fields open everything up and with it come the views. The drop down to Kirk o' Shotts is great fun, but watch out for just a little bit of less than perfect road surface in places on the way down.

and action. Everything seems easier and you get the feeling you have now reached the real turn for home, if not exactly the final furlong. Welcome back onto the fast main roads. First, though, almost immediately there is the rise up between the houses of Salsburgh to be taken, but it is nothing to fear and especially so if you have kept a tail wind for the home run up your sleeve. I get the feeling that before the parallel-running M-8 was constructed, the road we are now on was the former main route through to the east. Again, this would make it another blast from the past from the golden age of motoring.

We're not long in clearing this rise, and as we say goodbye to another small mining town, we now make serious tracks for home. A long, gradual, fast flow down, takes us on our way towards the Newhouse interchange. Back through the same flat, vast country that took us to Forth, only this time we have a lot more gradient on our side, and hopefully a tail wind to gee us along. This is the start of the very speedy return that I promised you right at the start, and if a good taily is blowing, then by God you will be getting a helluva return for next to no effort. This might not be the most stunning landscape you've ever ridden through, but it will be one of the fastest and most fun-filled.

Although the road flattens as it approaches Newhouse, you will still be effortlessly hammering it along, and just so's you know, there is a wee snack bar there if you need it. Despite this being a B-road up until the interchange, quite a few big trucks will have been passing your way, going to God knows where, but this will be nought compared to what you meet when you get through it. On passing through the roundabout, we flip onto the A-775 and have reached serious, and I do mean serious, modern commerce here. The Co-op has got a main distribution depot right beside a Malcolm's yard half the size of Texas. The Terex factory after Malcolm's, is about three-quarters the size of Alaska.

That's just some of the players within Newhouse Industrial Estate that sits beside another perfectly-angled (for our purposes) slope, carrying us to our next settlement of Holytown. It's all change again. We leave behind the open prairie, which was just magic because there was nothing to inhibit our progress whatsoever, and now enter small town main streets. These are magic, too, because they not only give the feeling of speed, but as roundabouts seriously outnumber traffic lights in this quarter, there is also little to suffocate our progress. Unless it is rush hour, that is, when getting past Bellshill can require some unorthodox use of the

Approaching Kirk o' Shotts, and just after we pass it we rejoin more modern roads as the long journey back home begins in earnest. I think this great old landmark was recently saved from demolition, and I'm glad that it was.

You join the B-7066 just after Kirk o' Shotts, and once you do you notice a definite pick up in speed and demeanour as the modern road lets its presence be felt. This is you on the long pull-up through Salsburgh, but once that's cleared then, boy, what a ride home if the wind is behind you.

road and pavement.

So we hit Holytown first, about 2 miles after Newhouse, and fly down through the well-worn Main Street. The

Going down Main Street Mossend and although it's still the same road you're on, it has now become the A-775. You're back into the old industrial heartlands of Lanarkshire big-time here. You can even to this day feel the industrial might of yesteryear still hanging in the air.

good news is the slope that has aided us ever since Salsburgh, will continue to do so right till we reach the far end of Uddingston. This means we are seriously moving right down through the tripartite of settlements, consisting of Holytown, Mossend, and Bellshill. All three

On the road between Salsburgh and Newhouse (still the B-7066), and it's long, straight, downhill, and open all the way. With a tail wind, you will be effortlessly flying on this stretch and also well beyond it, right through Holytown, Bellshill, and even to the far end of Tannochside.

This is the busy, blowy, dusty, and to be honest fairly unpleasant stretch of road between Tannochside and Glasgow's east end, the A-74, and the new M-74 runs beside it nowadays. It doesn't last too long, however, before the relative sanctuary of the London Road is reached (though it's still the A-74) and you're inside the boundaries of dear old Mother Glasgow.

THE FORTH RUN

wear that tough North Lanarkshire garb of small, hardy, brown buildings that hunker down and brave the worst that the harsh Scottish climate can throw at them year after year. Although all three initially were mining towns, they became reliant on the steel industry in more recent times, feeding off the massive Ravenscraig Steel Works in nearby Motherwell till it closed.

In fact, Mossend does still have its big rail freight terminal that you'll see on the right-hand side as you whizz past. It's about here that you'll start to meet numerous roundabouts. These become more intensified as you near Bellshill, where you lose the old main street riding, with more modern roads and their roundabouts taking you away from Bellshill centre, skirting the edge on less charming highways. One is Gartcosh Walk, which brings you past the impressive big Bellshill West Church, not long before you make your way across the huge interchange over the A-725. It is now the A-721 New Edinburgh Road that fires you straight and fast down through the outlying schemes of Uddingston. Its elongated line is followed all the way through to the end.

The old Toon is nearing fast, but first we have to negotiate a bit of no man's land when we unfortunately finally leave our friendly slope and the A-721 behind. The initial stretch on the A-74 is open, busy, noisy, dirty, and gritty. I batter along it as fast as I can, and the same goes for its latter stages, the Hamilton Road. When the major junction at the beginning of Glasgow is reached, go left following the signs for Bridgeton and the City Centre, staying on the A-74. This is you now onto London Road and it gets a lot easier from here on in. Initially it is long, straight, commercial-lined dual carriageway, but traffic is

Celtic Park is approached on the London Road, and it means that you're nearing Glasgow centre. It has been virtually the one road you have been on since you passed Kirk o' Shotts and this has helped maintain a very speedy return. Of all the runs I do, Forth has the fastest return journey by far. It makes it something to look forward to, and you can stay more or less on this one road all the way in to Glasgow Cross, if it suits. I prefer to bank away left at Bridgeton, and cross the Clyde there before returning back to Paisley on Paisley Road West.

a lot lighter and so, too, is the mood.

This style appears seemingly endless at first, and it's not until you start nearing Celtic Park that the east end housing schemes are encountered. Now, if you've read the rest of the runs in the book, you can probably guess my aim here is to make my way towards the start of Paisley Road West to get me home. Being in the city, of course, means there are numerous permutations to do this. However, for expediency, I will tootle along the most direct and straightforward route and allow you to suit yourself when you are returning. From London Road, at the front door of Celtic, continue straight down till you arrive at Bridgeton Cross. This allows you to use a new secure cycle lane on the way there. When you reach the cross, turn left at the underground station and old bandstand. The union flag flies proudly from the orange hall across the road.

From there, turn right onto James Street to begin heading south for Ballater Street and the New Gorbals. Shiny as a new pin are the modern houses of this much maligned scheme. No more the place to avoid, on the contrary, it is a much sought-after residential area now;

if you can afford it, of course. For the record, you're still on the A-74, but officially not for long, because it soon becomes the A-8 even before it carries you through the rough-looking old buildings on Nelson Street. Paisley Road, and then its continuation of Paisley Road West, follow automatically once the M-8 is passed under, and I'm at last on the home straight.

The familiarity of the long avenue westwards is always a welcome sight to this tired rider, who more often than not can't wait to sink his teeth into his Cornish pasty once he gets home. That won't be too long in coming, as I'm only about 8, mostly flat, miles from my front door. The tail wind, if you have one, will fire you right through the tenements of Ibrox and will be a more than welcome hand to help you up and over the Corkerhill rise. As always, tired or not, keep your wits about you at the shops around Berryknowes and Hillington, before clearing the long, gradual rise of Barshaw.

The climbing of the hard, steep, twisting ramp of the Munt, on the way up to Glenburn, signals the end of all the hard work for another day, and the last few yards are used as a warm-down.

And so another long ride comes to an end. A very interesting one, I hope you found. We've not quite finished with that neck of the woods totally yet, but for the next outing we will be heading in a more southerly direction, when we go right into the heart of covenanting country. Hope you can join me for that one, too. So until the next time, as always, stay safe on the bike.

Liam Boy

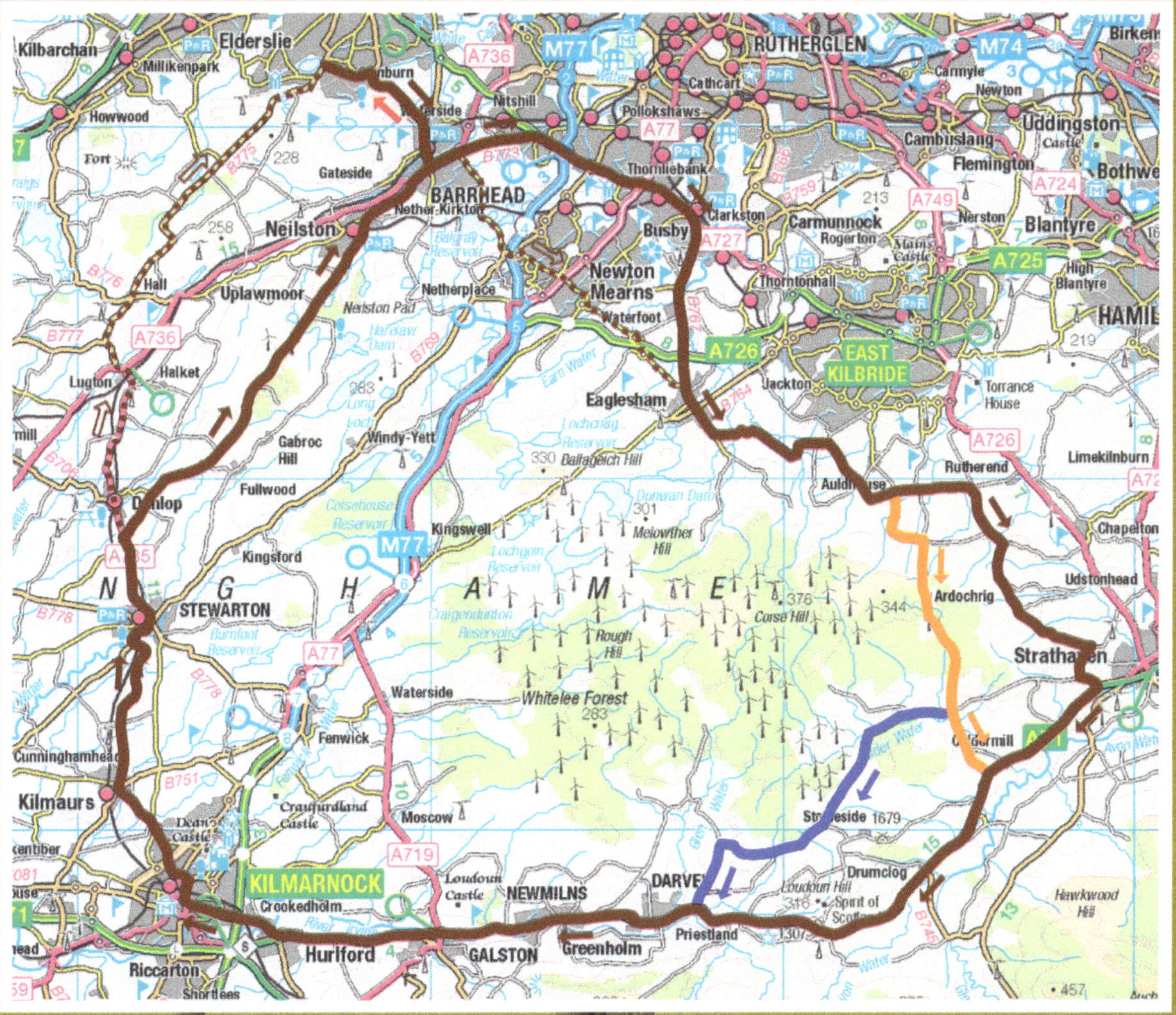

LOUDOUN VALLEY RUN

VIA STRATHAVEN)	(VIA DRUMCLOG)	(VIA DARVEL)
62.7 MILES	57.1 MILES	55 MILES
4.03 HOURS	3.42 HOURS	3.37 HOURS
ASCENT 2720 FEET	ASCENT 2640 FEET	ASCENT 2640 FEET
2668 CALORIES BURNED	2590 CALORIES BURNED	2501 CALORIES BURNED

OS LANDRANGER MAPS 64, 71, 70

ROUTE SUMMARY

Barrhead
A-726
(East Kilbride Rd)
East Wood Toll
Clarkston Toll
Waterfoot
Eaglesham
(Cycle Route)

Auldhouse
Strathaven
A-71 (West)

Drumclog
Darvel
Hurlford
Crookedholm
Kilmarnock
Kilmaurs
Stewarton
Neilston
Barrhead
Paisley

ALTERNATIVE START

Barrhead
Aurs Rd
(Barrhead Dams)
Mearns Cross
Mearnskirk
Humbie Road

DRUMCLOG DIRECT

Ardochrig Rd
Tackshouse Farm
Crossroads

Minor Rd (South)
A-71(West)
Drumclog

DARVEL DIRECT

Minor Rd (West)
High Hareshaw Farm
Underlaw Farm
Darvel

LOUDOUN VALLEY RUN

COVENANTERS COUNTRY

Character, I said character. That is what this run has aplenty. Good, gritty East Ayrshire character at that, with a fair chunk of South Lanarkshire grit thrown in for good measure. That's what we encounter as we make a big sweeping southward arc. One that takes us amongst the high ground between Eaglesham and Strathaven, then over to Kilmarnock on the A-71, going via Darvel and perhaps Drumclog enroute. And as we come very close to the site of a famous Covenanter victory, it's about time I mentioned just what they were all about as well. The jaunt round Kilmarnock centre has a most enjoyable exit, before we return back via Kilmaurs, then Neilston and Barrhead. This brings the run up to about the 60-mile mark.

One word of caution, however, is the busyness of the 71 between Galston and Hurlford. Some may find this just a bit too busy and tight for their liking, and therefore may wish to return via the A-719 when they reach Galston. This puts you back up onto the old A-77 and gives you a choice of either going left or right when you reach that, depending on what suits you best. So, that's what's waiting for us this time out – the ruggedness of the Loudon Valley and the quaint wee towns sitting in its bed. Don't forget your climbing legs, as there is a fair bit of that to do early doors and on the home stretch, too. Ready?

Now, the start for this one is exactly the same as for the previous run to Forth… as far as Eaglesham Village anyway. So once again it is towards Barrhead we make tracks. That means all the upping and downing on the Capplethill Road will make up our early warm up, and that's just peachy. The traffic which has always accompanied us on this stretch will soon be a thing of the past, as they are constructing an extension to the cycle lane at the time of writing[1]. If you've read the Forth run, you will realise what is involved, but if not or you need a recap, then here goes.

---

1 - They started work on the cycle track in January 2014.

Balgray Reservoir is misty and still as the Aurs Road is ridden, heading for Eaglesham via Mearnskirk and the Humbie Road. It is always a treat to ride through the Barrhead Dams, and even the sway of the road adds to the pleasure.

After gaining Main Street, Barrhead, from the Allan's Corner roundabout at the end of Cross Arthurlie Street, you have a choice of two routes to Eaglesham. This choice is upon you when you come to the lights at the junction with Ralston Road at the Arthurlie Club. You can carry straight on and gain Eaglesham via the A-726 main East Kilbride Road, which is the shorter, easier, though much busier option. Or you can turn right and, by going through Auchenback, gain the Aurs Road, which will carry you through the dams and up into Newton Mearns. After the short hop over to Mearnskirk, Eaglesham is gained via the Humbie Road. This is the tougher, slightly longer, but quieter and more scenic approach. As we went by the dams first the last time, we'll nip along the East Kilbride road first this time round.

EAGLESHAM VIA A-726

Carry on down the Main Street in Barrhead to the Dovecoathall roundabout, and take the second exit onto the Darnley/Parkhouse Road. The end of this meets the A-726 bound for East Kilbride. Turn right onto the busy dual carriageway, which will remain so as it slowly climbs past, but stays detached from, Arden, Darnley, and Thornliebank. Only once through the big Eastwood Toll roundabout and onto the Eastwood Mains Road does it become single carriageway, as you then get up close and personal with glorious Giffnock. Coming up, though, is Clarkston Toll, where the usual life or death dash across this real busy roundabout must be made.

Then you can breathe a bit easier, especially when you get through the next roundabout coming up, which is the Sheddens.

On this occasion, we are not taking the first left for East Kilbride, but are going straight ahead onto the B-767 and making a beeline for Eaglesham. You're in for a treat on this one, because it is one long, bolt straight, flat, fabulous road ahead of you now. When you finally pass Williamwood High School, after running the long length of the bungalows, you're into East Renfrewshire's rural quaintness. The farms and fields just keep coming, as you purr along serenely. It's only when passing through wonderful Waterfoot, right by the banks of the River White Cart, that the long, straight line of the road gets broken. But that's only temporary, for normal service is resumed the moment you start to head out of the village.

Once again, you're on a great long length of tar, which is aided and abetted by a sensational stone wall running most of its length. Rich fields and moo cows on the right, and rich homes on the left, along with a slow speed limit the entire length of the 767, makes it all calm and surreal to ride from start to finish. The big Belle Craig

Just approaching the end of Balgray Reservoir, where the Aurs Road is at its very best in just the way it double bends away from the dams and lifts you up into Newton Mearns.

LOUDOUN VALLEY RUN

The Barrhead Dams and Humbie Road aren't the only way to get to Eaglesham. It can also be accessed by first of all heading for Clarkston Toll and then taking the B-767 Eaglesham Road that will run you long and straight to the village. This takes you through bonny Waterfoot enroute. Despite its long, flat, and straight demeanour, it is quite an interesting road in its own right.

roundabout supporting the bypass must nowadays be rounded, before shortly entering Eaglesham itself. As you do enter, the Humbie Road feeds in from the right-hand side, and this, too, can be used to gain the village thus far.

EAGLESHAM VIA THE HUMBIE RD

If you don't fancy the hustle and bustle of the main road approach, then by all means treat yourself to a wee trip up through the Barrhead Dams. From the Main Street at the Arthurlie Club, turn right, then left, and head up Arthurlie Avenue, before climbing up and enjoying the great Glasgow views on Fenwick Drive. The end of this carries you conveniently onto Aurs Road and it's a tough wee pull-up to reach the reservoirs. The sensational swerve through them is followed by a more modern drop and long rise to Mearns Cross. A left/right quick one-two, finds you speeding along the Eaglesham Road and arriving at Mearnskirk. Another quick one-two, right/left this time, finds the start of the Humbie, and the very accurate direction sign informs you it's 2¾ miles to Eaglesham.

On reaching the village, you of course meet up with the other route and then drop prettily down to the old centre crossroads on Gilmour Street. Now, on the last run you might remember I didn't advise carrying straight on and using the back roads between here and Strathaven, as they were too windy and time-consuming when doing the 80-mile run to Forth. However, not only is this run at least 20 miles shorter, but also by using these back roads, which are also part of the national cycle route, you run very conveniently onto the best way to Drumclog and Darvel. So, this time I thoroughly do recommend going straight on at the crossroads, and following the signs for Strathaven when you do.

As I've said before, expect to be charmed by this village centre with its beautiful old black and white-painted buildings. Also in the last run, I mentioned how the village had been planned out by the 10th Earl of Eglington and how he had made a bloody good job of it. The Earl was a Montgomery, who has a street named after him. It's the one that runs off the crossroads to the right and takes

The old quaint crossroads signpost in Eaglesham points us in the right direction, which will take us to Strathaven via the Auldhouse back roads. Whitewashed and pretty, the village is always a treat to ride through, and within the graveyard of the church in the picture is a memorial to two Covenanting martyrs.

you onto the wonderful Eaglesham Moor Road. The local parish church sits on this road, just up on the left, and within it is a lovely wee graveyard containing a memorial stone. This stone is dedicated to two men, Robert Lockart and Gabriel Thompson, who were executed in 1685 for attending a Covenanters' conventicle – an illegal open air church service.

It's hardly surprising, as Renfrewshire, Lanarkshire, and Ayrshire were Covenanting strongholds. All around Eaglesham are places where these conventicles took place. Nearby Picketlaw was so named after the guards or pickets that were strategically placed to act as lookouts while a conventicle took place. The two executed men had the misfortune to meet with Stuart Dragoons as they were returning from one such conventicle. The dragoons, along with about another 6000 Highlanders, had been brought down from the Highlands and placed in the south west, sometimes lodging with suspected Covenanting families, to prevent illegal gatherings taking place.

This was during a period known as the killing time, when on-the-spot executions were carried out. The superior Government forces didn't get it all their own way all the time, as we shall shortly discover, but first we have to get over to Drumclog Hamlet to find out about that. We do that by carrying on at the Gilmour Street crossroads, where we get our first real look at the moorland to the south of Eaglesham. That is exactly where we are heading, but not on this road as it is a dead end. So, we must resort to the back roads for Strathaven first. The road sign says 10 miles to there. The cycle route sign says it's 9! Whichever it is, it's a lot of jinking about in anyone's book.

It starts off good fun, though, with a long drop down to Millhall Farmstead, and a delightful hop over the Ardoch Burn sets us up for more of the same. More of the same exactly, for shortly there will be an almost identical scenario when we cross the Threepland Burn at Millhouse Farm and make our way along the Millhall Road. Jumping over these beautiful wee brooks on beautiful wee bridges is a great way to go anywhere. Some open-field riding carries us between the two, and then some more on the gradual rising Shields Road brings us to the T-junction with the Burnhouse Road. All places in all directions are well signposted here, and we want right to stay on the correct course.

Fast and flowing is your isolation on this road, for about a mile or so, till you meet the Auldhouse Road at the next

Crossing over the Polnoon Water at Millhall, shortly after entering into the myriad of single-track back roads between Eaglesham and Strathaven. This particular spot is a very pretty one and quiet, too, as you are now following the national cycle route.

junction. All is open and hedgerow up to here, and will continue to be so for the duration of your ride through the Auldhouse back roads, call them what you will. As for Auldhouse Road itself, you're hardly on it when you're off it. That's because in no time at all you meet a pretty wee Y-junction, which again is well signposted, and we go left up the ramp and onto the Millwell Road. There's a big swing required to take you round past Raahead Farm[2], whose dairy herd might be lined up, close enough to touch in their trough, and who will spontaneously and wholeheartedly moo at your efforts.

The more egotistical amongst you will no doubt feel buoyed up by this attention, as you find yourself once again on the long, straight section of the Millwell. This is the one that will run you straight as a die for a couple of miles onto the East Kilbride Road, should you so wish that. That was the way we went when heading for Forth. This time, however, we want to follow the arrows

---

2 - A slight word of caution here as the road surface is pretty poor and muddy on this stretch.

LOUDOUN VALLEY RUN

for the cycle route. That will either be the one at Laigh Cleughearn Farm or the one a mile or so down the road at Millwell Farm.

It all depends on how you wish to tackle the Loudoun Valley that will determine whether you take the first right at Laigh Cleughearn or the third right at Millwell. That's because you can either ride the entire length of the Loudoun Valley low down on the A-71 all the way from Strathaven to Kilmarnock, or cut out Strathaven altogether by heading onto the high ground which sits right above you to the south at this point and take a more direct line for Drumclog, or even Darvel for that matter. This will also cut out a lot of the early A-71, which although a great road to ride, it is still an A-road and some may wish to avoid that as much as they can. It isn't overly busy, the 71 – well, not till you get to Galston – but quite a lot of heavy lorries use it, and that can be a little unnerving for some.

Strathaven and the A-71 aren't the only way to reach Drumclog, if you come through the Auldhouse back roads. You can also use the great Ardochrig Road, which you join from the Millwell Road, to climb high and quietly up to the Whitelee Forest. Carry straight on at the crossroads past Tackhouse Farm, which then takes you more directly to the A-71 just east of the village.

There are three main routes that I generally use when doing this run. The first is, as already mentioned, to head for Strathaven via the back roads,[3] and then run the whole length of the A71 to Hurlford. The other two routes use the Ardochrig Road to begin with, which avoids Strathaven completely, as it is a shortcut over to the Loudoun Valley. But once up on the Whitelee Moor past high Tackhouse Farm, the routes split. One branches off right for Darvel, staying on the high back roads for some considerable time and missing out about half the riding on the A-71. The other, the Drumclog route, sort of splits the other two in the middle and gives both a taste of the high ground riding and also the early and most dramatic part of the 71.

Now, take it from me, all three routes are great and have their own special charms. However, as far as I can tell, the Darvel route seems to be the most popular choice for bike riders, though I'm only gauging that by the amount of riders I meet on the road. I assume that they actually do drop down to Darvel, because it is possible to ride the length of the Loudoun on the high farm roads till you reach the A-719, which as previously stated will run you up to the old A-77. I don't use that way on this run myself, but do so on the next one, and I will describe it in that outing.

In the meantime, I will describe the three routes I normally use when riding the Loudoun Valley, covering Strathaven first, and it goes without saying that I recommend you try all three to see what suits you best. So now we must return to our last stated position beside Leigh Cleughearn Farm, on the Millwell Road, amongst the Auldhouse back roads.

STRATHAVEN

If you intend to go via Strathaven, it's best not to turn right at Laigh Cleughearn Farm. Instead, carry straight on down the Millwell Road for just over a mile till you reach Millwell Farm itself, and turn right there. For although it is possible to reach Strathaven by turning right at Laigh Cleughearn, the road over from the crossroads at Skeoch Farm to Cladance Farm is simply bloody awful. There's no other way to describe it. By going via Millwell, you will avoid that stretch. And although the Millwell way isn't exactly perfect itself[4], it's a damn sight better. So it's best to fire straight down through little Leaburn and hang a right at the farm, where a blue cycle route direction sign aids your way.

So far so good, and it's going to get better. Now begins a long draw up into the flat, still, quiet high fields around the Cairnduff Farms. Whenever you need one, like when you reach the split in the road at Dykehead Farm, you will find a welcome, strategically-placed, wee blue sign to

---

3 - You can, of course, use the main A-726 to access Strathaven, if you so wish.

4 - Even that road just before Cladance Farm at one point is about 98% crater, 2% tarmac. You have been warned.

Passing the Nether Lethame Farm duck pond, just before the long drop down into Strathaven is started. The sight of this wee pond always delights me, and just for the record you are still on the national cycle route.

keep you on the right road. This is necessary up here, as there is nothing else to guide you.

The road meanders most pleasantly between North and High Cairnduff Farms, before the beautiful, long, beech hedgerows at South Cairnduff run you back out into the open fields. You can see the vehicles on the main A-726 away to the east at this point, and also the orange windsock from Strathaven Airfield fluttering perhaps on your right.

Another blue direction sign, sitting under an overhanging Scots pine at the end of a line of glorious big beech trees, tells you to turn right. This takes you past Nether Lethame Farm with its lovely wee duck pond, leading you onto the lovely Lethame Road itself. This provides an indication of what to expect in picturesque Strathaven, as you fall down a most beautiful street, passing homes of quality and looks. John Hastie Park sits close to the bottom of the Lethame. Hastie was a local grocer and businessman who made good, and left the town not only the park but also a great wee museum that sits close to the bottom of the Lethame Road, too[5]. It is housed in a delightful old building that was built in 1915, so says the ornate plaque high on the wall.

Unfortunately, it appears to be closed at the moment, with no indication when, if at all, it will open again. Now this is a pity, because the museum told not only of Strathaven's past, but also about the Battle of Drumclog in 1659. We have still to reach that small strong

---

5 - If you turn left at the bottom of Lethame Road onto the Threestanes Road, the museum sits just along on the right.

Covenanter enclave, but will do so shortly. As you will find out, Strathaven and its inhabitants also played an important role in that monumental day. Perhaps this early militancy was what encouraged some of the town's inhabitants to rebel almost 200 years later in 1821, in what became known as the "Uprising that never was" or the Radical War[6]. One local man, James Wilson, was hanged for his insurrection and this was linked to the armed clash that I spoke about in the Falkirk run, that took place up on the Bonnymuir above Bonnybridge.

Once in and about Strathaven centre, the tight, narrow, old streets charm every inch of the way, and we immediately pick up Townhead Street (after turning right at the lights at the bottom of Lethame) and start to run out west. The bright orange façade of the Bucks Head Hotel is typical of Strathaven and just beyond it, meeting the big white road sign and mini roundabout means you've joined the A-71. Long, flat, and straight into the bargain, this big girl stretches out in front of you as you pick up speed quite noticeably after spending so long on the back roads[7]. And now begins in earnest the 20 or so miles (approximately) over to Kilmarnock.

Straight away you will notice the wonderful Muirkirk Road breaking off away to the left. At the same time, the first in a series of wonderful bridges are seen, these

Just about to enter Strathaven by coming down the long, dropping Lethame Road, and it makes for a fine, fast entry into this very well-to-do looking village. The centre has a feeling of hustle and bustle about it, but it's still pretty and quaint all the same. You will really enjoy this descent.

---

6 - The Radical War was a workers' uprising and had nothing to do with religion.

7 - To be honest with you, if you intend to go via Strathaven, then I recommend using the main A-726 as opposed to the back roads, as it is the quicker, slicker option.

LOUDOUN VALLEY RUN

Sitting at the traffic lights right at the bottom of the Lethame Road, after coming in with quite a swoop, and looking across into Common Green which is the centre of the village. There is plenty in there if you need anything, but if not then simply turn right, which will run you out onto the A-71 for Kilmarnock.

belonging to the old Strathaven to Darvel rail line that closed in 1939, and this will be your constant companion along the way for a while. The 71 won't stay a straight, boring road for long, I'm happy to say, because she starts to bend, dip, curve, and dance her way westwards very shortly, and will continue to do so from time to time. As she does, she carries you through quite a rich flat plain, with the added interest of the hills to the south making a splendid backdrop. There now comes a slight dip down over the Calder Water and then a rise through tiny Caldermill thereafter.

Just as you cross the Calder, you will see a real old relic of a road bridge to your right, showing that it isn't just the rail bridges in this valley that are show-stoppers, though there is one of those just downstream at this point as well. Now, just after you leave Caldermill, you will see a great road sweeping down off the high moor from the right, which then joins the A-71. This road is a continuation of the Ardochrig Road, which can be used to get here from the Millwell Road at Laigh Cleughearn Farm near Auldhouse, and thus avoids Strathaven altogether. It is a much more direct route to Drumclog or even Darvel, if you should so wish.

DRUMCLOG – DARVEL

Now it's fair to say that the best way to do this run, and as far as I can tell the most popular, is not to make tracks for Strathaven, but instead gain the high ground lying to the south of the Loudoun Valley by climbing up on the great Ardochrig Road from the Millwell. You can either turn right at the farmstead of Laigh Cleughearn or take the next right onto the start of the Ardochrig itself; it doesn't really matter. Both roads will meet when they reach the crossroads at the big, white sprawling Skeoch Farm. Continue to climb up on this slim slither of grey tar, getting ever higher and wilder, towards the wind turbines and conifers that dominate the moor above.

Ever more wild and scatty gets the landscape the higher you go, and although it's predominately a long, easy draw, the Ardochrig, it does steepen just before it tops out at the Whitelee Forest. Congratulations, you're up! Now it's time to enjoy a great, but barren-looking jaunt along a road that has recently been tarred, and glides and curves wonderfully. Pylons and pines aplenty, though not much else is up here. There is a great wee bridge to take you over the Little Calder, though, and when you do emerge from the quite extensive forest, you get a good open field view, just before the short, steep pull-up to the highly-perched Tackshouse Farm.

Only just beyond this, you come to a crossroads and it's make-your-mind-up time again. You can go straight ahead and join the A-71 before Drumclog and run the majority of the main road, or you can turn right and stay high all the way to Darvel. Although Darvel is quieter and more popular, Drumclog by the 71 is a great way to go, too.

No country back road this, it's the A-71 taking us west from Strathaven – noticeably fast, if you've just emerged from the single-track cycle route roads. The 71, although it looks straight and bare here, actually curves and entertains far more than you would imagine, before you reach Drumclog.

173

DRUMCLOG DIRECT

So, from the crossroads past Tackshouse, continue straight on, dropping down and over the Calder Water, and enjoy the sight of its wonderfully carved-out valley. The rise up the other side takes you first past North then South Brownhill Farms. The latter has a most wonderful, large, and busy duck pond. This is followed by a great, leafy-lane ride, which ends with the final fantastic swoop down to meet the A71 on the Loudoun Valley's high floor. "That was the business", no two ways, as they say. We now rejoin the Strathaven route, and with our tails well up, continue to follow the 71 west.

And well it leads us, with more jinking and dancing along so merrily, taking us shortly into the hamlet of Drumclog. The beautiful parish church holds court right on the main road, and inside its grounds are the remains of a memorial stone that once stood on High Drumclog Moor, before it was damaged by lightning and moved here. The stone was erected in 1839 and commemorates a battle that took place on Sunday, the 1st of June, 1679, between local Covenanters and Government troops, under the command of one Captain John Graham of Claverhouse.

He was later to become known as "Bonnie Dundee" to fellow Jacobites, when he took up the fight for the Stuart cause after the invasion by William of Orange. But he was known as "Bluidy Clavers" by the Covenanters, who he was sent into the Southwest to suppress. So, just who were the Covenanters, and why were they being so brutally treated? Incredibly, they were merely Scottish Presbyterians, who took their name from the covenant signed by Israel in the Old Testament, and who only wanted to pray in their own manner. The problem was that they were defying the King, Charles II, whose father Charles I had laid down a different liturgy[8] (prayer book), and therefore it was a capital offence to defy the King.

This had not always been the case; far from it. Ever since the Reformation of 1560, the Protestants had for the most part held sway in Scotland. However, due to outside Catholic threats from France or Anglican threats from England, it was felt or deemed necessary for Presbyterians to sign an oath or covenant to uphold their religion, and to act and do whatever was necessary to protect their faith. The first one was signed in 1557 and was known as the Lords of the Congregation. This was as a direct result of a fear of becoming a mere province of France, after the infant Mary Stuart (later Mary Queen of Scots) was shipped off to France in a political deal.

The second covenant was signed in 1581, and this was more to counter any English takeover of the Kirk[9]. This was the most important covenant and was known as the King's Confession, or better still, the National Covenant. A third covenant, signed much later in 1643, was really a treaty between Scotland and England. The reason this came about was because the Covenanters had been requested to provide military aid for their Presbyterian brethren amongst the English Parliamentarians, who had lost the first civil war to Charles I and his Royalists. This the Scots agreed to do, so long as their religious ways were adopted south of the border.

It was this meddling in England's religious affairs that was to cost the Covenanters dearly in the long run. For although the army they sent south in 1643 helped defeat Charles and put the Parliamentarians in charge, it ultimately led to them falling out and fighting with their former allies, who by this time were under the command of Oliver Cromwell and his New Model Army. He, as they were to find out, really wasn't the man you wanted to be facing. This was indeed most ironic, because it was Charles I who had been the enemy of them both in the first place, and the man who in 1637 had kicked off the recent trouble with his insistence on issuing the Scots with a new prayer book. It was this meddling by Charles in the Kirk's affairs that began the initial hostilities.

It came about because in 1637 Charles was King of both England and Scotland, and head of the Church of England but not the Church of Scotland. When he tried to introduce a new prayer book north of the border, he met fierce resistance. His aim was to try and retain the old traditional Anglican ways, to bring about a uniform way of preaching in both his kingdoms, and thus supress any rise in Protestantism by both the Puritans in England and the Presbyterians in Scotland. The Scots decided to revive the old national Covenant from 1581 when they felt the threat, and raised an army which defeated Charles in what became known as the War of the Bishops in 1640.

---

8 - Liturgy is a definite and proscribed way of public worship. The Covenanters preferred to use their own style and prayer book, as opposed to the one which was forced upon them by both Charles I and II.

9 - John Knox had died in 1572, so the Kirk had lost its captain, so to speak, and may have felt vulnerable due to this.

LOUDOUN VALLEY RUN

This was a slow burning catalyst to the Civil Wars in Scotland, England, and Ireland[10]. In Scotland, the Covenanters faced the Charles-supporting Royalist Catholic and Episcopalian forces, who were led by the dashing and able James Graham, 1st Marquis of Montrose. He was supported by Highland clans and Irish troops under the command of Alasdair Mac Colla. Although the Royalists had numerous early victories, mostly due to Montrose's leadership and the Irish soldiers fighting ability over hastily arranged and makeshift Covenanter forces, they were finally defeated in 1645 at Philiphaugh near Selkirk. The Civil War in Scotland lasted three years, ending in 1647.

Charles lost his head in January 1649, but not before he sent his son (who would later become Charles II) away to the safety of France. The future should have been rosy for the Covenanters. They had been the de facto Government in Scotland for 13 years from 1638 to 1651, under Archibald Campbell, 1st Marquis of Argyll. They now had their brothers-in-arms, the Parliamentarians (Roundheads), in charge in England. However, they distrusted the English, and this would lead to all-out war between the two. The Covenanters agreed a deal with the exiled Charles II, who was 20 years old at the time and by now residing in Breda in the Netherlands[11].

This was a most unlikely alliance[12] in which the Scots would fight for his cause to get him back on the throne, if he would implement and support their Covenant. Charles agreed to this, as he thought it the only way he could regain the throne. This was really a marriage of convenience. Charles sailed to Scotland and landed in June 1650, but they were defeated by Cromwell at the Battle of Dunbar in September of that year, which weakened the Covenanters' power. Any power they had left was totally destroyed with the defeat at Worcester in September 1651, exactly a year after Dunbar. Charles was lucky to escape to France. Cromwell now occupied southern Scotland, and the Kirk lost all its civil powers as the country was forced into a temporary union with England.

However, the worst was yet to come for the Covenanters, because after the turmoil that was caused by Cromwell's death[13], Charles II was restored to the throne in May 1660.[14] He turned against his former allies, who fought so gamely for him at Worcester, by outlawing the Covenant oaths in 1662 and reinstated episcopacy. He also appointed the unpopular James Sharp as Archbishop of St. Andrews. Any Protestant ministers who refused to recognise the Episcopal Bishops were outlawed, and it was these rebel ministers who began to preach in secret at the open air conventicles. Charles cracked down on them harshly, fearing the Covenanters would organise and rebel against him.

When Charles met John Graham (Bluidy Clavers/Bonnie Dundee), he was immediately taken by him, which allowed Graham to rise quickly through the ranks. It was he (Graham) who Charles trusted with quelling any unrest in the Southwest. There was some rebellion in 1666 which ended in what became known as the Pentland Rising, but this was more a reaction to the harsh measures the people were facing than anything else. Most Covenanters still professed a loyalty to the King and simply wanted to pray in their own way. It was against this backdrop that people made their way to High Drumclog for a conventicle on that first Sunday in June 1679, little realising they were about to witness history.

Admittedly, there had been a couple of major unsettling incidents just before Drumclog that did greatly heighten tension. The first was the murder of Archbishop James Sharp on Magus Moor[15] just outside of St Andrews, by a group of Covenanters in April that year. Barely a month later, Sir Robert Hamilton led 70 armed horsemen[16] into Rutherglen, and denounced and then burned all Acts passed by the Government and Privy Council since 1660.[17] On hearing of this, John Graham – who was at Falkirk at the time – was furious and intended to make the Covenanters pay for such an affront.

The Rutherglen Declaration took place on the 29th May of that month, only two days before the Drumclog

---

10 - This was the Confederate War.

11 - This would become known as the Treaty of Breda.

12 - Morally they were poles apart.

13 - He died on the 3rd of September, 1658.

14 - This was on his 30th birthday.

15 - Sharp had this coming. He offered mercy to 6 Covenanters at the Pentland Rising, only to go back on his word and have them killed when they surrendered.

16 - At least two of the men with him had been at Magus Moor.

17 - This became known as the Rutherglen Declaration.

conventicle was due to take place. It appears that Bluidy Clavers had been tipped off about the prayer meeting and that's why he headed for Strathaven. Now, there are various accounts about what happened next, but I'm inclined to believe the one that I read when I was in the John Hastie Museum in Strathaven. In there were the very swords that were used in the battle, and also an account of how Bonnie Dundee and his men stayed overnight in the town before launching their attack the next day. Although this smacks of arrogance by Graham and also a bit of naivety, I am inclined to believe he did.

The reason I do so is because it seems that the Covenanters were aware that Graham was going to attack them, as they, too, had been tipped off in advance. The people of Drumclog and Strathaven were very close, not only in distance but also in belief. The tip-off would have come from the townspeople of Strathaven, who would have known the reason for his overnight stay. The congregation at High Drumclog were not taken by surprise by his arrival, far from it. The preacher that day was one Thomas Douglas, already a wanted man with a price on his head[18]. When a shot fired by a lookout warned them of Dundee's approach, he famously finished his sermon with the words, "Well, you have had the theory, now you are going to have the practice. You know your duty, self defence is always lawful."

If John Graham had expected to find them praying, he was in for a shock. The King's men were about 150 in number, on horseback, and well armed with musket and pike. The Covenanters were about double that number, but mostly poorly armed with makeshift weapons and only 50 on horseback. They were led by Robert Hamilton. However, they knew the terrain well and very cleverly took up a good strategic defensive position behind an awkward marshy bog. This made it difficult for the King's men to engage them properly. After a few early skirmishes, a flanking movement by the Covenanters – led by William Cleland – came round and engaged the dragoons. Despite coming under heavy fire from the King's men, they pressed home their attack.

From his vantage point, Graham could see his men being routed, and sent in his cavalry. This was a mistake, as they soon became hindered by the bog. Realising his chance for victory was gone, Graham actually offered the Covenanters a flag of truce, which was rejected out of hand. In the ensuing turmoil, John Graham, Captain of the King's men – the one and only Bluidy Clavers, scourge of the Covenanters – was lucky to escape with his life. They almost got him when William Cleland grabbed his horse's bridle and another man, farmer Thomas Findlay, speared his horse with a pike. However, Dundee forced his horse on and managed to get away.

Respite was short-lived for the troops, however. For when they reached what they thought was the sanctuary of Strathaven, they came under attack again. Dundee again had to flee, as even more of his men were killed there.[19] A great day for the Covenanters was over, and this unexpected victory did begin an uprising of sorts. This was short-lived, however, when they were heavily defeated a few weeks later at the Battle of Bothwell Bridge. This was mainly due to them spending more time fighting amongst themselves, as opposed to preparing for the inevitable counterattack. As we pass through Bothwell on the next run, I will cover that battle in more detail then.

I want to end this rather long history lesson, if I may, by saying a few words about John Graham of Claverhouse, Bonnie Dundee, or Bluidy Clavers, call him what you will. He was a major player in the Covenanting Wars and is often portrayed as a man who went about his business with a ruthless streak. However, his personal letters at the time show this to be anything but the case, as he often asked for leniency to be shown to captured Covenanters. I also heard a story that he actually left his wedding reception, which was being held in Paisley, to break up a conventicle that was taking place nearby at the time. This attempt was unsuccessful, they say. However, he actually married Lady Jean Cochrane, who was from a very strong local Covenanter family[20]. So I find it hard to believe that the wedding day incident is true.

With that one left hanging in the air, we are at last back to the run in hand, which will see us flying out the other side of bonnie wee Drumclog. And when we do, we find the road sign saying 5 miles to Darvel and 15 to Kilmarnock. Fast and straight, that's what follows, till a curving wooded section is met. Through the trees the wonderful silhouette of Loudoun Hill is spied, it helping to add to the already rugged character of the surrounding countryside. It's hardly surprising, as you are up over

---

18 - There was a price of 3000 Scots Merks on his head.

19 - The dragoons lost 36 men at Drumclog and another 12 in Strathaven.

20 - They were the Cochranes from Johnstone.

LOUDOUN VALLEY RUN

Just about to enter Drumclog, which still has an air of historical importance about it for such a small place. To this very day, on the first Sunday in June, the local kirk – whose tower can be seen in the photo – still holds a service to commemorate the Covenanter victory that took place near here in 1679.

200 metres high at this point, on a great wee stretch of road known as the Windy Wizen. It's wonderful up here, where the pyramid-shaped volcanic plug of Loudoun shows its rocky south face close up.

You only really become aware of the height you are up when you begin the great swoop into the head of the Irvine Valley. This at first takes you down to the white and isolated Loudoun Hill Hotel, across from which can be seen the remains of a once great rail bridge that spanned a road. It breaks my heart to see these things gone and removed. A second swoop down brings you into the village of Priestland, which nowadays is merely an eastern extension of Darvel. A gentle curve down its main street, dotted in delight in places, brings you right onto the banks of the River Irvine below. A short flow takes you to the Darvel name sign.

When you reach it, if you take a look to your right, you will see a steep brae coming down the hill. This is the way you will arrive if you decide to stay high when you reach the crossroads just after Tackshouse Farm. It will allow you to avoid a lot of the A-71, as you ride high in the valley, and also gives great views of Loudoun Hill on the way down.

DARVEL DIRECT

When you reach the crossroads just after Tackshouse, instead of going straight on for Drumclog, turn right if you intend to make directly for Darvel. Right away, you find yourself on some fine, wild moor road riding, as the road caresses the rough pastures right beside the meandering Calder Water. You soon cross it on a fine old bridge, as you get ever higher and drawn up towards the West Browncastle wind farm, now with enough turbines to power NASA. They won't spoil your fun too much, for if you're like me, you'll be in your element by now as you hit the long, narrow straight up towards Hareshawhill Farm. It ain't pretty, that's for sure, just conifers, turbines, and pylons, but the road is good and the height is good and eventually you flip over into the Loudoun itself. A great swerve down past the farm at Fore Hareshaw,[21] leads into mega-rough windswept terrain, through which you manoeuvre. The great rear views of Loudoun Hill do somewhat compensate for the scantiness that surrounds you.

On the A-71 here, heading west and just about to cross the boundary from Lanarkshire into Ayrshire, where you get your first glimpse today of the striking Loudoun Hill. You are also quite high up on this stretch of the A-road, which is wonderfully named.

"Never mind the quality, feel the bloody width," that's what I say, as it's a long marvellous drop all the way to Darvel to come, and then some. I always take the next left turn, though you can go straight on and finish up in the same place. In fact, you can use these back roads to avoid any contact with the A-71 completely. It would require a lot of meandering and perhaps either a good look at the maps or a bit of trial and error, but it can be done.

I prefer to drop down to Darvel, and that's how I will take you on this run. When you make the left

---

21 - A left turn at this farm will lead to the actual sight of the Battle of Drumclog, which is marked by another monument which was put there in 1839 to replace the one hit by lightning.

At the beginning of the long descent down into the Loudoun Valley towns from the high ground, and this very long drop is another highlight of the run. You can not only see the change of terrain round about you, but also how the valley itself opens up away towards the coast in the distance.

On the final approach into Priestland then Darvel, after the long and glorious descent down on the A-71, which is a rather fine and dramatic fall, I might add. It's all change now, because you go from the windswept, barren, high moorland onto the valley floor with its continuous procession of small settlements.

turn, you will immediately notice a much richer feel to the landscape as you fly down this narrow lane past Underlaw Farm. This richness is supported by the quilted patchwork of fields facing you on the slopes on the southern side of the valley.

Be ready for the severe sweeping bend at the bottom of this straight, which carries you round and onto another great straight that runs parallel with the valley floor. You incidentally get a great view of the A-71 on the way down, and also a good look at all the valley's dips and rises as you make your way along here. Simply batter right through the wee crossroads ahead and you soon find yourself firing down the ramp-like finish to the back roads. You'll arrive at the Darvel sign on the A-71 with both hands on the brake levers.

This is all three routes back together again, and there will be no more splitting of the route from now on.

Welcome to the Lang Toon. Quite an appropriate name, you will find. It has to be said that a lot of the houses that line the Main Street are a brown or drab grey colour, and it gives a rather oppressive look to the place.

The area was also known for its lace-making – an industry that was brought to this valley in a big way by a man called Alex Morton. There is a monument to him as you leave the town. Numerous mills produced the lace which was sent worldwide, especially to India, until the demise of the industry was all but complete by the late 70s. Despite the worldwide market, Alex isn't the town's most famous son, not by a long way. That accolade belongs to Alexander Fleming, he of penicillin fame. He's even got his face on the fivers! More upmarket, middle class housing takes over just before you leave Darvel, on a toughish wee climb. This allows views back down to the valley floor, in what must be the Irvine Valley at its narrowest.

It's only a short, green hop over to Newmilns, and the height gained when leaving Darvel allows a delightful drop into a town of quite different character. The gentle, curving fall in soon reveals an aged town just oozing with charm, and with buildings that are so old you could be forgiven for wondering what century you're in. There's the black and white Loudoun Arms Hotel from the 18th century, along with the little white kirk, with its bell tower

Just like Drumclog, the A-71 isn't the only way to reach Darvel, because a high-level moorland approach can also be used to reach this town. When you get to Tackhouse Farm, after climbing high on the Ardochrig Road, don't carry straight on at the crossroads. Instead, turn right and follow the road up past the Calder Water, which is seen in the picture, and continue on past the Whitelee wind farm. This takes you very high along the south side of the valley, before dropping you down very dramatically to the very start of Darvel itself on the Kirkland Road. This is, in my opinion, the best route of them all.

LOUDOUN VALLEY RUN

Loudoun Hill is seen beyond Fore Hareshaw Farm as the descent down into the valley begins. It's all fun from hereon in, such is the reward for all the hard climbing that's gone before.

and stepped gable ends. These are just two of the many that are crammed into ye olde town centre here. There is the layout of the town to be taken into consideration as well. Some houses seem to sit high on raised ground just as you begin to leave town – a most unusual sight, and one that reminds me of coastal regions.

There is also a strong early Protestant presence attached to Newmilns, as French Huguenot refugees settled here in the late 1500s and introduced weaving to the town. The star man, however, has to be local farmer Murdoch Nisbet, who around 1520 was the first man to produce the New Testament in the Scots language. At the time, it was illegal for any layman to own a bible, and this crime was actually punishable by death. Murdoch had to flee the country, though he did return in time. He had relatives who were at both Drumclog and Bothwell Brig, along with many others from Newmilns.

You leave Newmilns by a council estate, and find yourself well and truly anchored to the valley floor from now on. Not only that, but the Irvine Valley starts to open up big time, and you are no longer in any rural landscape. You've hit the built-up and least charming

Loudoun Hill looks fabulous from near High Drumclog. The hill itself is the centrepiece of this whole area, and never fails to impress from any angle.

There is still on High Drumclog Muir a memorial to the battle that took place here in June 1657, though you have to double back from Fore Hareshaw Farm to see it. This monument replaced the original that was struck by lightning; though some of the original can still be seen inside the grounds of Drumclog Parish Church.

LOUDOUN VALLEY RUN

Just beginning the final, very steep drop down to Darvel, and the minute you hit the valley floor you're right at the start of the town. Just like coming in on the A-71, you are completely out of the rural and into the urban.

part, to be honest. You'll pass numerous land uses from schools to the Loudoun Gowf[22] Club, as well as some green fields, all on your way to Galston. It's fast, flat, and a little bit furious as you run up to the big roundabout that guards Galston's gateway.

Now I always go straight on here when doing this run, and return home through Kilmarnock. However, the road ahead does get even busier, so if you want to avoid that you can turn right at the roundabout and take the A-719 home via Moscow. This is probably your best bet if you stay on the south side of Glasgow.

It's not an easy route to return by the Moscow road, but it leads onto the old A-77 and works well for any south side-based riders. I use the A-719 when returning home on our next and final run, and will cover that way next time. But Kilmarnock has always been my preference when covering the Loudoun Valley, so I go straight ahead at the Galston roundabout.

At first I enjoy the way that the houses of Galston open and spread out to the left of you. In a way, the town sort of bares its soul. After that, this road can become a bit of a chore, till you reach Hurlford anyway. It does get noticeably busier than before and the surrounds become rough and ready in places. Not to mention a longish draw up through the fields just before Hurlford, which is open and exposed to any south westerly wind.

Tough going, indeed, and I'm always glad to get into the shelter of the Hurlford houses. When I do, it's a run down the Galston Road to the roundabout at the far end

After Darvel comes Newmilns and, boy, is it old-looking. There are some fine buildings lining the Main Street here, that are very aged in appearance, which is hardly surprising as it's an old textile town going way back.

of this old, small mining town – a town that took its name from a nearby ford in the River Irvine. No need to ford it nowadays, of course, because when you turn right at the roundabout, you cross the Irvine by a beautiful bridge as you enter Crookedholm. Very pretty she is, too, with her church spires and glistening Irvine running away and under the glorious big railway viaduct off to your left. A climb up through Crookedholm's houses, then a roll down under the railway, followed by a crossing over of the A-77, finds you in Kilmarnock.

Heavy, I said heavy, that's Kilmarnock. Heavy industry of the heaviest kind. I'm talking locomotives here. Coal mines, Massey Ferguson tractors, throw in some textiles and Stoddard Carpets for good measure, that's

When going along Darvel's long straight Main Street, expect to meet a fair bit of traffic on the way, which is hardly surprising as the A-71 is a primary route, don't forget. It's more or less this busy all the way now till you leave Kilmarnock.

---

22 - Yes, that is the correct spelling.

After Galston, the turn off the A-71 is made into Crookedholm where you immediately cross over the River Irvine rather picturesquely. Shortly you will enter Kilmarnock, when you cross over the A-77 rather unpicturesquely.

Kilmarnock. Bold John Barleycorn into the bargain, until Johnnie Walker pulled out fairly recently under a cloud of controversy. Quite an array, I think you'll agree. Not that the road that carries you all the way to the town centre lets you know this.

You are on the rather leafy and pleasant B-7073 London Road, which takes you past the Foxbar Hotel. And it's not

Looking back, having just gone under Kilmarnock railway station by one of it fine old tunnels. This is an unbelievably pleasurable manoeuvre for such a simple task.

every day you pass a hotel that has its name painted on the wall outside with a brush. Perhaps it's something to do with Basil Brush.

In total contrast, the town centre itself is a bit of a hideous one-way system, taking you round the modern, and less said about the better, shopping centre.[23] It will be mega-busy and tight, but fairly slow and safe if you want to follow it all the way round. Now this is a bit of a pain for me, because it is a long way for a short cut, as I am actually close to my exit road when I arrive, but have to circumnavigate the whole one-way system to reach it. The road I want is the A-735 for Kilmaurs. Admittedly, it is well signposted as you make your way round the one-way, so route finding is the least of your worries.

Finding the right road back to Stewarton and Kilmaurs isn't a problem, once you emerge from below Kilmarnock rail station, as it's signposted straight away. Simply follow the signs and you can't go wrong.

And that is just as well, for it is so busy, you will be more concerned with watching all the traffic around you instead of looking out for directions.

Having been a bit hard on poor old Kilmarnock's centre there, I must say that there is a lovely and quaint exit from the place, going under the old rail tunnel beside its grand old station. This again is well signposted, and puts you automatically on the right road for Kilmaurs. With a bit of experience, you can avoid the one-way system completely by cutting along the pavement to your right when you come to the one-way, which is part of a cycle route. This is a very good and safe shortcut,

---

23 - I think Kilmarnock was voted the worst place to shop in 2006.

LOUDOUN VALLEY RUN

Heading out of town through Kilmarnock's tough-looking housing schemes on the Kilmaurs Road. The Onthank estate, made infamous by the BBC's The Scheme documentary, sits just off to the right here.

Again, in complete contrast to Kilmarnock's tough housing schemes, you end up riding into Kilmaurs on probably Ayrshire's quaintest-looking street. It's called Townend.

which uses the pavement to put you on the right road for Kilmaurs. It won't take you long to suss out this unconventional alternative route.

So, after clearing the hustle and bustle of the centre, you find yourself on the south side of town and making your way out on the 735. A very large, busy roundabout that services what's known as the Western Road must be gotten round first, before you can run out of town on the Kilmaurs Road, through the tough-looking housing schemes. You've got Altonhill on the left and the Knockinlaw on the right. Just behind Knockinlaw sits the now infamous Onthank estate, which gained notoriety when it appeared in the 2010 television programme, *The Scheme*.

Don't panic, because serenity lies just along the road from here, in the shape of the fields and mossy stone walls that lead to Kilmaurs. That's good, but it's nought compared to the village itself, and especially Townend, which is the street that will carry you in.

I'm not saying this is the quaintest street in the whole of Ayrshire, but it's certainly in the top one. I'm always expecting to see Rabbie Burns himself come donnerin' roon the corner. Small, nestling cottages huddle together and guide you up the brae and round the corner towards the village centre – a village that felt the full force of the Government measures to quell the Covenanting movement. Highland troops, put here by Charles II, inflicted many barbarous acts on their reluctant hosts. Some people were burned until they told where their savings were hidden. Even poor families had to buy tobacco and liquor for the Highlanders. The Highlanders

In just about a mile after leaving Kilmarnock on the Kilmaurs Road, you see the church tower belonging to the village as you approach it, and what a transformation from the hardness of Killie; this could not be any different. Suddenly, once more it's soft, pretty, rural Ayrshire at its best.

On the road between Kilmaurs and Stewarton (the A-735), you're back into the rich dairy fields, and sweeping and bending between them on the way to the next small town that's only a few miles away and can be seen in the distance.

Stewarton's centre crossroads provides an option or two for the return route home, depending on where you live, of course. I will turn left for Paisley, but you can return to Barrhead or Glasgow's south side by continuing straight on and taking the B-769 all the way back to the Barrhead Dams, and ultimately the Spiersbridge roundabout at Thornliebank. It is a fine road to return on, offering great views of the city from its highest vantage point.

would even cut and wound villagers for sheer devilment, and destroyed property and cattle as they pleased.

In later times, it was a prosperous place, however, and was known for bonnet-making, shoes, and especially cutlery. For our purposes, despite the pleasing look of the place, it signals the start of a tough run home. The climbing begins within the village and this is the first of many hills that must be ridden to reach Paisley. This is you climbing out on Townhead and it leads almost immediately onto more of the same.

This is me now on the home straight, so to speak, and it is a hard finish to come. Not for the first time, but for the first time in a long time, we are once more gliding

A fantastic view of Glasgow and the Campsie Fells over the Barrhead Dams is had, after taking the B-769 road from Stewarton. This return will suit if you are a southside-based rider.

the blanket green through the undulations of Ayrshire. Not easy terrain, no, but pretty all the same, this quilted patchwork of green fields through which our grey guide, the A-735, takes us.

When the road finally levels out high, it will swerve and swerve, and swerve some more, before a dip down and a climb up takes you into Stewarton. The crossroads at the centre of the Bonnet Toon is soon found after going under its magnificent railway viaduct. This small enclave, as its nickname suggests, was also involved in the making of such hats and, like its near neighbour Kilmaurs, also suffered badly during Covenanting times.

A left turn at the crossroads keeps us on the A-735, and it's out under the railway we go. Another wee pull-up follows, and then we're on the road to Dunlop, of course. But on this occasion, we won't actually go through it.

If you decide to the take the A-735 from Stewarton and are Paisley-bound, then there are still a couple of options open to you about which way to return home. Before you reach Dunlop, you will see a sign saying 7 miles to Neilston, and this great wee B-road, the Kingston Road, is a fabulous rollercoaster ride home. It will ultimately run you into Barrhead, and is used by myself on occasion as an alternative to returning via the Gleniffer Braes.

Ordinarily, at least 9 times out of 10, I would. However, I will keep that return route for the last run home, and this time I will come back on the great road down to Neilston. The right turn for this will be coming up shortly. It involves a most dramatic descent through that East Renfrewshire dynamic duo of Neilston and Barrhead. This way would also suit any rider who happens to live in south west Glasgow. Turn right at the sign which indicates its 7 miles to Neilston, and start to make your way through the fields. All is fine and pastoral to start off with, as only a slight rise is needed to get you

LOUDOUN VALLEY RUN

A couple of fans come out to cheer me on my way as I make tracks for Neilston Village on the Kingston Road. The Tour de France boys get an army of adoring fans clapping and cheering them up the Col de Tourmalet, but I've got to settle for a couple of Shetland ponies.

going onto the long straight that will carry you past the back road into Dunlop and then toward what little is left of the old Howie's of Dunlop factory[24] that stood up ahead on the right.

It's so far so good, and so far so pleasant. This will last a little bit longer, until the road starts a fairly tough wee climb just after the landfill site at the entrance to Craignaught Farm. Just grind this one out, which ends when you pass a high-perched cottage, and get ready for one helluva treat and payback. You can actually see Dumgoyne Hill when the view finally opens up in front of you, though this unfortunately is seen through four new wind turbines that have sprung up along the Neilston Road.

It's a fantastic fast entry into Neilston on the Kingston Road, and is a fitting end to such a fine road. It is always a very frantic, open, airy, and tumbling jaunt down this rolling B-road, and one that is enjoyed every time it's ridden.

---

24 - It made animal feed.

Some glorious upping and downing is to be had on the drop down to Neilston on the Kingston Road. The views just get better and better the closer you get to the village. It's simply thrill-a-minute all the way down.

rise ahead. More recently-planted turbines are passed close by and more seen away to the right, white and wallowing in the wind, until you are level with the Craighall Dam on the right.

At this point, dear old Mother Glasgow will look formidable in the distance, as down the Kingston Road you plummet, flying past Neilston Quarry before shooting into the village at a helluva speed. This frantic pace only slowly blows itself out as you approach the junction with Main Street. Across the road sits the delightful looking parish church, with a wonderful Celtic cross headstone just inside its gates. Don't worry, this break in the momentum will only be temporary, because when you turn right for Barrhead, guess what? You're on another screamer of a descent; this one is bolt straight and with great views of Glasgow dead ahead, and the Fereneze Hills which fall steeply and finely green, away to your left.

From now until Neilston, the road will undulate like hell – mostly in your favour – as you fly down a series of real rolling rises and dips. The road falls frantic and fast down towards the Commore Dam, where you have to be careful as you negotiate the chicane which carries you over the small burn that feeds it. It's very easy to overcook this one, as you try to keep up as much momentum as possible to give you a good run at the

A great bit of swerving fast fun can be had when you get into the bungalows, so get the old centre of gravity down low for maximum control on these ones. It's still steep, brilliant bending down through the houses, till you meet the busy T-junction with Kelburn Street, the A-736, where you must stop. In fact, even Kelburn Street is a drop-and-a-half down to Allan's Corner roundabout. Just watch out here for all the traffic that will be coming and going from the big Tesco's supermarket on the left.

LOUDOUN VALLEY RUN

This fine-looking Celtic cross stands in the churchyard of Neilston Parish Church, which sits across from the end of the Kingston Road where it meets the Main Street in Neilston. You can actually see it from the road through the gates of the church, and that is what drew my attention to it.

When you reach Neilston, you're not finished with the descending just yet, not by a long chalk. For there is still a brilliant dive down into Barrhead on the Neilston Road to come, and this one matches anything that has gone before. It is an absolute fun-filled screamer that will take you all the way into Barrhead centre itself. The new traffic lights on Kelburn Street do check the run somewhat, however.

Don't forget, of course, that the Gleniffer Braes Road (the B-775) is still a great way to return from Ayrshire, and the fall from the top of them into Glenburn is a particularly wonderful finish for me personally. You never tire of the view of the Clyde Valley that opens up to you as the descent begins.

This always seems to be a mega happening place. Busy, too, will be the easy wee drop down onto Cross Arthurlie Street, and the dropping doesn't end till you get under the rail bridge. Quite a way to get here, I think you'll find.

All that's left for me is the long run down Paisley Road onto the rollercoaster that is the Capelthill. No doubt by the time you read this, the new cycle lane will be operational, and its lower section now negates any need to negotiate the upping and downing on the Capelthill Road's lower stretches. This cycle lane runs beside those beautiful Brownside Braes meadows, and very conveniently leads me onto Glenburn Road, where I'm only a street or two away from home.

So that's it for this time. A tough, gritty run through the old Covenanting country was promised, and that's exactly what you got. Hope you enjoyed the history as much as the run, as there was quite a lot of it in there. There will be a bit more of the same to come in our next and last outing, so I hope you can make it then, too. Till then, you know the drill: be good, be bad, be indifferent, just don't get caught

Liam Boy.

A fitting final view of Stanely Reservoir, Paisley, and Glasgow, from the top of the Gleniffer Braes, and all the hard work is over for another day. The freewheel down is very often a welcome respite at the end of a long hard run.

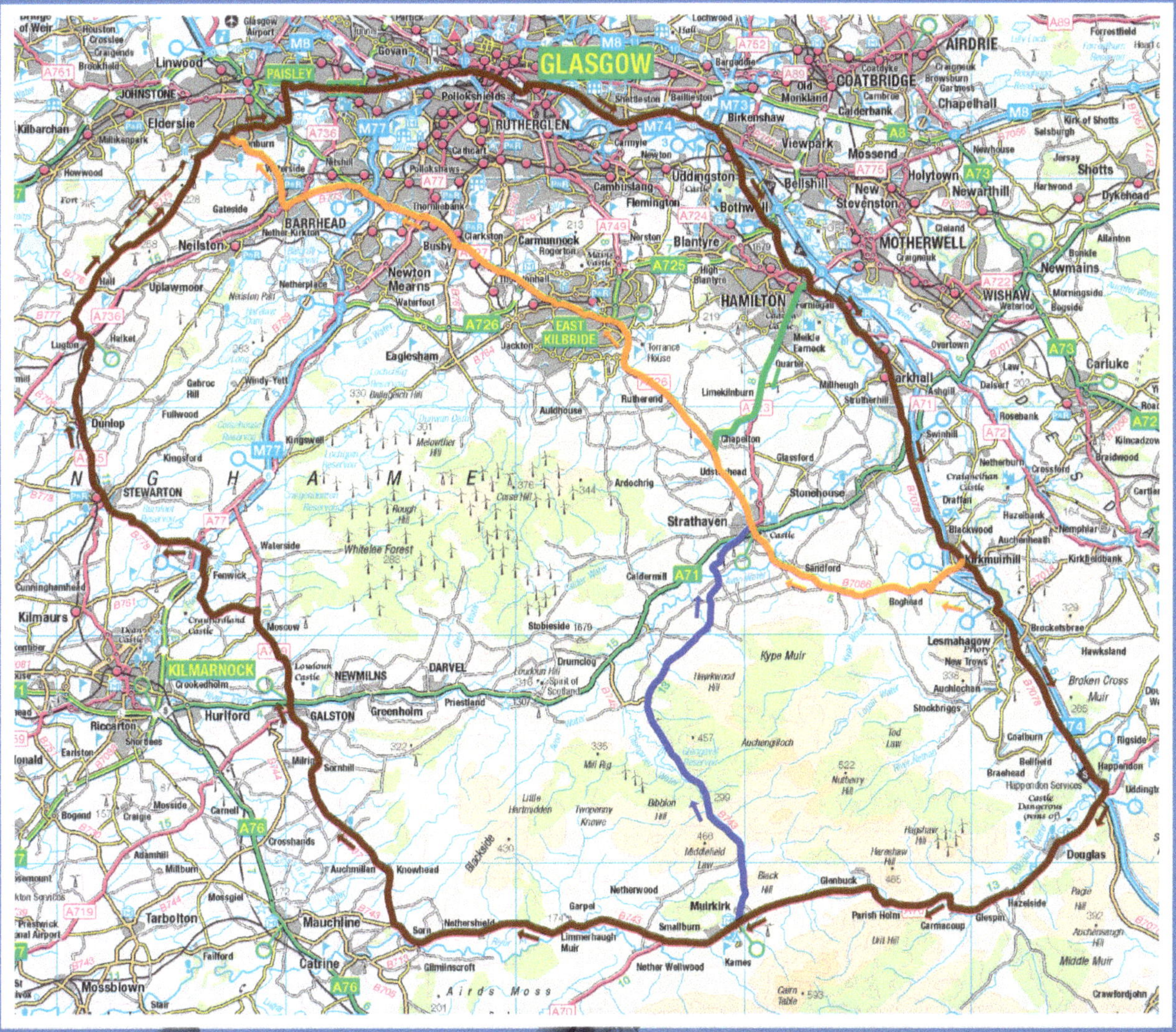

THE DOUGLAS RUN

RETURN VIA	SORN	MUIRKIRK	BLACKWOOD	HAMILTON
	90.6 MILES	85.4 MILES	59.5 MILES	47.9 MILES
	5.46 HOURS	5.09 HOURS	4.01 HOURS	3.11 HOURS
ASCENT	3920 FEET	2980 FEET	1960 FEET	1520 FEET
CALORIES BURNED	4015	3186	2256	2079

O'S LANDRANGER MAPS 64, 71, 70

ROUTE SUMMARY

Paisley Rd West
London Rd
Bothwell

HAMILTON RETURN

Hamilton Hamilton
Larkhall Chapelton

BLACKWOOD RETURN

Blackwood E. Kilbride Blackwood
Douglas Barrhead Strathaven

MUIRKIRK RETURN

Muirkirk Paisley E. Kilbride Muirkirk
Sorn   Barrhead Strathaven
Galston   Paisley E Kilbride
Fenwick   Clarkston Toll
Stewarton   Hurlet
Dunlop   Barrhead
Lugton   Paisley
Sergeantlaw
Paisley

THE DOUGLAS RUN

WHERE MINERS WALKED

Now, our last sortie takes us south, carrying us in a similar big sweeping arc to the last run. This one does, however, take us further south, and deeper into both South Lanarkshire and East Ayrshire, and is therefore a longer, more sustained and serious run than the Loudoun Valley jaunt. For me, it can have the same tough finish, returning back through all the small settlements of Ayrshire and its rolling terrain, though not necessarily. The overall route involves heading for Glasgow's east end and then making our way down through Bothwell, Hamilton, and Larkhall, before continuing down the old A74 as far as Douglas, then returning west along the A-70 through Muirkirk and Sorn. The route back is via Galston, Fenwick, and Stewarton, before finishing off on the great Sergeantlaw Road on the Gleniffer Braes.

The full run comes in for me at about 92 miles, which is not only quite a distance, but also contains, I think, about the toughest and most arduous finish of all the runs I do.

The long road back from Sorn is not for the faint-hearted. But there is an alternative return route to the Sorn one, and that is to take the road over to Strathaven when you get to Muirkirk. This is the B-743, and is an absolute belter. Not only that, but it allows an easier finish back down through East Kilbride, so I suspect this will be the more popular of the two options for most bike riders, as opposed to doing the whole circuit.

As I have done both many times, and I know others like to do both as well, I'll cover the two of them and you can make up your own mind. In fact, there are numerous permutations to this one, including heading for Sorn first and then returning from Muirkirk, or vice versa. Additionally, there are also plenty of opportunities on the Hamilton/Douglas stretch to swing in towards Strathaven early, and therefore cut the run short to suit. This can be useful should the conditions not be to your liking, but will still give a good lengthy day out. For example, if you swing in when you reach Blackwood, the return to Paisley still racks up around 59 miles.

Even the Muirkirk shortcut isn't saving a lot of miles, despite a lot less climbing on the home leg; it comes in at 86 miles for me. As for the run itself, I usually do it clockwise, though not always. No matter which way you do it, just like the last run, we will be going through staunch Covenanter country. And also just like the last run, I will be covering some more of their brutal bloody history.

So, that is what's waiting for us this time – a great run, yes, but one with an arduous section or two in its midst, requiring a fair bit of endurance and stamina in reserve if you don't want to end up suffering too badly a long way from home.

Bearing that in mind, it's stomach in, chest out, keeping a stiff upper lip, as we manoeuvre the old bike out the door for the last time. And let me just say thanks for sticking with me throughout the whole book, and that you can hold your head high and feel proud after completing so many long and tough runs. If you were a bit unfit to begin with, you may have thought that covering such distances was either impossible or certainly beyond you personally. Well, now you know differently. From the fitness you have gained and will continue to keep, you will benefit tremendously health-wise in the long run. I say that with some confidence, because if you've come this far then you've clearly got the cycling bug, and it won't be leaving you any time soon.

Right, as we're heading for Glasgow, you know the drill – its Paisley Road West here we come. On this occasion, I'll stick to Paisley's quieter south side roads like Lochfield and then Hawkhead to avoid the town centre, and these take me very nicely, thank you very much, out at Barshaw Park. Now begins the long journey out east, first through the not-so-busy bungalows of Ralston, before crossing the city line and meeting a bit more resistance in the shape of traffic lights and the traffic they are meant to control. You know by now that I always exercise a bit of caution when passing any area on PRW that contains shops and commerce, and the first row of stores at Hillington comes into that category.

The quick, free-flowing purr along to the bottom of the Berryknowes Road follows, where sure as hell this busy bottleneck will slow down your progress. However, once through, comes the quick up and over by Corkerhill, and after Craigton's wonderful brown tenements, the Helen Street roundabout, which although busy, never really causes too many problems. Hello, Ibrox – the old stadium front resplendent as ever in its red brick garb. The fast fire down through the Cessnock stretch always boosts morale, then a few more hold-ups are sure to follow at Paisley Road Toll.

The plan here is to gain the London Road right at its start at Bridgeton Cross, so we make our way along Ballater Street, passing the Gorbals to get there. But first the one way system swings us alongside the Clyde's south bank, and a dive under the Central's rail bridge is required, before breaking off first left on Bridge Street (going round Oxford and South Portland), till we are able to gain Ballater itself. Now, we shortly reach the lights at Glasgow Green and shoot straight across onto James Street. The cross itself is at the end of this street, and can be reached by either jumping on the pavement, which is a cycle lane and slightly more direct, or by sticking to the road proper and taking the first left.

At Bridgeton station, we turn right onto the lengthy Londoner (the A-74), which of course has been the main road south from Scotland since just about roads began. This main artery has obviously been upgraded as time has passed, and is now motorway further south for the most part. I just wonder how close this modern road's route is to the original that headed south all those centuries ago. It's hard to believe it, but like every other road it started off as a dirt track[1].

Now, the moment you turn onto London Road, Paradise itself – the modern Celtic Park – comes into view. To reach it, you can use the natty wee cycle track that takes up space on the right-hand side of the road, if you so wish, but it runs out quite quickly and it's hard then to get back over to the left, so I don't recommend it.

There has been a lot of construction work going on outside the ground since early 2014, but the stadium itself was the handiwork of the Bunnet who Dunnit, Fergus McCann. Not only that, but he also saved the old Hoops from extinction into the bargain. Despite this, he left five years later almost unnoticed, such was his lack of rapport with all connected with the club. It's hard to fathom how such a successful individual could be so unpopular at the same time. Anyway, that is now confined to recent history, as all around the east end is changing fast, real fast. For cycling, the Sir Chris Hoy velodrome is right across the road in the impressive Emirates Stadium.

We do, however, get just a slight taste of 60s/70s

---

1 - Roman roads being an exception.

DOUGLAS RUN

At the Bridgeton Cross bandstand, and just about to join the London Road. From here on down to Douglas, it is literally the one road, so there should be no route-finding problems of any great difficulty.

Glasgow as we depart over the Springfield Road and head out towards the city's eastern boundary. The houses of Parkhead, Braidfauld, and Fullarton, keep us company as far as the roundabouts which harbour an oasis of modern commerce, such as a Travel Inn and the ubiquitous Arnold Clark car dealership, and beyond we find older, heavier commerce for company, all the way out to the edge of town. The next long straight section of road is lined with businesses of a different nature, and again speaks more of old Glasgow than new, wat with haulage companies and the like. However, the whole road seems surprisingly neat and tidy.

We take our leave of the city about a mile after the lights where London Road meets Hamilton Road, and straight ahead Mount Vernon Avenue joins the party just to add a bit more buzz to the junction. Not that it needs it, for its helluva busy at the best of times. We now join grittyville, when we take Hamilton Road and head out east under the rail bridge. We used this road, though in the opposite direction, when returning from Forth, and I mentioned then how it is a busy, dirty, noisy, stretch of dual carriageway that I can't wait to get off. Well, going this way is no different. The only saving grace it has is the old Mail Coach Inn. Given its name, location, and looks, I assume it was used in the distant past by horse-drawn coaches delivering mail or whatever.

The good news is there is usually plenty of room, so drivers give you a sizeable body swerve, but I'm still glad to get off it when we reach the motorway and boundary sign, where there is a noticeable drop in volume. Hey

When going along Uddingston Main Street, keep an eye open on the left-hand side for the Tunnocks factory just as you go through the cross. This place is as synonymous with Scotland as shortbread and bagpipes.

presto! The A-74 has now become the M-74, which we cross over as we enter South Lanarkshire and Uddingston on the slightly more serene B-7071, and begin the long line of red into the town. The busy dual baby that we have just ridden only lasts for 2 miles, and ends as we cross the motorway. There is a hotel along this road called Redstone's, which is hardly surprising, as all the big leafy villas here are of a bright red persuasion.

I must say, it's a very nice entry into a town that proudly has Tunnocks as its main resident. You can actually see the factory, with its bright red name and logo, as you fly through the crossroads along Main Street[2]. The town centre is an elongated procession of more red stone and stores, and includes a small bike shop, which could come in handy. Between Uddingston and Bothwell is a short strip of uninspiring brown belt, which is followed almost immediately by an avenue of old, white, modest council stock that greets your arrival into the town. These sit on the left side, and the wall surrounding the old Bothwell Castle and golf course sits on the right.

A long, dour, straight run-in it is, too, but once into the town centre, past the Bothwell Bridge Hotel, it's a different matter altogether. The beautiful, big, square bell tower of the local parish church looks down on the swerving Main Street as it curves and carries you round past and through a delight of doors. One of these is the Douglas Arms pub, which is the first mention of this major family in Scottish history. We are heading south to

---

2 - It sits just to the left.

the town of Douglas, of course, and it was from the river that runs through it, the Douglas Water (Dark Stream), that both the town and the clan took their name.

The plaque on the pub wall says the name was first used by a William de Douglas who held land there in the late 12th century. Certainly, it was about that time the name first came to be used, but more of that later. We've still got a fair bit to go to reach there, as we continue our way through pretty Bothwell, now beloved by football stars from both Celtic and Rangers alike. Hard to believe this was an old mining town with three medium sized pits, in Victorian times. It was the housing built to accommodate the workers from these pits which built up Bothwell in the first place. That magnate's magnate from Coatbridge, William Baird – he of the massive Gartsherrie foundry fame – owned two of the three mines.

We leave the village on a great long straight drop down towards the River Clyde, meeting Bothwell Bridge when we get there. A large stone monument commemorates the battle that took place there on the 22nd of June ,1679, between Scottish Covenanters and Government forces. If you've read the Loudoun Valley run, you will know why this battle took place; if not, then it was exactly three weeks to the day that a group of Covenanters, praying on nearby High Drumclog Moor, unexpectedly defeated mounted dragoons under the command of John Graham, Earl of Claverhouse, and started a mini revolution to boot. Graham, of course, known to many as Bonnie Dundee or Bluidy Clavers – depending on what side you were on – was himself almost captured and killed at Drumclog.

The Covenanters were only praying in their own style, and nothing more. However, this style had been outlawed by King Charles I in 1637. Now that his son Charles II was on the throne, he imposed his father's laws vigorously. On hearing of the defeat at Drumclog, Charles sent his son, James Scott, 1st Duke of Monmouth, to quell any unrest in the Southwest. He had John Graham as his second in command, and made sure he was ready for action with a well organised small army. The Covenanters, on the other hand, were anything but well organised. Certainly, many came to swell their ranks on hearing of the Drumclog victory, but most of the time at Bothwell was spent falling out and arguing amongst themselves.

Their leader, Robert Hamilton, was not for compromise, and disowned any moderate ministers who had accepted an earlier amnesty from the King. This caused further division within the ranks of the rebels and was a recipe for disaster. Disaster was quick when it came. The Government troops, who numbered about 5000, were positioned on the Bothwell side of the Clyde; the Covenanters, who numbered around 6000, were on the Hamilton side, with the conflict centred on the bridge itself. The rebels held the bridge well during the early exchanges, and were led by one of their few competent military men, David Hackston. He had been personally involved in the murder of Archbishop James Sharp near St Andrews only a couple of months earlier.

However when lack of ammunition forced them to abandon their barricade at the bridge, Monmouth's men quickly gained the south bank and drew up for battle. To the Covenanters credit, they too were ready to engage; well, the rank and file were, but most of their leaders disappeared pronto. The hero of Drumclog, William Cleland, tried to find replacement officers at very short notice, but without any leadership on the field, they were quickly surrounded and defeated. There were few casualties on the Government side, with around 700 reported dead for the rebels.

Perhaps death wasn't such a bad outcome, because the 1200 survivors who were taken prisoner then spent a harsh winter imprisoned at Greyfriars kirkyard in Edinburgh, before being transported overseas to the colonies. This effectively put an end to the rebellion, but some extreme and armed Covenanter elements remained at large, principally those followers of the hard-line Reverend Richard Cameron.

As we pull up away from the Clyde and enter Hamilton, I have to say that I admire the old Covenanters for standing up for their beliefs. It's hard not to admire them when you consider the terrible persecution they suffered for it. There are one or two other stories of that nature still to come, but now we find ourselves running alongside the Hamilton racecourse, on a road that's as long and as straight as a road can be[3].

It runs us towards Hamilton centre, and as we near the end of it, we pass one of Dougie Parks' car dealerships. This is a man whose name is synonymous with the town, principally through his fleet of coaches. We arrive at a roundabout and it's from here that we aim to make our way directly across town and leave on the A-72, taking us past the Avonbridge Hotel. I have to be honest and say here that it is probably the lesser evil to stick to the main ring road and follow it down and round, then up again to gain the 72. I say that because for years I have tried every way I could think of to ride through the town centre, to avoid traffic and losing height, but have never found a satisfactory way yet.

The Hamilton one-way system has always forced me to either jump on pavements, or ride down one-way streets the wrong way, or do some other daft manoeuvre to get me across town. So nowadays, I save myself a lot of grief and just bite the bullet and fall fast onto Palace Grounds Road and then get the hell back up onto the start of Carlisle Road (the A-72) as fast as I can. The one saving grace of going this way is the great views you get over to Motherwell on the way down.

Hamilton itself was originally known as Cadzow, changing its name during the reign of James II, when it was named after James Hamilton, 1st Lord of Hamilton, who married the King's daughter. The town has been linked to the famous family ever since.

Passing by one of the many car dealerships in Hamilton, and for once I don't think this one is owned by Dougie Park. You're on the A-724 Burnbank Road. After a quick dive down and round the one-way system, you head out on the road to Larkhall, the B-7078.

3 - This is you on the Bothwell Road, Hamilton, still the B-7071.

Heading south on the B-7078 and approaching the roundabout on the A-71. The long haul down has begun in earnest here, and in fact you've gained quite a bit of height at this point. You cash it all in on the big fall down to Blackwood, coming up next.

Now, there is an option to head for Strathaven on the Low Waters Road (the A-723) from Hamilton centre, and this is the first good option of cutting the run short, should you so wish. The climb up on the Low Waters is a great one, and a good wee run in itself, coming in about the 47-mile mark for me. If that's not your intention today, then make your way out of town on the A-72, and just after you pass the Avonbridge Hotel you'll see a big sprawling ostentatious house on the left. When you climb up after crossing the Avon, you enter tiny Ferniegair, which contains the entrance to the magnificent Chatelherault, the old hunting lodge of the Hamiltons.

There are more great views across the shallow valley to Motherwell as we speed towards Larkhall. We're sitting high, moving flat and fast, and sandwiched between the railway and a big long stone wall here. All very atmospheric, I must say, and I like this stretch. We hit the open fields, and just before reaching Larkhall itself, the 72 branches off left for Lanark, while we go straight on and onto the B-7078, still the Carlisle Road. A slight rise takes us into Larkhall town. A long drawn-out affair it is, too, much more elongated than you would imagine, and a place that has an industrial past like many round about it. It's an old mining and textile town, and certainly some of the houses that run off the main street have a real miners' row look to them.

I'm particularly thinking of the homes on Macneil Street, which is on the right when you reach the prominent crossroads and lights just after the Trinity Parish Church. Now Macneil Street, if followed, will also lead to Strathaven, and is the second available shortcut on this run, if you so fancy it for whatever reason. I like this road, which leads to Glassford Village, and a great wee back road cuts over to Chapelton and cuts out Strathaven altogether. It's a great road home, which is there if you need it. As for the rest of the town, everything certainly looks solid and strong, and none more so than the great old Trinity Parish Church itself, snoozing idly on the right. Make sure you tiptoe past, so's not to wake it up.

At the end of town, a long, rising, and twisting exit is made on the Machan Road.

This is one that I like, despite its length and continuous gradient. And by taking of it, we leave behind a town with a reputation for being of a serious blue-nosed persuasion.

Back into the fields we go, on a road lined with those great old South Lanarkshire lampposts from yesteryear. Sadly, near and far, there are plenty of wind turbines hereabouts as well now, as we rise gently up towards the big roundabout that is fed by the A-71. From here, the journey south towards Blackwood is a high and open affair; well, it is till the final approach to the town is made.

The long road down to Douglas has started in earnest, and as you fall long and fast off the high ground towards Blackwood, the modern M-74 is just to your left at this point.

We actually cross over it at the bottom of the descent, to enter the town, which we have sort of visited before, due to it being joined at the hip with Kirkmuirhill. Blackwood seems to be the more modern-looking side of the equation, with its plush bungalows and a primary school that looks just out of the wrapper. A quick whizz

When you reach Blackwood/Kirkmuirhill, you can cut the run short by cutting back to Strathaven on the B-7086. If you do, expect to enjoy curving bends through the pleasant, green, dairy fields like this on the way.

down the main Carlisle Road takes us onto familiar territory when we pass the sign for the B-7086, which was the road we came to reach here from Strathaven when doing the run to Forth. This is another early cut-out option if you don't fancy going all the way down to Douglas on the day, and is a circuit I have used many times in the past.

If I take it, it gives a round trip back to Paisley of about 59 miles, and makes a most pleasant and pastoral plough home. It is also just about the last chance you have for cutting it short, certainly on a main road.

Now despite this town's tired look, due to lack of employment since the mining stopped, it does hold a fine position amongst the surrounding countryside. Most prominent, as I've mentioned before, is the well sited local parish church, sitting right in the centre of the striking Y-junction that splits the Lanark Road from the Carlisle Road. The hills of the Nethan Valley look just so green and serene away to the left, and quite dramatic in their steep slant.

But it's south out of the town we continue and once more find ourselves on a long, soulless road beside the main M-74. Only, this time we are running down its east side. As you leave Kirkmuirhill, you will notice a brand new, tarred cycle path on the left. Very inviting it looks, too, but sadly it lasts no time and you're back on the road. This is the first of another three sections of road like this. The first one isn't too bad in road surface, and it comprises a long gentle rise then fall all the way down to a roundabout which is signed for Lesmahagow and Coalburn. At this point, you must re-cross the M-74 onto its west side. The moment you do, you are taking a major step back in time.

You now run onto the old A-74 itself no less[4], and will continue to stay on it all the way down to Douglas. Admittedly, you are now rolling on British transport history, but other than that it will prove to be hard-going for most of the way. Nowadays, it's the A-9 heading north that gets the bad reputation, but it's kids stuff compared to the old 74 in its heyday, as any old trucker of repute will tell you. Most will have stories galore of all the crashes they have seen over the years on this road. There was never a dull moment, I have been reliably informed.

So, off we go, snaking long and slender southwards for approximately 7½ miles, and as you do, just get ready to

4 - Technically you are still on the B-7078.

Going over the M-74 just outside Lesmahagow, as you must cross over it at this point to stay on the road down. For a motorway, it makes for quite a striking sight.

dour this one out. The main problem is the road surface, which isn't potholed *per se*, but merely rough; very rough in a lot of places. It's an 18 carat gold boneshaker, with no respite on some stretches. In others, however, with a bit of experience and ingenuity, you can seek out a slightly smoother line, which may be in the gutter or along the central white line, and will prove to be good experience should you wish to take part in the Paris Roubaix road race, though not much else.

The first section ends when we hit the roundabout and re-cross the 74. The stretch to come can be so long, dour, and arduous that it could put you off doing the run this way ever again. The good news is it's quiet, very quiet and roomy, so whatever traffic there is will be well away from you. The scenery isn't too great till you get past the old mining areas of Lesmahagow and Coalburn, but then Border hills and valleys start to put in an appearance and cheer the place up. To begin with, we have the option to either continue straight down the old highway, or to break off left and go through Lesmahagow itself.

I usually just charge straight on, which is faster. But it isn't easy; after the dip down and long pull-up away from the River Nethan, the road surface is probably at its worst here. It's shake, rattle, and roll for the next mile

You are now following in the tyre tracks of British motoring folklore, as you find yourself now on a stretch of the old A-74 (now the B-7078) at Lesmahagow. However, that is all that you can say in support of this stretch, for it has a road surface as rough as a badger's bum, and it's shake, rattle, and roll all the way here. Try your best to find any smooth runnels of surface that you can.

or so, as you pass the rest of the town and seek out any line of relatively smoother tar to make life just a little bit less jarring. It does improve the further south you get, where away to the right can be spied an old pit bing in the distance, just to remind you of this place's industrial past[5].

Flat and bleak and dour is the going hereabouts, and it's simply a case of getting through it. Don't worry, for there isn't too much more of this to come, and when you do get to Douglas the riding will improve immensely. This arduous section ends when you come to a T-junction right alongside the main motorway, and you then go under the M-74 and continue on down its eastern side. Only just over a mile to go now, and the countryside gets more wooded and pretty as you make your way past a big truck stop, with no limit to the amount, variation, and colour of the lorries parked up.[6]

Finally, thank God, a long, languid, easy section drops us down to the picturesque Douglas Water. Suddenly you're in a different world – well nearly, because as beautiful as this spot is, with the river murmuring away through the fields eastward and the cattle munching quietly away, we've still got one bit of new road to take to reach Douglas.

We hit it when we turn right at the roundabout[7], which we must do, joining the A-70 for Douglas which is still 2 miles away. Not only is there an unattractive new stretch of road ahead of us, but it comes in the shape of a long pull-up which we could well do without. "Ouch." I said, "Ouch." Yes, it's a bit of a muscle-burner this one, but take heart, for it's just about to get seriously better when you clear the rise. At the top, you start to meet woods and walls, the big, stone, moss-covered variety – all very nice and impressive they are, too – and then the countdown

5 - You're just about level with Coalburn here.

6 - This is Happendon services

7 - It's signed for Ayr A-70.

markers to Douglas aren't long in coming. You enter the town, passing the wonderfully named Colonel's Entry on the right.

Douglas is small, curvy and very old pretty; hardly surprising when you realise just how far back it goes. Ahead you soon meet the most exquisite looking little white post office that sets the scene to come. It couldn't be more charming as, buoyed up by it and the rest around, you bank left and drop down through the village Main Street. Shortly, we will head out west and follow the Douglas Water west; as already mentioned, the town derived its name from the river itself. In turn, the Clan Douglas took their name from the town when they settled hereabouts in the 12th century. They were probably of French descent initially, I dare say. The town in turn then blossomed as it serviced nearby Castle Douglas.

Swerving through Douglas on its Main Street will only take a minute or two, for although it is pretty it is also very small. The wee general store that sits on the left has a good coffee and tea machine, all the same.

The stretch of the old A-74 is soon coming to an end here, thank goodness, as you near the turn for Douglas. It has started to become a bit more scenic again as well, for just south of Lesmahagow was old coal mining country whose terrain added to the misery. Doing this stretch could actually put you off doing the Douglas run ever again, but don't worry, it's just about to get seriously good.

The village has a monument to a man named James Gavin, a tailor and Covenanter, who was seized by the authorities and refused to renounce his faith. As punishment, they cut off his ears with his own tailoring scissors, before sending him off to the West Indies for a life of slavery. As for the Douglas family, they were for a long time main players in Scottish politics, often thought to be the real power behind the King at times. The clan was linked very closely to both Wallace and The Bruce, and they were considered such a threat to the monarchy in the reign of James II that both the 6th and 8th Earls were killed during that period.[8]

The clan's most infamous son has to be Archibald the Grim, the 3rd Earl of Douglas (The Black Douglas), who became even more powerful than the King at the time, Robert III. He was a big, strong, powerful man, who had the unenviable task of controlling the difficult Galloway region. This he successfully did, and drove the English out into the bargain. Stories and rhymes about him survive to this day.

In the village, there's a great wee general store, with a tea and coffee machine to boot should you require some sustenance at this stage, which for me is about 40 miles into the run. I often stop there as I like the place, and after a quick cuppa I'm on my way again pronto. You will have noticed throughout the books that I never mention cafés or café stops.

Some guys like to use them, usually group riders, but as I'm a lone ranger then I never do. It is, of course, personal choice whether you want to yourself, however when doing such long runs, I find them just too time-consuming. Anyway, it's not long till you've swept round the rest of town and now begin the great passage through and along the Douglas Valley itself. This can be a beautiful green serene ride on a lovely day, despite the fact that we're up quite a height and that the valley has been heavily mined in the past. The upper parts that is, as the lower is very green and pastoral.

The road will be the real star of the show, however, as

---

8 - The young 6th Earl, William, was a victim at the infamous black dinner in Edinburgh. He was only 16 when he was murdered along with his younger brother, David.

After leaving Douglas, the journey back west along the A-70 makes for a very pleasant change to the long, hard road south, and what follows next is what makes the Douglas run all worthwhile. The jaunt is about to get very pleasant for the first time today, starting here.

It jumps and jives along with the flow
Leading where we want to go
Pleasing bikers fast and slow
Leading us to Muirkirk so.

Glespin looking its best. I say that with some honesty, because the first time I ever rode through the place, the rain and wind had just come on strong and it looked truly dismaL.

Doing so in quite some style, I hasten to add, as this is the payback we get for all that bloody awful road-riding we suffered on the way down past lovely Lesmahagow. This is a completely different kettle of fish, and it's this stretch from here to Muirkirk that makes it all worthwhile to come this way. It's a broad shallow affair early doors, the old Douglas, and after a few early curves, it's by a long and easy gait that the A-70 carries us away westward. Spirits lifted? You bet! So much so that I'll probably start singing again, all the way through the many wonderful curves and swerves of this rather quiet road. Quiet indeed for an A-road, but a little bit trucky all the same.

The funny thing is that most of the trucks that use it seem to be going in the opposite direction, I always find. Believe that if you will. Anyway, trucks or no trucks, nothing will spoil the fun of riding this one, not even the sight of Glespin on a dreich day. You arrive in this small isolated mining village after about 2 miles from Douglas, and I'm going to be a wee bit hard on old Glespin here, because the first time I ever did this run was the first time

DOUGLAS RUN

A delightful bending stretch of the A-70 just to the west of Douglas.

which doesn't do the run any harm. Neither, too, does Glenbuck Loch itself, which is a smallish, wooded, pretty and enclosed water, that must have appeared on some calendar or another at one time, I'm willing to wager. Before you reach it, though, you pick up the remains of a rail line that would have been used to ferry coal and ore from Muirkirk, which is, of course, our intended destination.

The skirt round the side of the loch is a delightful donner and carries us from South Lanarkshire into its fellow mining neighbour, East Ayrshire. Once again, the valley beyond here will begin to open up and become more muir-like (moor-like) in its appearance. We are now on the run in to Muirkirk, and shortly pass the site of the old Ponesk open cast mine. Some of its slag heaps can still be seen scarring the hillside above. The ground becomes generally rougher and the road becomes generally straighter as it continually rises towards the now visible and distant houses of Muirkirk itself.

A real feel of its industrial past gets you even before you arrive in the village, because there are clearly disused rail lines on both sides of the road and you pass through what was an old rail bridge, with an isolated row of

I had ever set eyes on the place. Just before I arrived, the weather took a turn for the worst and I saw it against a background of grey clouds and through driving slanting rain. I must say a more dismal sight and place to live, under those conditions, would be hard to find.

It doesn't look too bad in the sun, mind you, and I think it's probably just the greyness of the front terrace houses that gives the place such a dull appearance, especially in the rain. The front terrace is all you really see of the place, as you fly through unhindered and continue on up the valley. Still, the road shines in its swaying shift as the valley gets rougher and tighter, and we enter a sort of gorge-type stretch of the road. We get very close to the Douglas Water and skirt the edge of some rounded hills that come right into our personal space. Despite being rounded, they are craggy and bold, and this – along with some old ruins beside the river – makes for a most scenic and dramatic passage through this beautiful wooded glade.

The road remains just a little hemmed in on the next stretch, taking us up to Glenbuck. The hills have backed off a fair bit, but are still near enough to the road to make us take evasive action to avoid the closest of them,

On the A-70 here, still heading west and following the Douglas Water between Douglas and Glespin. It's great easy riding on this stretch, where the valley floor is still quite wide at this point.

either miners' or rail workers' cottages right beside it. Just beyond them, a steel plaque on a small wall tells you Muirkirk was a village of Covenanting martyrs. Glenbuck Loch is the source of the River Ayr, and already it is becoming a sizeable water that sits down on the left; numerous old bridge stanchions belonging to the railway can be still be seen standing above it. Also down there is

On the final approach into Muirkirk, keep your eyes open for these rather striking standing stones that sit down beside the infant River Ayr. Behind them stands the remains of an old rail bridge, which is not the only one you will find around here. It signifies the industrial importance once enjoyed by the town you are about to ride into.

a ring of standing stones, though I've no idea just how old they are. And at last, with about 51 miles on the clock, we arrive in Muirkirk.

It's a sizeable enough wee place of about 2000 residents, with a couple of good general stores to satisfy our needs. But for our purposes, it offers another major choice in what way we return home from this one. Very quickly

Coming into the centre of Muirkirk, once you reach the traffic lights ahead, it's make your mind up time. You can either turn right onto the B-743 and head over to Strathaven and East Kilbride, or continue straight on for Sorn and do the full run. A well-stocked wee Co-op sits just on the other side of the lights.

we meet the junction with the great B-743, which will take you over to Strathaven, and at this point you have the main choice of the whole run, in my opinion, as to which route to return on. Straight ahead will be for Sorn and completing the whole circuit. It leads to a tough home run, with about 41 miles for me to go personally. The Strathaven way is approximately 6 miles shorter, but offers an easier return and also the chance to ride one of the best roads in the whole area.

Hardly surprising then to find that it is used by many local riders – including me on many occasions – though, so too is the Sorn route. I'll cover the Strathaven route first and then the Sorn one, and you can make up your own mind.

MUIRKIRK TO STRATHAVEN B-743

Turn right onto the B-743, pull up slightly out of town, and get ready for some seriously good tarmac here. 14 miles to Strathaven, the sign says, and it's away we go. Out on the Glasgow Road, curving past the top houses and cemetery on the way, where there isn't actually much pulling up to do, as Muirkirk sits so highly perched itself[9]. Bang! Before you know it, you're already up on the moor and it feels like you've stolen a free climb here. Right away you're in amongst the sheep fields and hills, and all you have to do now is follow the road, as it only gently rises ahead of you through more of the same. Simple as that. No great effort required here, it's just pure enjoyment the whole way[10].

---

9 - It sits about 220 metres high.

10 - The poor early road surface does take the shine off things somewhat.

DOUGLAS RUN

This is the memorial garden in the centre of Muirkirk to commemorate all the poor miners who lost their lives down the mines. The roll of honour would match any WWI memorial, so great were the losses.

The early snaking bends keep it all interesting till you're up among the hill farms. Here, pointed Middlefield Law might just give you a wink. Now it's all open and airy and you don't have a carey[11]. If you aren't struggling or canned at this stage, then you will be seriously enjoying yourself, take my word for it. The 743 is an out-of-this-world road to ride, and it is very difficult to ignore it when doing Douglas. I dare say that's what makes it so popular. Its wonderful open swaying flow continues till you run into the large conifer plantation[12] that surrounds Dungavel Hill. You enter it after passing beneath the gentle slope of the finely-named Dippal Rig.

The road continues to slenderly please, only now it does so amongst the tightly packed pines, before suddenly there opens up a most wonderful sight ahead, including Glengavel Reservoir, beyond which sits Loudoun Hill. Now it's a game of two halves, with open heath on the left and the trees covering all the right side. The road slips past the reservoir with a fine shimmy, and now allows a panorama of the Loudoun Valley to be viewed. A fine, broad, fertile specimen she is, too, the old Loudoun, with our star man Loudoun Hill stealing the show centre stage. Now begins the long and very drawn-out descent down towards Strathaven.

On the B-743 climbing out of Muirkirk and heading for Strathaven, though admittedly there isn't a lot of climbing to do. It's a fantastic road to ride, and everything about it will please and delight. An easy, none-too-hard rhythm and tempo will pull you up wonderfully to its high point.

In its early stages, we shortly pass the former Dungavel Prison. It was originally a hunting lodge belonging to the Hamilton family, though nowadays it has the unpalatable task of being a detention centre for people who are on the brink of being deported back to where they came from. Their attempt at political asylum has been unsuccessful, and I can only assume that things back home must be pretty bad. Desperate isn't the word to describe their situation, and one I would wish on nobody.

Another view of the memorial garden in Muirkirk, which is a place that also tells the history of the village – not only industrial, but also going way back to the Covenanter times. It is well worth a visit.

---

11 - Pardon the awful rhyme there.

12 - In doing so, you re-enter South Lanarkshire.

Taking the bends past Glengavel Reservoir on the B-743, where Loudoun Hill puts in an appearance just before the long fall down to Strathaven begins. This is an out-of-this-world situation at this point, and the bends themselves make it ever so special.

You're well on your way into the Loudoun once you pass Dungavel, but it's still a good 6 miles to Strathaven itself. 6 miles of very slowly changing landscape, which soon has a totally different look from the area we ran through on the 743 only a few miles back.

Now it's big, broad, richer fields on a flat plain that we find ourselves amongst, making our way through beautiful curving beech hedges as we go, before we cross the old Roman road a couple of miles out of town. Then we enjoy an interesting crossing of the Avon Water, by a green-railed bridge, and a windy wooded pull-up. This only leaves the crossing over of the old disused rail line, by a fine old bridge, before completing the final stretch into town. You now approach Strathaven from the west, through low broad fields, and enter the town just before you meet the A-71 coming in from Kilmarnock.

When you do, immediately take the left turn at the wee mini roundabout, to run you down Townhead Street. This carries you very pleasantly into the bonnie town centre, where you will meet a set of lights just after the Bucks Head Hotel. There is, for me at least, a choice of two routes home from here. I can, if I wish, turn left at the lights onto Lethame Street, and from there follow the signs for the cycle route[13], which will take me to Eaglesham via the Auldhouse back roads.

If you've read the last couple of runs, you will know about these roads, which continue single track for about 9 miles till Eaglesham itself is reached. I've mentioned before that I don't usually use them when doing the very long runs, because I feel they are slow and time consuming. Occasionally, I do use them, and when I reach Eaglesham, I then return home via the Humbie Road and the Barrhead Dams. Mostly, however, it is via East Kilbride and the now infamous A-726 that I make my exit on this run. To do that, continue straight on at the lights and whizz round the bend onto the Glasgow Road.

This will take you out of town on a slight rise, and be ready to be seriously entertained again. As I've mentioned before in previous runs, I absolutely love riding the road back from Strathaven to East Kilbride. Despite this being an A-road and one that has just been labelled about the most dangerous in the country – hence the reason I referred to it as being the infamous A-726 a little bit earlier – you won't be disappointed. Once you clear the rise when you pass Cloverhill, it carries you high, flat, and flowing through the broad plain that leads over to Chapelton.

I think I already mentioned as well that on a winter's eve, there can be a real still hard quietness to this road, one that I really enjoy whenever I ride it, despite the cold. A swerving drop runs you very nicely into Chapelton Village and it doesn't take much effort to propel you out the other side. The road between here and East Kilbride runs through slightly lower-lying ground than what we've just ridden, but despite this it starts to get rougher. Certainly the closer you get to E.K. it does. It straightens out a fair bit on the way there as well, and at the bottom of the long drop ahead, there is a chance to head for Eaglesham on the Millwell Road, just at the little white cottage on the left.

I usually charge straight ahead into E.K. and like to enjoy the bends and drop in height that takes me there. Soon, I find myself on the mega-long, straight dual carriageway that is the Queensway. The section from St Leonards to Peel Park isn't too bad, I find. Yes, it's busy enough, but not overly so. And with plenty of room to spare, it's never that scary. Not the most picturesque stretch of road you are likely to ride, mind you, but it's a New Town and therefore expected to be an eyesore. However, I find that the stretch of road between E.K. and Busby can be a little too fast and hairy for my, and most other riders', liking.

It's a shorty that stretch, thank God, as soon into dear old Glasgow town we re-enter, only skirting the edge this time, though. It's the helter-skelter dive and twist under the rail bridge at Busby station that allows us then to get up to the Sheddens and Clarkston Toll roundabouts. This is the last wee climb for a while, as it now follows

---

13 - It's also sign posted for the airfield.

DOUGLAS RUN

If you decide not to take the B-743 for Strathaven, then the alternative is to stay on the A-70 and make your way out of Muirkirk on it heading west. This photo was taken just after the B-743 had been passed, and therefore we are still near the middle of the village. The road to Sorn begins with a fine, swaying gait.

the busy straight fall down through Giffnock, then the lang drap doon through the Darnley. The 726 is arguably at her busiest here, and that's saying something, so keep your wits about you and keep smiling. To that great old staggered junction that is the Hurlet, she takes us, where I break left for Barrhead and am almost home.

I carry on up the Glasgow Road till I hit the new roundabout at the junction with Blackbyres Road and turn right onto it. It does have many nice touches, the old Blackbyres, despite having so much industrialisation attached to it. The rail bridge you nip under has character enough, and the farm of Blackbyres itself is a fine example of old British if ever there was one. When I leave Barrhead, it's on the fine Caplethill Road as always. But now, even before I finish writing, the new extended cycle track is open for business. It will carry you smoothly and safely all the way from the edge of Barrhead right onto Glenburn Road.

I only require to turn a quick corner or three to arrive back home, and that would complete my journey if I decided to bail out early at Muirkirk when doing the long and mighty Douglas run. That would rack up about 85 miles all in, and is a great way to finish the run. It's not the full circuit, however, and if you want to do that instead of returning via Strathaven, then we need to return to Muirkirk. Before we do, however, it has to be said that going to and returning from Muirkirk is a fantastic run in itself. It gives the opportunity of riding the great B-743 twice in quick succession, and is a real favourite of mine and many others. I include the details here.

MUIRKIRK RUN

68.8 MILES
4.22 HOURS,
ASCENT 2600 FEET
2988 CALORIES BURNED.

SORN

So, if you are in the mood for doing the whole circuit, then carry straight on past the cut-off for Strathaven. As you do, you will notice right at the junction a memorial to all the men and boys who were killed in the mines here. It is a fine statue and plaque, which sits in a sort of garden of remembrance, not only to the lost men, but to the history and industry of old. That, I assure you, was quite extensive, to say the least. In fact, a visit into the Miners' Memorial Garden will be very enlightening, not only about the old industries but also the village history, including their proud Covenanting past.

The village began to grow round about the kirk, which was built in 1631 up here on the muir – hence the name. It was a fertile recruiting ground for the Covenanting cause and was, as the plaque entering the village told you, the scene of much Protestant martyrdom. None more so than John Brown, who was executed in front of his wife on the night of 30th April, 1685, by none other than Bluidy Clavers himself and his men, for refusing to swear an oath of allegiance to the King[14]. The night before his death, the renowned preacher, the Reverend Alexander Peden, had spent the night in his household. Peden, a leading Covenanting preacher, was also known as Prophet Peden.

Peden had not only predicted Brown's killing that very morning, but also when he married the couple

---

14 - This was the 1684 oath of abjuration.

some three years earlier. Stories of Clavers taunting Brown's wife Isabel after the murder are almost certainly untrue.[15] Another big name from Ayrshire who had links to the village, though at a later time, was one John (Tar) McAdam. He was involved with an ironworks here and also built one of his early prototype roads from the village to an industrial site just to the south. He was the first man to incorporate a camber into a road to assist drainage, and also used a build-up of small materials in the road's construction. Ironically, he never actually used tar himself in the construction of any of his roads. He only gained the nickname through his association with a tar works.

The most famous mine in Muirkirk was the Kames mine, lying just to the west. It produced very high grade coal that was used by steam locomotives. It was always regarded as a safe mine until Tuesday, 19th November, 1957, when an explosion caused by firedamp killed 17 miners. Smoking had been allowed even at the coal face up until that point, but afterwards the taking of matches down the mine resulted in dismissal. The pit finally closed in 1968, ending mining in the village once and for all. There is, believe it or not, a totem pole that you pass as you come in from the east[16] which depicts the village's industrial past. But now, of course, we want to head out west.

The road leads away through the village with a similar swaying dance to the one that it led you in by, and that's as good a start as any. We pass the old Kames Social Club, a real blast from the past, and also other parts that have an old ragged look to them, along with the town's outlying suburb of Smallburn, on the way out. There is also what is known as the Covenanters layby, which tells us more about the village's history. There now follows a longish easy rise, taking us higher on towards Airdsmoss. No sooner has the road levelled than we come to a major right turn for us, which is the B-743 signed for Sorn. This we take, of course, and we're onto the wild high roads.

The young River Ayr becomes our companion again, once more close up and curvy, and right in the centre of one of its bold meanders sits a monument. The Airdsmoss is flat, fertile, and silent – a vast plain of silence. The monument you see[17] is not be confused with one that sits just to the south (closer to the Cumnock Road), which tells of another Covenanters battle with the forces of the Crown. For on Airdsmoss on the 22nd July, 1680, hard-line preacher the Reverend Richard Cameron was killed, along with his brother and some of his supporters, when they were attacked by troops led by Major Andrew Bruce. Cameron was a man who showed no allegiance to the King, and was in fact outwardly hostile to the Crown. His supporters were likewise hard-line.

He had been touring the area and building up his support ever since returning from a brief stay in Holland. He had a price of 5000 Merks on his head. It appears that on this occasion he had been betrayed by a local laird who told the authorities of his whereabouts. The fighting was heated, bloody but brief, lasting for about 15 minutes. The Government forces were over 100 strong, the Covenanters numbered around 70, though the troops were naturally better trained. Despite losing their leaders, many Covenanters managed to escape and also killed 28 soldiers into the bargain. The captured were hung in Edinburgh later. Richard Cameron's legacy lived on, and his followers became known as Cameronians.

The next few miles (it's about 7 to Sorn), will be spent up here on the moss, where the early stages beside the river find you riding through a narrow, fieldy, fertile plain, containing sheep for the most part. It's wild and

Shortly after leaving Muirkirk, you take a right turn off the A-70 and you're onto the B-743. You are carried onto the Airdsmoss, where you meet the young River Ayr again, and you both take off in the same direction. This wild area is also steeped in Scottish Covenanting history.

15 - The stories of the taunting only appeared years later, and were written by men who were not present at the time.

16 - There's also another one on the west side in the Covenanters layby.

17 - This is in fact a monument depicting where once stood the house of Bauld Laprirk. He was a friend of Robert Burns.

pretty all at the same time. Then after a punchy wee pull-up, you're out onto the open moor itself. The road, now long and straight, is only interrupted by the need to cross the occasional burn. You're up a fair old height here, about 224 metres, but despite this no view of Ayr Bay or the Clyde coast is to be had, as we're still too far away for that yet. The high riding, past farms and their fields, will continue till the drop down to Sorn begins, and "full on screamer" doesn't begin to describe it.

After all these miles, you'll be glad you're not climbing the bloody thing, because long and steeply you fall, down and into the prettiest of villages Ayrshire has to offer. In you go, running the long straight length of the Main Street, past numerous white homes, till you pick up the now more mature and wood-lined River Ayr running right beside the road. Nowadays, the name sign just says Sorn; however, in times past, I think that even the official name sign actually said Sorn a Covenanting village, or words to that effect. This is hardly surprising, because from here hailed Alexander Peden, the prophesising preacher himself.

He was a leading light in the Covenanting cause, who was born in the nearby farm of Auchincloich, and was initially a teacher in Tarbolton. He was the man who prophesised John Brown's death, of course. After being ordained in 1660, he became the minister at New Luce in Galloway, before being forced to go on the run 1663. For ten years he roamed far and wide, including Ireland, narrowly escaping capture on numerous occasions. He wore a cloth mask and wig a lot of the time, to hide his identity[18]. He was finally captured in June 1673 near Ballantrae, holding a conventicle.

He was sentenced to over four years on Bass Rock, followed by fifteen months in the Tolbooth in Edinburgh. After that, he was to be shipped to the America's. However, after being taken to London by boat, the captain of the American ship which was to deport him, on hearing the reason for his deportation, released him. Peden made his way back north and ended his days by living in a cave by the side of the Lugar Water near Sorn[19]. At the time of the Battle of Bothwell Bridge, Peden was safely 40 miles away, realising what punishment would be meted out to those who were captured. His time in captivity had taught him well, so he wisely stayed away. Even after his death, he was hounded by the authorities, who dug up his body from Auchinleck kirkyard with the intention of hanging it from the gallows in Cumnock. The 2nd Earl of Dumfries had this stopped[20].

Nowadays, the village is peaceful and as said, oh so pretty. The latter part of the Main Street is nothing short of a fairytale setting. There is an old, steep, stone, hump-backed bridge crossing the river, across from the old kirkyard. Beside the bridge is a cottage, belonging to either Hansel or Gretel, and containing their chicken coop. All this is looked over by the resplendent Sorn Castle, which sits a river's bend away downstream; the river itself is a beautiful curving shining bar at this point.

Now, I always steel myself well as I leave Sorn, for I know what is to come. Get ready yourself, chaps, because it's going to be tough. Damn tough.

Expect a lot of high, barren, moorland riding like this as you steam along the B-743 Sorn-bound. There is one short steep pull-up fairly early on, but after that no real problems. The drop down into Sorn Village itself is a really dramatic screamer.

I'm talking about the whole route back to Paisley, not just the road over to Galston. It can be hard enough going in itself, though, and it begins on the short, steep, sharp brae out of the village, before we turn right across from the gatehouse to the castle and onto the B-7037. A climb starts us off on what will prove to be a great, though long, undulating road over. Up through the trees at first, and then begins a few more rises for us to struggle over on the long high traverse to Sornhill. When we gain top height, there will be great views over to the high peaks of Arran,

---

18 - The mask and wig can still be seen in Edinburgh's Museum of Scotland.

19 - This cave is actually marked on the OS map.

20 - His remains now lie in Cumnock.

At the far end of Sorn Village is its oldest part, and it really does look like something out of Hansel and Gretel. It is most picturesquely quaint and pleasing on the eye. Just be careful you don't run over a chicken.

as through field and farmland we get carried. Some of it is quite rough early on, but becomes richer, broader, and rolling later.

You soon pass a sign post for Auchencloich, which I think is the very farmstead where Alex Peden was born. The road does contain some beautiful touches, in the shape of Meikleyard Farm and also as it flows through a great beech hedge-lined chicane, before finally the lofty white row of Sornhill cottages is reached. The road takes no evasive action to reach there, being long straight and true in its gait as far as Sornhill, and then continues in similar fashion beyond it at first. Now it's payback time for all the effort expended since Sorn, as the road will flow down, then up, and finally down again, all the way into the Irvine Valley and to the rather forgotten town of Galston.

The striking, circular, red-roofed church will probably catch your eye as you first enter, which is hardly surprising, as it looks like it belongs in Istanbul[21]. It's not the oldest or most important building in the town, however, because when we reach the bottom of Station Road, we abut with the A-719 in the shape of Wallace Street.

We will turn right to run us down through tight solid streets of red sandstone, but if we look to the left before we do, we will see Barr Castle. This is a five storey high tower house, also red in colour, which was built by the Lockhart family. They were strong supporters of the Reformation, and George Wishart[22] in 1545 and John Knox for three years from 1556, both preached there.

---

21 - This is Saint Sophia's.

22 - Wishart was burned at the stake for his beliefs.

DOUGLAS RUN

On the road back over from Sorn to Galston (the B-7037), great views are to be had of the high peaks of Arran, like this one in the late evening light. This is the beginning of the toughest return home that I do, and it's never easy even if you are in really good nick. The climbing starts even before you actually leave Sorn, and doesn't stop for me personally till I hit the top of the Gleniffer Braes.

Finally, the last vicar of Galston, Alexander Arbukill, closed the door on both Wishart and Knox. A plaque on the wall tells of their association with the tower.

We leave Galston when we cross the Irvine and approach the big roundabout on the A-71, with its mini tower in the centre. We came through it before when doing the Loudoun Valley run, and last time headed for Kilmarnock. This time, though, we go straight across on the A-719 and head for Moscow. Get ready to dig in again, for it can be a fairly arduous climb up and away from the Irvine Valley, taking you almost immediately past Loudoun Academy. This one is not easy, especially with so many miles in the legs already, so just sit down and dour it out. Dour out indeed, because after a brief level off, the road rears up again.

However, as you get near the top, there is a fantastic view waiting for you away to the west in the shape of Ayr Bay and the southern half of Arran. If you've left it late, you are in for a fantastic sunset over the isle on the rest of the run over to Stewarton. You continue to climb long and gradual, levelling out shortly before touching the top end of Moscow, passing through a crossroads, beyond which another long but gentler curving rise carries you up into a landscape of broad fertile fields. These continue along with a straight road till you near the hamlet of Waterside. Then it's dipping drops and curving downs that carry you over and up after the Craufurdland Water.

Waterside had a mill of some sort here at one time, judging by the buildings, street names, and the location. All is pretty and white within, and just before you clear the last house on the rise out, turn left for Fenwick[23]. When you pass the grand-looking white farmstead of Arness Farm, you've cleared the place. A short swerving swoop through the fields over to Fenwick follows, and it's best to take the first right after Bruntland Farm, the Raith Road, to save you some leg work[24]. This carries you by a

Running past the row of cottages in the hamlet of Sornhill on the B-7037, and it means that the first tough section of road is behind now, and there follows a lot of respite in the long, wonderful descent down into Galston.

23 - This was signposted at one time, but it appears the sign has gone missing now.

24 - This turning has also lost its signpost. Perhaps somebody's nicking them.

Barr Castle in Galston may be the town's oldest building, but even if not, it can still lay claim to fame that both George Wishart and John Knox preached there. That's some claim to fame, I have to say.

These riders (who I don't know) are on the tough pull-up out of Galston on the A-719. This is a climb that I always find very hard, and am glad when I'm up. The man at the back here, who has been dropped by his companions, informed me he was "knackered". I knew how he felt.

rise and a fall into the centre of the village.

As you do enter, you come up past the great old black and white parish church, dating from 1645. The first minister here was William Guthrie a strong supporter of the Covenant and a man who was imprisoned many times for it. The church graveyard is full of memorials to men who took the pledge and died for the cause. Their graves are clearly marked by green plates that sit atop their headstones. Fenwick also had the world's first workers co-operative, when a group of weavers got together in 1761 to arrange prices and such like. At the end of Kirkton Street you meet the Main Road, just across from ye olde splendid Kings Arms Hotel. On this occasion we don't overstay our welcome, because a right, followed by a left turn at the war memorial, sees us head out under the modern M-77 and soon we're flying towards Stewarton on the B-778.

Now follows a lot more energy-sapping riding and climbing between the hedgerows, skirting along country roads, where the climbing leads to a great feeling of height on this stretch. Arran, again resplendent ahead over the lush fields, and a big swinging bend is coming up to keep it all interesting. This is followed by another of those great descents into a deep-lying Ayrshire town. The one into Stewarton is up there with the best of them, and not even a modern traffic calming system can ruin it, though God knows it has a try. The drop down is fairly gentle and curvy outside the village, but once inside, it is a great fast fall all the way down till you have to brake hard when you

On the road between Moscow and Fenwick, and again this is in some glorious late evening sunshine. I've usually finished my run long before now, but it has to be said that there is a lot more in the way of pleasing scenery to be had if you return home round about dusk.

meet the back road coming in from Kilmarnock.

The magnificent big stone railway viaduct that Stewarton possesses looks awesome on the way in, as now you trundle down towards the crossroads in the middle of town. At last we're back on familiar territory when we head straight across, and after meeting a bit of tradition in the old Granary Inn and a bit of colour from the filling station, we're under the rail bridge and out on a climb. When you level off among the fields this time, then you know you're well on the way to Dunlop. Once again, it's only us and the fields and a breeze behind to carry us onto our next port of call. We shall ignore the right turn for Nielson this time and continue straight ahead for

From high up on the A-719 on the approach to Moscow, Ayr Bay can be spied away to the west in the distance, and it's always a sight that I personally relish. It looks particularly stunning on this occasion in the late evening, as I've left this return home very late indeed.

Approaching Fenwick in the gloaming, with Arran looking glorious behind.

Almost at the bottom of the fantastic swoop down into Stewarton, and what a fast fall down it is. Its great railway viaduct can just about be made out in the background. The road over from Fenwick is the usual Ayrshire style of tough upping and downing.

delightful Dunlop.

This is entered with a most dramatic curve and dive down and under the railway, before it's up and round and through the most charming of settings. The old cottages and their red barn doors attached, along with the sweep of the road, always make it fun. Good, too, is the knowledge that a great wee bit of respite is to come in the hill that takes us down fast and out of the place. What goes down must come up, of course, as old Sir Isaac[25] would have told you, or something like that. For there now follows a sharp wee pull-up, which lasts till you're over the rail lines and then it's easy street again. A fairly high purr through the fields follows, with great views away to the west, before the long welcome drop down to

---

25 - Sir Isaac Newton, that is.

DOUGLAS RUN

On this occasion, the Sergeantlaw Road is preferred to the B-775 Gleniffer Road on the final approach to Paisley, and although tougher and a little bit slower than the main road, it has its good points, too. Ahead, in the distance, can be seen the final rise up in the road leading to Sergeantlaw Farm itself.

Lugton begins.

It's another drop and swerve under another rail bridge that fires you down fast and fearless into Lugton and onto the right hand bend that brings you to the Irvine Road. A right turn at the Canny Man sees you on the B-777 Beith Road, but not for long, because the next right turn takes you onto our old favourite stalwart – the Gleniffer Braes Road. 6 miles to Gleniffer Braes says the sign, but we're not out the woods yet, not by a long chalk. That old tiger of a sting in the tail, the long drawn-out pull-up past Hall Farm is still to come. It isn't long till it's upon you, and even the lush green surrounds and the familiar sight of the farm buildings don't help to make it seem any easier.

It can be a real long suffering experience at times, one that every rider from my area has had to endure many, many times, and will no doubt endure again. The steepest part is the first, thank God, and it isn't this hill's steepness that is the problem, it's the length of the bugger. So, dig in and just get up it. Just keep your eye on that front wheel and don't look too far ahead, remember, for therein lies despair. When you finally clear it, there's not much flat to work with, only just enough to roll you past old Muirhouse Farm, with great views across the whole of the braes in front of you.

Then comes the big left sweep of a bend at the end of Sergeantlaw Road, which can see you plummet down and then sweep right to begin the long straight ride over the braes on the B-775. On this occasion, however, we're going straight on and taking the Sergeantlaw. This great wee hill road will be our guide back this time, and as it sits higher than the Gleniffer Road, it provides really good views along the way. Admittedly, it's more rough and ready all around, but that's what you get on the high ground and that's just fine. The early straighter sections soon give way to bends that dance and jink out of site as you pass High Plymuir.

Soon you're running high and open towards the crossroads, where sits the great old farmhouse of Middleton. Once through, you only rise slightly before the exciting and hairy long drop down to Mossneuk Farm begins. But before it does, you get a great classic

The Clyde Valley comes into view just before the final ramp-like drop down on the Sergeantlaw Road is taken. At the bottom, we meet the B-775 Gleniffer Road, which is where it all started as we headed up for our first run to Turnberry and Girvan. It means we've just gone round in the circle game, and thanks for coming.

view of the Sergeantlaw's last rise away in the distance, as the road climbs up to Sergeantlaw Farm itself. Quite a sight it makes, rising like a lightning conductor to the highly-perched farm, which shares the road's name. And when you reach it, a tough wee customer it can prove to be for a last climb of the day, as you pull up the 100 feet of ascent or so on rotten old tarmac.

On passing the pylon ahead, you clear the climb and then nothing short of a toboggan-type descent of near Olympic proportions lies ahead. Tally ho! Right down through the small clump of conifers and then flying down, holding on for dear life, as you drop off bump after bump after bump, whilst getting thrown around by the road's surface for good measure. The old iron railings keep you tightly hemmed as you rush to the top of the final ramp-like drop that awaits you at the end. Below the full flat force of Foxbar, Stanley Reservoir and Strathclyde for that matter suddenly appears to welcome you back home, as steeply downhill, hard on the brakes you drop, meeting the Gleniffer Road at the bottom.

You must stop here – if you know what's good for you, that is. And to be honest, you'll be glad of the rest. A right turn sees you back on the steep stuff again, but not nearly as hairy a drop now, and the last bend sees us re-enter Glenburn. On doing so, we've come down the road and brae where it all began, as we made our way up that very same hill heading for Turnberry. It means at last we have finally come full circle.

A quick right turn at the Shieling filling station means I'm safely down, and can at last relax and take my hands off the brake levers. And just in case you haven't noticed, you've just gone round in the circle game…

Liam Boy

APPENDICES

LOCAL TRAINING RUNS

Below are a number of training runs, and the local testing run that I and many other riders from this area use. If they are handy, you may wish to use them yourself or, if not, you can devise your own. These are useful to build up stamina for the longer runs, and can also be used when time is tight or you are just in the mood for a shorter jaunt.

I describe them, very briefly, in the direction I normally do them in. But as they are all loops, they can be just as easily done in the opposite direction. They all, apart from the test run, have at least one good climb in them, to maximise the benefit. All runs are contained within the O'S Landranger 64 map, unless otherwise stated.

ROWBANK RESERVOIR

16.7 MILES
1.07 HOURS
ASCENT 980 FT
713 CALS

This is a great short and very picturesque training run that packs a fair climb in its armour, and one I like to do often. After gaining Howwood on the Beith Road (the A-737), turn left up the Bowfield Road (the B-776) and, after a fantastic long climb, run past the beautiful Rowbank Reservoir. Continue on up to the crossroads at Hall Farm, where a left turn onto the B-775 will run you back to Paisley along the top of the Gleniffer Braes.

FERENEZE HILLS

10.9 MILES
0.50 MINS
ASCENT 860 FT
574 CALS

This is a great quick but hard wee run I like to do, especially if I'm short for time. It involves heading into Barrhead and along Paisley Road, then turning right before the rail bridge and running up to Gateside. Continue up onto the steep side of the Fereneze Hills, which are similar and therefore good training for Arran's roads. The gradient gets up to about 15%. The height gained actually allows views of Ailsa Craig. Continue right to the end of Fereneze Road, until you meet Shilford Road. Turn right and come back over by Middleton Farm, where you descend to the B-775, where a right turn will return you back down Gleniffer Braes.

LOCHLIBO ROAD

15.2 MILES
1.03 HOUR
ASCENT 840 FT
608 CALS

This run also involves running up Paisley Road, Barrhead, but this time continue on to the end until Allan's Corner roundabout. Turn right onto Kelburn Street and climb out of town onto the great Lochlibo (Irvine) Road, the A-736. The Fereneze Hills look awesome, as does the big white Nielson Mill, which is where the road starts to climb up to Shilford Hamlet. When you reach Uplawmoor, turn right at Caldwell Golf Club onto the B-776, and again climb hard to Hall Farm on the B-775. From there, turn right and return back over the Gleniffer Road and Braes to Paisley.

DUNLOP

21.7 MILES
1.29 HOURS
1320 FT/ASC
929 CALS

The Dunlop run is another good climbing one, which follows the same start as the Lochlibo Road run all the way to the top of Kelburn Street, Barrhead. This time take the left fork for Nielson and not the Irvine Road, and climb long and great up into Nielson Village itself. From there, turn left onto the Kingston Road and undulate wildly and upward into the wild country leading to Dunlop. You can either go right to the end of this road and turn right on the A-735 and enter Dunlop that way, or take the right turn before the end, which will lead to the village centre by a slightly shorter route. Return back through Lugton and then the B-775 over glorious Gleniffer.

STEWARTON

> 28 MILES
> 2.11 HOURS
> ASCENT 1680 FT
> 1320 CALS

The Stewarton run entails heading up through the Barrhead Dams on the Aurs Road, until you meet with the lights at the bottom of the Stewarton Road (the B-769) and then turning right. This will carry you straight to the Ayrshire village with a real tough climb along the way, but a great descent down to finish. This is another high moor road and, when going clockwise, allows another long distance view of Ailsa Craig. On reaching Stewarton, turn right at the centre crossroads and return back through Dunlop and Lugton on the A-735, before that old stalwart the B-775, carries you back to Paisley via bonnie Gleniffer.

EAGLESHAM MOOR ROAD

> 29.8 MILES
> 2.15 HOURS
> ASCENT 1380 FT
> 1231 CALS

Without doubt, this is a superb run. One that's long enough to be a run in its own right and was denied to us for years because of heavy traffic on the A-77, until the new M-77 and A-726 Eaglesham bypass were opened. It is enjoyed by many south side riders and why not? Not only is it A-1, but it just falls in handy for good measure. It entails heading for Eaglesham through Barrhead and then along the Humbie Road, or by using Clarkston Toll. Turn right at the Gilmour Street crossroads in Eaglesham centre and climb initially up Montgomery Street (the B-764), running you up and onto Eaglesham Moor. All's quiet nowadays, with no more thundering dumper trucks; in fact, there is a cycle lane marked out on the road and you may even enjoy the call of the curlew in summer.

Wonderful rise follows wonderful rise until, at the crest of the road, you can see the sea. When you hit the old A-77 (which has a superb cycle lane, too), turn right and return down to Mearns Cross and back by the Barrhead Dams, if it suits. I personally prefer to turn left earlier than that, using the Malletsheugh Road and then come back in down the Springhill Road, Barrhead.

CLUNE BRAE

> 29.8 MILES
> 2.08 HOURS
> 1120 FT/ASC
> 1165 CALS
> O'S MAPS 64, 63.

This run is probably the most famous training run in the whole area, and used by local groups as well as individual riders. It entails heading for Bishopton and then dropping down onto the busy A-8 which takes you to the big Woodhall roundabout. You can either stay on the A-8 or head through Woodhall to take you to the bottom of the Clune Brae. There is a bit of a shortcut when using the Woodhall route, which entails taking a left turn at Woodhall station and climbing steeply up to the middle of the Clune on Heggies Avenue.

If you don't take the shortcut, expect to meet the Clune at its steepest early doors. From the roundabout at the top of the brae, continue to climb, though much more gently, till you are on the road to Kilmacolm. Continue to run right through millionaire's row on the A-761, which allows you a fantastic flier of a fall towards Bridge of Weir. Personally, I prefer to return from Bridge of Weir by Kilbarchan, which requires another short sharp shock of a climb, but gives a great descent into that old weaving village on the other side as compensation. From Kilbarchan, I return along the Beith Road, Johnstone, before taking the Glenpatrick Road, Elderslie, up to Foxbar Road and into Paisley that way.

LOCHER BRIDGE

27.1 MILES
1.52 HOURS
1300 FT/ASC
1181 CALS

This is about the best way to see rural Renfrewshire wearing its prettiest petticoat. This one involves heading for Kilmacolm on the A-761 and then, at the crossroads in the centre, turn left onto the Lochwinnoch Road, the B-786, and climb very highly on that road. It carries you over the Locher Burn, before the road drops splendidly and dramatically down towards Lochwinnoch. Before you reach the top end of that village, however, turn left onto the Howwood (Bridesmill) Road and, after a double whammy climb, descend like a banshee into the centre of that village. A run back to Johnstone then follows on the Beith Road, before the Abbey Road and then Glenpatrick Road, Elderslie, are used to return to south Paisley.

HOUSTON ROAD: TEST RUN

7.3 MILES
60 FT/ASC

Now this is not a training run per se. Rather, this road, the Houston Road (also known as the Georgetown) is used by many riders as a test run. Principally this is because it is one of the few flat roads in the whole area. It is also used by local clubs as a short time trial route. On occasion you may need a flat stretch of road, several miles long, to let you work out your average heart rate and help you set certain training zones on your computer. If you are not attempting to do this, then you need not bother with the Houston Road.

Some guys will actually trip out a certain distance on this road and leave a marker by the side of the road, such as a traffic cone, to let them know exactly where it is for future reference. Others just use their computer trip distance. The road runs off the Barnsford Road, which is the A-726 behind Glasgow Airport, up to the roundabout at Crosslee and back down again. On the whole a seven mile stretch, wherethere is really only a dip and rise as you pass Loanhead Cottages.

THE BIKE

As I mentioned in the opening run, it can be difficult to know which bike to go for early on, as you simply don't know what you're about yet. If you already have a machine in the garage or one that you haven't used in a while, then simply dust it down, oil it up, and use it to get you going. The price of bikes has shot up in recent years, and unjustifiably so. There is no need to go high-end, top dollar unless you intend to race. Just remember that the difference between a top machine costing thousands and a level-entry one costing hundreds is two miles an hour on a hilly course, with the difference being reduced to negligible on a flat course.

A level-entry machine is more than adequate for non-racing recreational riders, and a lot of the runs in the book can be easily ridden on the modern, lightweight, slick hybrid bikes, but my preference is for the racer. I actually did the Clyde coast run many times on a GT Talera mountain bike before I bought my first roadie, which was a Greg Lemond Reno. So a level-entry machine is a good way to start. And if you do decide to buy one that is a lot higher spec in the future, the level-entry one will make a good winter training bike, which is a good thing to have, as you will find out in time.

Despite what I have already said, I will finish this brief piece of advice by saying that when doing a long run on a top-end, high spec bike, the difference it can make – even from a mid-range descent machine – is quite noticeable. And although it will come down to personal circumstances, such as justification and cost, I would say that if you do decide to splash out and treat yourself to a really good machine, it will be money well spent, especially in the long run. I thoroughly recommend you do.

My two machines, which were used when writing the book, are pictured below. On the left is the trusted trainer, the Dolan, which is pictured at Wemyss Bay station, just before a jaunt over to the Isle of Bute. It is carbon fibre with a Shimano gruppo made up mostly of an ultegra/105 mix. It sports the essential mudguards, of course.

To the right is the pride of the fleet Eddy Merckx Cima, sporting wall-to-wall dura ace. On this occasion she is on Largs pier.

ESSENTIAL EQUIPMENT

SADDLE BAGS

The photograph shows the two saddle bags which I use, along with their contents and the pumps that I carry on a ride, the lights, and also the home-based track pump I use. Both my bags are Top Peak, though there are numerous other good brands on the market, mostly about a similar price of between £15 to £20. I just like the internal pockets or attachments that come with the Top Peak for keeping money and keys in, etc. The difference between the one on my training bike and my best bike is size. The training bike one is slightly larger to accommodate a beanie hat and thin pair of gloves during the winter time.

The contents are, for the most part, identical, though the multi-tool and patch kits in the smaller bag are more compact. In fact, the only additional thing I carry in the training bag a lot of the time is a couple of cable ties in case my mudguards start giving me gip. Other than that, they are as near as dammit the same.

I did try out some very lightweight expensive compact tubes from Continental in the small bag at one point (they cost £11 each), but they proved to be far too susceptible to punctures, even when you only rode over a small stone, so I don't use them now and don't recommend you do either. Stick to the standard tubes and you'll be fine. The list that I carry is as follows:

- Spare tube
- Tyre levers
- Multi-tool (with chain splitter)
- Two pre-glued patch kits (winter ones in a more waterproof cover)
- Two cable ties (training bike only)
- House keys
- Money bag (I always carry 7 tenners & 7 fivers)

NB. I only use the pre-glued patches to get me home. If I intend to continue to use a tube that has punctured, I have a more traditional puncture repair kit at home, which I will use on occasion to provide a more dependable, solid, and lasting repair.

PUMPS

Both on-bike pumps are Mt Zefals, which are the big babies on the block. I take them instead of the more lightweight pumps, because when push comes to shove they do the business without the strain and effort required when using a mini-pump; therefore, they are my preference. Park Tool do a similar model to Zefal which, although it has a better frame-fitting set-up, the pump action isn't to my liking and therefore I prefer the Mt Zefal.

I also recommend buying a track pump for the house, as it is good practice to check your tyre inflation before every run, and a bike-mounted pump is not adequate for this regular operation. Buying a good track pump, costing between £30 to £40, will save you a lot of time and elbow grease in the short run, never mind the long run. Get one pronto.

LIGHTS

Nowadays you may see some road riders using a flashing rear light even when they are out for a daytime jaunt. I personally don't use them all the time, but do so when the weather turns bad or if I am riding on a busy road. I will, of course, carry lights on a run that I know will end after dark.

My front light is a re-chargeable Cat Eye Nano Shot + and I have two rear lights. Both are Top Peak, as I tend to find their mounting system safe and secure. The larger of the two lights can either be mounted on the frame or clipped into the rear of the saddle bag, but the smaller one can only be mounted on the frame. It weighs nothing, and is ideal to carry on a long run on a day when you suspect the weather might turn bad and you might want to become more visible in the rain.

On top of that, for the winter I also bought a small flashing light that you fit to the top of your helmet. The idea here is the higher the light sits, the better. However, just to prove that nothing can guarantee your safety, the only time I have ever been brushed by a car was very recently when I was wearing a yellow hi-vis rain jacket and using a flashing rear light. It happened just as I neared the top of the Rest and Be Thankful. In this instance, though, I have a sneaky suspicion the driver was either stoned or drunk, just by the way he drove (he never stopped) after the incident. So it's better to carry a lot of luck as opposed to anything else.

NB. Also please note the rolled-up hi-vis rain jacket and cotton cap that I carry on many long runs, if there is even a hint of bad weather in the forecast. It's a good insurance policy to do so.

SADDLE HEIGHT

I am of the opinion that the most important thing to get right if you are bike riding for any distance at all is your saddle height. Once you get that right then the rest can follow on. That is how I work it. Not only that, but the type of saddle you have can be the real make-or-break component on your bike; if it is uncomfortable even after quite a distance, then it can put you off riding the bike altogether. Simply put, if your saddle is uncomfortable, it doesn't matter how good the rest of the bike components are as they won't even enter into it. Most serious bike commentators will tell you that the frame is the most important part of the bike, which is true in many respects, but you could also put up an argument for the saddle.

There is a chance that the saddle which comes with your bike may suit you, especially if you ride only fairly short distances. However, there is also a high chance that it will not, especially if riding long distances. That's when you have a problem. You have to find a replacement, and this can be a long expensive search for some.

Seeking advice from fellow riders with a lot of experience can help, as can going online and reading reviews of saddles, and such like. One guy whose advice I like to take is Aussie bike-fitting guru, Steve Hogg, who is a man I will refer to several times with regards to fitting of bikes and components. But for the moment let's deal with getting the saddle height correct first, because without that it won't matter if you do have one that is suitable, as you won't be getting the best out of it.

If you ever have to get on a strange bike at short notice (such as a hired machine), or for any other reason you don't have time to do a proper job of setting your saddle height, then a good quick fix is to sit on the bike and – with your heel on one of the pedals – put the pedal in the furthest positon from you (i.e. not straight down but slightly forward). Adjust the saddle height til your leg is bolt straight, and when you move the ball of your foot onto the pedal, there will be as near as dammit the correct amount of bend at the knee to ensure a reasonable fit. That, as stated, is fine as a quick fix. However we want something much more exact and accurate for our purposes, and for that I use and recommend the Greg Lemond method.

GREG LEMOND SADDLE HEIGHT METHOD

This simple but accurate way of getting the correct saddle height was devised by the great man himself, way back when they still used pedals with straps and clips and people still listened to LP records. I mention this because I will, as far as possible, give you the method he used as he described it then, along with some modern substitutes where necessary for you to get the correct height. So here goes.

Greg says stand with your back to a wall, wearing only socks and your riding shorts. Take an LP (long playing) record and, with the side of it placed right along the back wall, jam it as hard as you can into your crotch just the way the saddle would do if you were sitting on your bike.

Measure the distance from the floor to the top of the LP and record this in millimetres. Now get out the old calculator and multiply this number by 0.883. With the number which the calculator gives you (also in millimetres), measure from the centre of the crank bolt to the top of your saddle in line with the seat post – and this is your saddle height (Photo).

I use a flat blade screwdriver to ensure the ruler is in the centre of the crank bolt. Greg also says to subtract 2 millimetres if you are using clipless pedals. Don't forget that this was back in the days when a lot of guys weren't using clipless, even top pros like Shaun Kelly. As just about everyone uses clipless now, remember to subtract the 2 millimetres before setting the saddle height.

Also back in those days just about every household had a stack of LP records, nowadays I doubt if few households even have one. So we need a replacement for the LP. You can go into a second hand record store and get an old LP to do the job, or you can use a square or rectangular piece of very thin wood measuring 10 x 10 inches or 8 x 10 inches, or the cover of a hard-backed book, or one part of a plastic folder (the type you get in W H Smiths) – any of these will suffice. Also, if you don't have anyone to help with taking your leg measurement, it can be helpful to buy a long metal ruler about 2½ to 3 feet long, which will make the job easier if you're doing it single-handed. I bought one from B&Q just for this alone, and thoroughly recommend it. So that is the way I get my seat height.

I also recommend that before you do anything, you ensure your saddle is sitting straight by using a small

spirit level; if you don't have one, it is worth your while getting one for this job alone. You may find that you will need it quite frequently as you adjust saddle height and fore aft position, which we will deal with shortly. Next I recommend you set your cleat position on your shoes first, and then adjust your saddle's fore and aft position.

CLEAT POSITION

One of the most important things to get correct nowadays is the position of your cleats on the bottom of your cycling shoes. I will give another simple method of getting a good starting position, which – like all the other adjustment techniques in the book – requires no previous experience, special training, or specialised expensive equipment to enable a successful operation.

Once the basic set-up position is achieved, I will also talk about a more advanced position, courtesy of Mr Steve Hogg, that dynamic Digger (Aussie) whose advice is always worth having. This operation is probably made a little bit easier if you have an indoor trainer to sit you and the bike on, but it can just as easily be performed when sitting on the bike and using one hand to lean against a wall. So once again, here goes.

The idea is to position the cleat on the shoe, so that the ball of the foot sits over the pedal axle when riding. For expediency, this position will from now on be referred to as BOFOPA. The easiest way to do this is to first remove your shoes and socks, then locate what is known as your 1st MTP (metatarsophalangeal) joint. This is the big, bony, first knuckle joint that sits between the foot and big toe. Mark a small line across this (photo 1). The ball of your foot is obviously on the bottom of your foot, but the 1st MTP joint sits directly above it on the top, so we use it as our guide to make the job easier.

Now we want to mark the part of the outside of the cycling shoe which has the 1st MTP joint right below it.

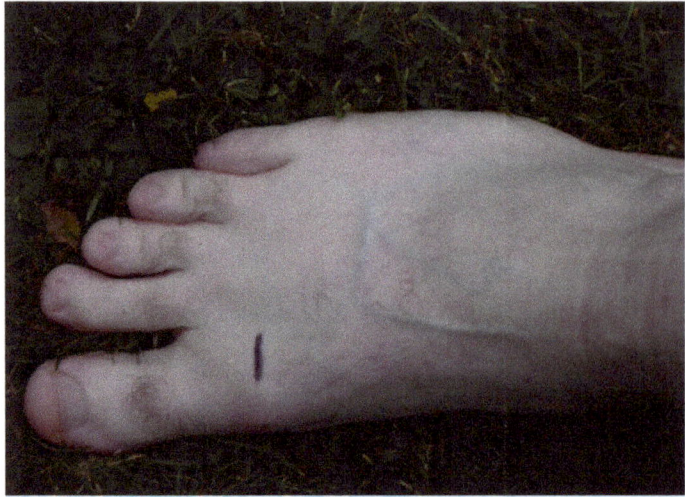

Photo 1

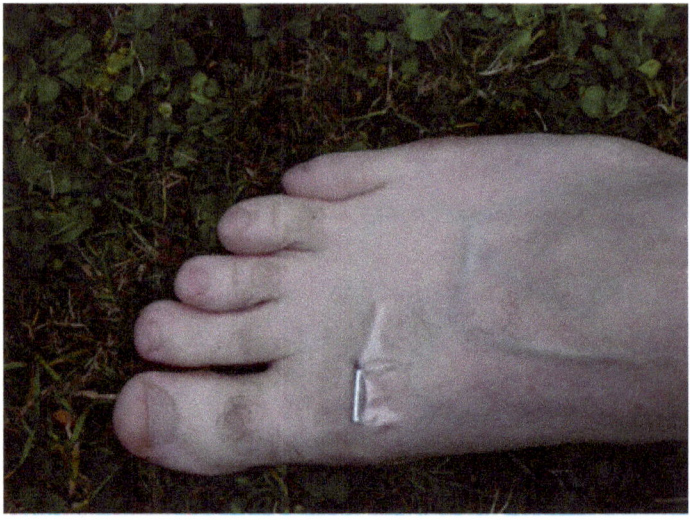

Photo 2

You could just put your shoes back on, without wearing your socks, and try and feel for the joint from the outside then mark the shoe at that point. However to make finding the 1st MTP joint easier, it helps to sticky tape a small metal cable end/nipple (the type you have at the end of your brake and gear cables) to the line you have marked on your foot, then put your shoes back on, again without any socks (Photo 2). You will feel this from the outside of the shoe much easier, and can mark this point with a felt tip pen or a slither of tape or white adhesive paper (Photo 3). If you don't have any cable ends/nipples, then just something small and hard will do.

Once you have marked the shoe, attach the cleats to the bottom of the shoe and tighten them up, but not fully at this point, as there is still some adjusting and manoeuvring to do. Now get back on the bike, click into your pedals and position the cranks horizontally. Then manoeuvre your forward-facing shoe so that the mark on the shoe is in line with the pedal axle. Climb off and tighten the bolts on your cleats, then do the same with the other foot.

It is usually easier to take your foot out of the shoe and leave it in the pedal at this point, as this part of the operation can be a bit higgledy-piggledy, if you are doing it on your own. It is easier if there is someone to help you, but for most of us, it's a one man job.

The final slight adjustment is to ensure that your cleat is facing straight forward. So after you have removed it from the pedal, you may have to loosen the cleat very

Photo 3

slightly at this point, ensure it stays more of less where it is, then line it up with the marker lines on the bottom of the shoe. *Voilà*! Job done.

If you have a computer and are online, it may be worth your while to have a look at a website run by an Australian bike-fitter called Steve Hogg. He is a very well-known and respected man in the world of cycling. If you are not online (and many of us aren't), I will give you Steve's thoughts on cleat position. Steve says that the foot in cycling is a lever and not a very efficient one. That's because the piston (which in this case is the leg), is positioned at the end of the lever (foot). Problems can arise when you are cycling hard and applying a lot of force to the cranks, because then the heel can drop more than usual and you lose the BOFOPA position, as the foot tends to slide back.

He therefore advocates actually moving your foot forward of BOFOPA position when setting up your cleats, so as to counteract this movement by the foot under pressure. Steve also goes on to explain that some people are toe-down riders while others are heel-down riders. For each size of shoe he gives a range of adjustments. If you are a heel-down rider, he advises to use the greater length of adjustment. It will, of course, take you a little time to figure out what is your own personal pedalling style, and so BOFOPA is still a good place to start. Steve's recommended adjustments are as follows:

SHOE SIZE	APPROX. POSITION
36-38	7-9mm
39-41	8-10mm
42-43	9-11mm
44-45	10-12mm
46-47	11-14mm
48-50	12-16mm

Remember, we are moving the cleat back in the shoe, which in essence means we are moving the shoe forward to make our foot a more efficient lever. I am a size 43 and have moved my cleat back by 10mms. Again, the guidelines on the bottom of your shoe should help you achieve an accurate adjustment. Just get your BOFOPA positon first and take it from there.

SADDLE FORE-AFT POSITION

Getting your saddle in the correct fore-aft position comes next, and it will usually mean with most saddles (with only one exception I know) that the saddle height will need to be checked and most likely adjusted again.

Fore-aft is also easier (just like cleat position) to get right if you have an indoor trainer to put the bike on and then sit on, but it is more than doable with you just sitting on the bike and using one hand to lean against a wall, preferably indoors. The only piece of equipment you need is a plumb line, or as some call it a plump bob. If you don't have the real McCoy, you can make one with a piece of string and some metal washers. It only has to be about 3 feet long to do the job.

So get on the bike and do a few turns of the cranks (if you're on a trainer) just to get your feet settled in the right position. Then position the cranks horizontally. Try and put, then keep, your foot in the position it would be in during a normal pedal stroke. This is where the trainer is handy because you can concentrate and watch how your feet move before stopping to do the adjustment.

Now drop the plumb off the front of your forward protruding kneecap and let it fall to the inside of your shoe. Ideally it should just touch the end of the crank arm. If it doesn't, then adjust the saddle forwards or backwards till it does. That's it. This is a very good starting positon for most riders.

However, don't forget that this is only a *starting* position. Some guys, usually time triallists, will sit further forwards, whereas others may want to sit further back. Once the fore-aft position is set, once again check and re-adjust the saddle height if necessary. This will need to be done with most saddles unless you are using a Selle SMP saddle. I will deal with saddles themselves next.

STEM AND HANDLEBARS

STEM

Once saddle height, cleat position, and saddle fore-aft position have been adjusted, it's time to check the length of your stem. I use a very simple on-bike method to check if my stem length is correct, and so far it has served me well and I've had no back problems or shoulder pain.

First, get on the bike and ride along, either on a turbo trainer or out on the road, and put your hands into the hooks of the handlebars. Now tilt your head down at an angle of about 45 degrees, and try and see the hub in the centre of your front wheel. If your stem is the correct length for you, the hub should be obscured by your handlebars. If the hub can be seen in front of the bars, it means your stem is too short. If the hub can be seen behind the bars, it means the stem is too long. Replace accordingly.

HANDLEBARS

I will only go as far as to say that handlebar style and width are very much a matter of personal preference. I personally prefer a narrower bar, measuring about 40 centimetres from centre to centre. My advice is that if you are thinking of trying a different width and style from the one which came with your bike, buy cheap at first to find out what suits you best before digging deeper for a more expensive one. Carbon bars are really pricey. Aluminium is very cheap by comparison. Just remember, a lot of the pros prefer aluminium.

SADDLES

All I can do on saddles is to give some general advice, mostly based on personal experience. That's because finding the right saddle can be a very unique and personal thing. However, generally speaking, the more padding a saddle has the more comfortable it will be. You may find that some manufacturers do a specific saddle in more than one weight. If you are not racing, don't need to save weight, and are planning to do fairly long runs, then it's a good bet to go for the heavier, more padded one in the range. That said, padding isn't the be-all and end-all of more comfortable riding.

That's because you may suit a narrower or broader saddle, depending on the width of your pelvis. This won't be obvious until you have tried out a few for yourself. Again, you can go online and read horror stories of guys and girls who have spent a small fortune in search of the perfect saddle. I advise you to buy cheap at first until you find out what suits you best, then buy a better quality model in that style when you are sure you know what you are about – and have the funds, of course.

I am of quite stocky build, yet it seems that a narrow saddle suits me best. I found this out by accident when the saddle that came with my Trek mountain bike was narrow and padded. As I used the Trek for a bit of rare cycle touring (the battlefields in France), I soon became aware that even after days of riding, my bum still wasn't sore. About the same time, an expensive, lightly padded and broad Selle Italia saddle which I bought for my Eddy Merckx road bike, started to hurt like hell after about 60 miles. Through that, I learned the narrow job was for me.

Even Steve Hogg in his blog admits that he is wrong about people's pelvic size in about 25% of the cases he deals with. So it will come down to a bit of trial and error, especially when you start riding long. At the moment I am using a Selle SMP saddle on both my bikes. On the Merckx I am using the SMP Evolution, which is about the narrowest in the range. On my training bike I'm using the SMP Stratos, which is just the Evolution with more padding. Without any financial inducements, Steve Hogg recommends the Selle SMP on his website, and he rides one himself.

That said, they are not overly comfortable, as the whole centre section is cut out, and you literally ride on two rails. The nose on the SMP dips down noticeably, and it's one of the few saddles that is designed not to be set up horizontally, but to be tipped slightly nose down, anywhere between 1 and 5 degrees. If you do decide to invest in one, it's worth your while buying a digital spirit level to get the angle of degree of drop correct (this also requires some trial and error).

The SMP also has the advantage of being designed so that you do not need to readjust saddle height if you are adjusting fore-aft position. They are not cheap, costing well over £100 for the top ones, and they do take some getting used to, but at the moment that's my personal choice.

HEART RATE MONITOR INFO

I am about to give some general and also very specific information about using heart rate monitors. But before I do, I want to stress that you do not need to know this or even to use a heart rate monitor if you don't want to. It is not essential or even necessary that you do. Some, however, may be interested in using one as they find they are getting into their bike riding and would like to know more about the benefits of using one. So here it is.

As we are doing a lot of long endurance runs in the book, it helps to pace yourself well, so as not to run out of steam halfway there. It is actually easier to do this on your heavier training bike than your top-end machine (if you have one), as the extra weight keeps you from getting carried away and going too fast too soon. The main device for keeping yourself in check is the heart rate monitor, though power meters are becoming much more common. Now as I mentioned at the start, I know plenty of guys who ride long and never use one; that's fine. It's all a matter of personal choice.

I like to use them, and have invested in a fairly upmarket model – the Polar C.S. 600. This gives me plenty of information, though a lot of it I don't need. A basic model of heart rate monitor/cycle computer will suffice, giving you your current heart rate, distance covered, time ridden, current speed, etc., which will do the job for most people, especially if they are riding for recreation, no matter how long the distance. But even for recreational riding, some of the features on a more advanced model are handy and useful, especially if you are a distance man or woman.

The Polar which I have includes a feature which tells you which heart rate zone you are in. This is very useful for people who are racing and want to know what intensity they are training at, but is also handy when you are on a very long run and are trying to pace yourself. In fact, it is a good idea to take your resting heart rate in the morning, before getting out of bed, to judge just how fit and well rested you are on any given day. The fitter you get, the lower it should become. So if you find you're getting into your riding and want to judge your fitness, simply start taking your resting heart rate in the morning so that you have an idea of your resting rate.

As your fitness improves, the amount of heart beats per minute (bpm) should come down. If you start increasing the riding then this will happen and that is good, because it means you're getting fitter. The lower your resting bpm, then the harder and longer you can ride on any given day. However, after a period of long hard riding, you might find your morning heart rate goes up. Warning!!! Time to back off. Your body is telling you you've done too much and you need more rest. Getting fit has a very simple equation, it goes like this.

STRESS THE BODY-
REST AND RECOVER.

Hard training doesn't do you any good on its own; it simply exhausts you and wrecks your muscles. It is resting that rebuilds you and makes you fitter and stronger for the next doing. To improve, you must have both sides of the equation working in tandem. Too much exercise and you burn out. Too little and you become a couch potato.

As you are not a professional bike rider, don't forget to take in the big picture. Stress is stress. The body doesn't know if it's stress from riding, working, DIY, family quarrels, or whatever. It only knows it's getting stressed. So if your morning rate goes up and you haven't been riding a lot, don't forget to take into consideration everything else that's getting lumped onto your plate.

An easier ride on the old machine in those circumstances should reduce the stress levels most of the time, so a run where you stay in your recovery zone should be the tonic. How do you know what is your recovery zone? Well, that's where the old heart rate monitor comes in. Try not to go for the off button here, for this is a good thing to know, although not essential. I've mentioned Aussie Steve Hogg as the main man on the bike-fitting front, but it's Yankee Joe Friel from Boulder Colorado who is the main man on the training front. I first became aware of him when I bought his excellent book *The Cyclist's Training Bible*, though I was unaware it was a book aimed strictly at people who raced. It was the excellent cover photo of Marco Pantani flying up an Alpine bend that caught my eye.

At one time it was thought that the best way to define training zones was to find your maximum heart rate and then work out the zones from there. However, this required you to sprint up a hill at full pelt and almost bring on a heart attack, at least for some (Joe describes it as a gun to the head). There was also the old theory about subtracting your age from some number like 220 (or thereabouts), but this is wildly inaccurate. So Joe explains it's better to work out your training zones based on your lactate threshold (LT). Here's what's going on. When you are riding at a fairly slow to moderate pace, you are mostly using fat to provide the fuel and oxygen to assist this process, which is called being aerobic.

But once you increase the pace, you start to use more carbohydrate than fat to provide the fuel. When this happens, the muscles produce a by-product called lactic acid. At first the body is still able to flush away the lactic faster than it produces it, so you don't notice this. You are still using oxygen to assist the fuel supply process, and therefore still aerobic at this point. However there comes a point when you further increase your effort and the oxygen supply cannot keep up with demand, and you then cease being aerobic and become anaerobic. This is the point where you produce energy without using oxygen.

This is also the point when you cannot flush away the lactic as fast as you produce it, and it starts to accumulate in the muscles. It's this that gives you the burning sensation in your muscles when you are sprinting hard over a small hill. This is because you are now producing lactic faster than your body can get rid of it. The lactic acid seeps into the bloodstream and becomes lactate, which – being in the bloodstream – is actually measurable. You cannot ride anaerobically for very long as it's too bloody painful. You are riding at your maximum sustainable output just at the point where you are on the threshold of going from being aerobic to anaerobic. This is your lactate threshold (LT). Your heart rate at this point is what we want to find out and then use to determine our heart rate training zones.

Again, no specialised equipment is required here, only an HRM that records average heart rate. The plan is now to do a short time trial and to go as hard as you can and find out what is your average heart rate for that particular exertion[1]. Once we get the average heart rate, we will divide that by a certain number and this will determine our lactate threshold and from that we will determine our training zones. Joe gives several distances with corresponding numbers by which to divide your average heart rate. This also includes whether you did the time trial as part of a race or as an individual time trial.

As most of you won't probably be racing yet, I'll give the two shortest distances he recommends as an individual time trial – one in kilometres and one in miles, depending on what you prefer to use. Either one will do.

1) Ride a 5 kilometre TT and record your average heart rate then divide this by 1.04.

Or

2) Ride an 8 to 10 mile TT and record your average heart rate then divide this by 1.01.

So, for example, if you did a 10 mile time trial and your average heart rate was 177 BPM, divide this by 1.01 and this would give you 175 as your lactate threshold heart rate. So your corresponding zones would look like this:

1 - Recovery	2 - Aerobic	3 - Tempo	4 - Sub-Threshold	5 - Super-Threshold
115-143	144-156	157-163	164-174	175-178

If you have bought Joe's book, *The Cyclist's Training Bible*, it now becomes very easy to find out your training zones with the number the calculator gives you, because on page 27 of the version I have, all the corresponding heart rates and zones are given to you in a very well laid-out table. It may be worth buying the book for this alone. However you can work out the zones yourself, which are as follows, with the corresponding percentage heart rates of your lactate threshold heart rate in brackets.

1) Recovery: (65-81%) This is used for easy days after a previous day's hard ride or when you want to de-stress. It is also the zone to be in when recovering between hard training intervals. It is the ideal zone to be in when working on pedalling technique and such like.

2) Aerobic: (82-88%) This is the zone used for building up the endurance base, and the time spent in it is usually measured in hours. It is the most common zone we use when doing the long endurance runs in the book. It is a very valuable zone.

---

1. Make sure you are well rested on the day you do the TT and choose a flat course on a calm day, if you can manage it.

3) Tempo: (89-93%) A fast form of endurance, but one that is sustainable. It can be handy for building up an endurance base fairly quickly when you haven't got a lot of time to do very long endurance runs.

4) Sub Threshold: (94-100%) This is the fastest you can go and still be aerobic. This zone can be used for several minutes at a time and helps the body deal with lactate build-up and become more efficient at disposing of lactate. This is the highest of the aerobic zones. It is still fairly hard on the body, however, so use this zone wisely. If you are doing training intervals in this zone, it will take at least half to a quarter of the time you spent in the zone to recover before doing the next interval.

5a) Super Threshold: (100-102%)[2] This is you now in the red zone. You are now anaerobic and this is used to help the body deal with lactate build-up. It is very hard on the body, so only short bursts are usual in this zone. Recovery time when doing intervals in the 5a zone are about one to one-and-a-half times the interval time.

Some computers might allow five, three, or one training zone to be pre-programmed. However, even if yours doesn't, as long as you know what your personal numbers are, you can use them for more intelligent and efficient training. This is very useful, especially if training time is limited or you want to take your recreational riding to a higher level and start racing. But remember, none of the above is necessary or compulsory if you only want to ride for fun. That's for sure.

(Main source: *The Cyclist's Training Bible*, by Joe Friel)

---

2. Please note that zone 5 can actually be broken down into 3 separate zones. The other 2 are zone 5b) Aerobic Capacity: (103-105%) and zone 5c) Anaerobic Capacity: 106%+. These are very, very hard training zones, used by experienced athletes.

HYPNOSIS DOWNLOADS

UNCOMMON KNOWLEDGE

In route 6, the Toward Lighthouse and Loch Striven run, I mentioned a couple of fine fellows, Mark Tyrrell and Rodger Elliot, who along with their associates, call themselves Uncommon Knowledge or Hypnosis Downloads, if you like. They have built up over 800 very effective downloads and CDs to help anyone not only overcome a problem, but to also grow and expand in their lives. I must own about a dozen at least of their CDs and intend to invest in some more in the near future. I thoroughly recommend you give them a try if you need help in any area of your life, and can assure you that you should see quick results for very little outlay.

Each download costs approximately £12, though I prefer the CDs that come in at about £20. They cover just about everything you could think of and I've had a lot of success on a personal basis with most, though not all, of the ones that I've used. They can help in all areas of your life, with things from losing weight to relationships, from overcoming fears to difficult people. This includes sports performance, personal development, and health issues. They even have one to improve your eyesight. I've got that one and there has definitely been an improvement in my vision, especially in my dominant eye, though not quite to prescription glasses standard.

I've noticed that if you string together two or three really important ones, such as Believe in Yourself, General Anxiety Treatment and Self-Esteem Booster, then you will feel a sure gradual build-up of inner strength the more you use them. They will become the most relaxing and enjoyable part of the day, which is just fine, as constant repetition is the key to success here. Using these hypnosis CDs will make a difference; I can say that from experience, a very good experience at that.

I just want to point out that I am in no way connected to or get any financial support from this company, and am only passing on information that I know to be beneficial. So, as already mentioned, you've got nothing to lose, as the guys do a 90-day money back guarantee. I include their address and telephone number at the bottom. Tell them I sent you…Boom, Boom.

Uncommon Knowledge & Hypnosis Downloads
3rd floor, Boswell House, Argyll Square, Oban.
Argyll, UK
PA34 4BD
01273 776 770
www.hypnosisdownloads.com

INJURIES

Unfortunately, injuries from cycling may occur from time to time, either through a collision or a crash of some sort. Obviously we hope nothing too serious, of course, and it's fair to say the benefits outweigh the drawbacks in the vast majority of runs. Broken collarbones are fairly regular in the ranks of the professionals, but not so much with amateurs, and I've never had one in all the years I've ridden. You are more likely to sustain an injury through over-training than anything else and it's usually the poor old knees that give way, as they take all the pounding.

I usually find that easing up for a few days, or even a week or more till things ease off does the trick, but on occasion I've had to seek some professional help. There are many good physiotherapists out there, of course, but ideally it would be better to get one who knows about cycling as well. If you feel that you require the services of a physio, it might be a good idea to ask at your local bike store if they know of anyone who is a cycling-orientated physiotherapist, or even ask fellow riders.

I do know of one who treated me a few years back and who did a very good job, not only on my knee but also on my cleat position which eradicated any further problems. I contacted this gentleman when I was writing the book and offered him some free advertising along with a glowing reference, but he seemed reluctant for any publicity. So, for that reason alone, I did not include his details in this section.

One bit of advice I would give is if you don't have the money for a specialist and you are letting time alone make the repair, try a balm of some sort. Some guys swear by Tiger Balm, which costs about £7 for a small pot, though I have never used that myself. I have used Wood Lock Balm, which cost about £15 for a larger bottle, and acts like a sort of heat balm and massaging it in helps with easing the pain. Both these balms are used in Chinese medicine. I got mine in the Piazza shopping centre, Paisley, where a very helpful Chinese lady has a small store. You may want to give that a try.

DATA

Below the title of every run will be the information and statistics relating to that run, the details of which have been provided by my Polar C.S. 600 cycling computer. Below this again will be the relevant numbers for the Ordnance Survey Landranger maps that cover the area of the run. The details of the information is as follows:

MILES

The mileage for any given run will be from my front door, in Glenburn, South Paisley, to the destination and then back to my front door, unless stated. Obviously this exact distance is only relevant to me, but it should act as a fairly good indicator as to what is involved for anyone wishing to do the run from their home. In the case of starting from a ferry terminal, the distances will be exactly the same for all. I could have used a more central starting point for the runs, such as Paisley Cross or Paisley Gilmour St station, but most riders wouldn't be starting from there either. The mileage given is only meant as a ballpark figure. So if, for example, you live in Renfrew, you can subtract 6 miles from the Stirling run, but would have to add the same 6 miles for the Turnberry run. Adjust to suit.

HOURS

Hours is simply the time taken to do the run. This will be for a run when no photos were taken and stops were kept to a minimum, i.e. toilet breaks, etc. Despite this, these times are of course approximate, as you may ride at a completely different speed from me. I did consider using an average speed for all the runs, say somewhere around 14 mph, but some of the runs were done partly on single track road, which can slow you down considerably, and other runs involved a lot more climbing than ones of a similar distance, so again the time would differ greatly. Also which bike, training or top machine, traffic, weather, and especially wind strength and direction would also play a part in speed and time, as would how many miles you had done the previous day or two. So remember, the time for each run is merely approximate.

ASCENT IN FEET

This is the amount of climbing involved in any given run or variation of that run. The CS 600 will often give a difference of perhaps 80 to 100 feet of ascent in a run covering anywhere from between 60 to 100 miles, so it is a fairly accurate figure that you are given.

CALORIES/BURNED OR CALS

This again is an approximate figure, as the amount of calories burned per mile can vary greatly from individual to individual. Your age, VO2 Max, the speed you ride at, can all affect how many calories you burn. As a useful guide, if you are trying to lose weight by cycling and using a calorie controlled diet, and you don't have a computer that tells you how many calories you've burned, then 40 calories per mile is a good, fairly accurate figure to use to help you know how much energy you are using and burning off. That should be accurate enough to help in your weight loss.

O/S LANDRANGER MAPS

The numbers for the Ordnance Survey maps that will cover the whole run are given. Although it is handy to have these, they are not totally essential and a good road atlas should suffice for the most part. As each map costs about £8 each, you can save quite a few quid by simply using the road atlas. However, the more detailed maps are both handy and interesting to have, and I consider it worth the expense to get them. They will prove beneficial when you are sitting of an evening and looking to plan out runs in the future or, as stated in the text, you may want to see where you took a wrong turn on some small back road after a run has been completed.

PHOTOGRAPHY

I used two cameras to take all the photographs within the book – both compact digitals, small enough to fit into the rear pocket of my cycling jersey. They were the very small and formidable Panasonic Lumix DMC-FT2 (the T stands for tough) and also the slightly larger Nikon Coolpix P-7000. During the countless runs I made while writing the book, I took countless photographs and none have been enhanced in any way. I wanted it to be quite simply what you see is what you get.

Sometimes I have found that when you, say for example, look at a brochure for an area you wish to visit or perhaps to do a long distance ride or walk like the West Highland Way, the photographs in the brochure will have been taken by a very experienced skilful photographer.

They have waited for the light to be right – usually early morning or late evening, when most people will have ended their days walking or riding. And also they have taken up unusual positions and vantage points, sometimes with the aid of a tripod, often when the weather is at its best. So, of course, when you go and do the ride or walk, the area looks nothing like it did in the photos. Well, I didn't want that. All the photos were taken at the time of day most people would be doing the run and in the very weather that nature threw at me at the time. So again, what you will see is what you can expect to get at the time you come to do the ride yourself.

A word to the wise here, if you do decide to start taking photos yourself when you are out on the bike. It is much more time consuming than you would imagine to continually stop the bike and take photos. I am telling you this in case you wish to buy a camera yourself and record your runs as you go along. You probably won't notice when doing a mainland run, but if you are on an island or aiming for a specific ferry, then it is very prudent to watch the clock continuously or you may miss your ferry and end up being stranded overnight. If your computer has an average speed reading, it will be a good indicator of just how much slower you are going when you are using the camera a lot.

To speed things up, I did invest in a bracket to hold the camera in position on my handlebars and save me from continually stopping to take a shot. Although this did save some time, I don't recommend doing this, as too many of the shots were ruined by camera shake. Certainly this set-up could only be used with a tough camera variant, as the non-tough Nikon proved to be totally inadequate on the bracket, but even the majority of shots with the Panasonic turned out to be well below par. The larger Nikon had the advantage of a viewfinder and more powerful lens, but the Lumix had a better metering system, which coped far better with difficult conditions, such as shimmering sunlight on the Clyde.

WORKSHOP

The photo shows just some (though admittedly, the bulk) of my cleaning and maintenance tools. But as this is not a book on cycle maintenance, I will not go into any great depth on that subject.

However, learning to do your own repairs is very satisfying, convenient, and cost-effective. So I recommend fairly early on in your cycling life to get a good maintenance manual (the two I have are old but still handy), and start to build up the old tool box as you go along. If the worst comes to the worst and a repair goes badly wrong, you can always take it along to your local bike store and you're no worse off than if you had gone there in the first place.

The cleaning kit does not need to be one of the fancy brush sets that you can buy which are specific to bike cleaning. I find a sponge, a rag, and a small brush, will do most of the jobs better than the purpose-built stuff does, though some small specialised brushes are really handy for getting into awkward nooks and crannies. The basic cleaning kit is as follows:

CLEANING KIT

- Bucket
- Fairy liquid
- Sponge
- Rag
- Stiff, small sweeping brush
- Chain cleaner (a must-have)
- Liquid de-greaser for chain cleaner
- Spray degreaser for other parts
- Specialised small brushes for cogs and mechs (optional)
- Old toothbrush (will do in place of small specialised brushes)

WORKSHOP KIT:

- Workstand (optional, but good to have)
- Wheel truing stand (wheels can be trued in situ, but a proper stand is handy)
- Spare tubes
- Spare tyres
- Rim tape
- Puncture repair kit (old glue style)
- Handlebar cork
- Spare brake pads
- Brake cables
- Gear cables
- Cable ends
- Cable cutters
- Link pin pliers
- Pliers: normal and long-nosed
- Chain checker
- Chain wrench
- Spoke keys
- Assorted combination spanners and shifting spanner
- Assorted screwdrivers
- Lubes: both wet and dry
- Bearing grease
- Multi-tools
- Bottom bracket tools (various)
- Sprocket removal tool
- Allen keys
- Cone spanners
- Small wire brush (for cleaning bolts, etc)
- WD40 (or equivalent)
- Spirit level
- Digital spirit level (if you have a Selle SMP saddle)
- Torq wrenches (good to have)
- Insulating tape
- Oily rags (last but not least, you'll need one or two)

FURTHER READING

The Secret by Rhonda Byrne

The Cyclist's Training Bible by Joe Friel

The Artist's Way by Julia Cameron

The Secret Code of Success by Noah St John

Steve Hogg's online blog

ABOUT THE AUTHOR

"Just a guy who does a bit".

Liam is an ordinary bloke. When he decided one night that he needed to change his unhealthy lifestyle, he did so in a spectacular way and found a passion for cycling.

He is a taxi driver with an interest in lots of things; bikes, history, photography, psychology and more. If you are lucky enough to share his cab you could find yourself inspired and entertained by his philosophy. Maybe enough to even start a new journey of your own.

Liam's "bit" has taken him on a journey from his home in Paisley around Scotland on his bike. If you'd like to know more please contact him on his Facebook page at

Liam Farrell - The Circle Game

or e-mail him at

liamfarrellthecirclegame123@gmail.com.

www.ingramcontent.com/pod-product-compliance
Lightning Source LLC
Chambersburg PA
CBHW061141010526
44118CB00026B/2836